Defining Social Work in Aotearoa

Defining Social Work in Aotearoa

Forty Years of Pioneering Research and Teaching at Massey University

Michael Dale, Hannah Mooney & Kieran O'Donoghue

MASSEY UNIVERSITY PRESS

First published in 2017 by Massey University Press

Massey University Press, Private Bag 102904
North Shore Mail Centre, Auckland 0745
New Zealand
www.masseypress.ac.nz

Text copyright © Michael Dale, Hannah Mooney
and Kieran O'Donoghue, 2017
Images copyright © as credited, 2017

Design by Kate Barraclough

The moral right of the authors has been asserted.

A catalogue record for this book is available from the
National Library of New Zealand.

Printed and bound in China by Everbest Ltd.

ISBN: 978-0-9941300-9-9

Contents

Dedication

The authors dedicate this book to Mervyn Hancock and Ephra Garrett, who were the founding staff members and leaders of the social work programme at Massey University. Merv is widely recognised as the father of professional social work in Aotearoa New Zealand, while Ephra is clearly the whāea and midwife of social work. We hope that this book in some small way captures the aspirations, hopes, dreams and vision you had for social work in Aotearoa when you started the Massey University social work programme.

— Michael Dale, Hannah Mooney and Kieran O'Donoghue

Introduction

The social work profession is a bridge extended to those who are excluded, marginalised, lost and unloved within society. On a daily basis, social workers work on behalf of the public to assist individuals, groups, families, whānau and communities to change the stories and circumstances of their lives, as well as the way in which society positions them in the stories that are told about them.

Social work practice involves intervening in the social problems that impact on people's private lives. Through the decades, social workers have undertaken this work diligently, while pressed for time and having to navigate the competing demands of clients, their agencies, resources, the law and social policy. Social workers as a group are generally unassuming, service-orientated and focused on the needs of their clients, while working for change within bureaucratic, dehumanising and rationed systems. They are engaged in social change through mediating the aspirations of human rights and social justice within civil society. Nonetheless, the realities of their work loom large, and as professionals some are often marginalised, in a similar fashion to the clients they serve.

In Aotearoa New Zealand, the social work profession has been constructed from a range of attitudes to welfare, including indigenous and Western approaches (rising from settler notions of charity delivered primarily by religious organisations). The establishment of the welfare state saw the government become the main provider of social and welfare services, through the departments of Education (Child Welfare Division), Māori Affairs (Māori Welfare Office), Health, Social Security and Justice. Up until the Department of Social Welfare Act in 1971, social workers practised under a range of titles including Child Welfare Officer, Māori Welfare Officer and Field Officer (Nash, 2001).

The education and training of social workers has been integrally connected to the development of the social work profession. Initially, social workers were trained through an apprenticeship model, under the supervision of a more experienced or senior colleague. Formal social work education came in the form of the Diploma in Social Science that was offered by Victoria University of Wellington from 1950 (Nash, 1998a). The Victoria programme only took a dozen students each year. Because this programme was unable to meet demand for trained social workers, in the 1960s the government departments developed formal training centres at Tiromoana and Taranaki House, where new social workers undertook an eight-week programme in two blocks of four weeks, with a six-week break in between (Staniforth, 2015).

In 1964, the New Zealand Association of Social Workers (NZASW) was formed, with Merv Hancock as its founding president. The NZASW and Merv Hancock were committed to the professionalisation of social work, which included the development of formal qualifications, and they worked alongside the government to establish them. In 1975, Merv Hancock was employed in the Department of Sociology at Massey University to develop and lead a social work programme for the university. This book endeavours to tell the story of this work.

The social work staff of Massey University, like their colleagues in practice, have a passion for the work of educating and developing social work practitioners, and furthering the disciplinary knowledge basis of social work in Aotearoa New Zealand. They have done this while responding to significant changes in social conditions since the mid-1970s. In essence, this book is an attempt to record this effort, and to reflect on the impact it has had in furthering their aspirations for professional social work. In other words, this book aims to explore the contribution that the Massey University social work programme has made over its first 40 years in defining professional social work in Aotearoa New Zealand.

The question of the contribution, influence and impact of a university programme is a challenging one. Traditionally, an assessment of a university programme is based on the success of its graduates, the reputation of the programme nationally and internationally, the impact of staff and student research, and how well the programme, through service, contributes to its communities and country. In exploring the question of how the Massey programme has contributed to defining professional social work in Aotearoa New Zealand from 1975 to 2016, the authors undertook a review of the salient aspects of the history of Aotearoa New Zealand society and of the social work profession. We have also reviewed the history of the university, and the way in which the social work programme developed in terms of staffing, curriculum and programmes. Finally, we have attempted to capture the breadth and depth of research undertaken by the staff, students and alumni of the programme, as well as the specific accolades and honours awarded to staff, students and alumni.

The research methods employed were, firstly, an email questionnaire and oral history interviews with key informants (former staff and alumni). We also undertook an extensive review of social work literature, the social work records in Massey University Archives, the School of Social Work historical records and documents, library resources and online sources. The email questionnaire and oral history interviews explored the social work context, the Massey University context, the development of the social work programme, the contribution the programme has made to social work and social policy, and the future picture for the social work programme. Both the questionnaires and the interview transcripts were analysed, with the key themes and events being identified by close reading. This research was approved by the Massey University Human Ethics Committee.

The review of literature, archival material, records, documents and online material was also focused on the social work context, the Massey University context, the development of the social work programme, and the contribution the programme has made to social work and social policy. The initial searching and collation of staff lists and staff publications was undertaken by Amy Viles, a fourth-year Bachelor of Social Work student on a summer scholarship. Amy's search involved looking through the university calendars and university research and publication reports.

We particularly acknowledge the assistance of Doug Franz, Strategic Research Information Manager, who provided access to the university research reports, and Louis Changuion, the Massey University archivist, for access to the archives and providing copies of digital photos. The Massey University Library also assisted us by providing endnote libraries of the social work and social policy theses.

In terms of the social work context, we drew from a range of sources, with key sources being Mary Nash's PhD thesis on the history of social work education (Nash, 1998a), the ANZASW Digital History project (http://www.socialworkhistory.nz/) and the Research and Publishing Group of the New Zealand Ministry for Culture and Heritage's New Zealand History site (http://www.nzhistory.net.nz/). We also undertook a review of all of the issues of *New Zealand Social Work*, *Social Work Review* (and its later iteration *Aotearoa New Zealand Social Work Review)*, *Te Kōmako* and *Tu Mau*, and key social work and social policy texts (for example, *Social work in action*, *Social policy in Aotearoa New Zealand*, *New Zealand social work*, *Restorying social work supervision* and *Social*

The Social Science Tower (SST) opened in 1973 at Massey's Turitea Campus, Palmerston North. Social work has been based here for 40 years. **MASSEY UNIVERSITY ARCHIVES**

work theories in action). We also acknowledge the assistance of the Massey University alumni office, which provided us with information about the graduates of the programme and those who had been awarded honours.

In undertaking the research and writing for this book, we as authors were acutely aware of our own positioning as insiders, staff and graduates of the programme, and that our perspectives, experiences, worldviews and values influence the construction of the narrative in this book. Our biases are obvious; we are all invested in the social work programme at Massey University. We feel a sense of responsibility as the current custodians of this legacy to continue its work and build upon the foundations, established by Merv Hancock and Ephra Garrett, of a bicultural, critically reflective programme that engages with the social challenges of the day, that has practice relevance, challenges the social policy agenda, advances the profession of social work, and aspires to advance both human rights and social justice within Aotearoa New Zealand and internationally.

The audience we initially envisaged for this book was our alumni, social workers in Aotearoa New Zealand and social work students. As we researched the area of the history of social work schools and social work education programmes, we were unable to find any books which specifically captured the history and contribution of a social work school or programme within a university. We therefore became aware that there was a further possible audience for this book with our international colleagues within the International Association of Schools of Social Work. With our audience in mind, we decided that we would focus on the narrative and story, which means that we have kept in-text citations to a minimum and have chosen instead to have a full bibliography at the end of the book.

We have taken a chronological approach with the chapters, with each covering a particular period in the development of the programme. Within each chapter, we have set the scene of the period by discussing the social work and university context of the time, and then how the programme developed and contributed to social work practice and policy in that period. The book concludes with a review of the programme's journey in defining professional social work in Aotearoa New Zealand, and explores what the future holds for social work and social work education.

Chapter One
A new professional programme for a changing society, 1975–1982

This chapter discusses the establishment and development of the social work programme at Massey University within a broader social context. The chapter consists of three parts: the social work context; the development of the Massey social work programme; and the contribution of the new programme to the development of social work in Aotearoa New Zealand. This three-part structure is also used in subsequent chapters.

The social work context is explored in two distinct sections. The first examines the events that shaped the social and political character of Aotearoa New Zealand. This in turn provides the background for the second section, which discusses the development of the social work profession.

Matters pertaining to government, legislation and policy, bicultural development and social issues characterised the social and political context of this period. Politically, Prime Minister Robert Muldoon dominated, trying to hold society together by interventionist government and regulation in the face of a liberal, deregulating and internationally changing world.

The political climate

Robert Muldoon led the National Party to electoral victory in 1975, and his government lasted until 1984. Muldoon's administration was characterised by heavily interventionist economic policies; for example, by imposing a wage and price freeze, controlling rents, and attempting to reduce interest rates. The administration also invested in the ultimately unsuccessful Think Big strategy, which was intended to simultaneously decrease the country's reliance on imports and address unemployment (King, 2004, pp. 488–489).

The second oil shock of the 1970s was associated with a reduction in supply linked to the Iranian revolution, but it was also driven by strong global oil demand. Oil prices began to rise rapidly in mid-1979, more than doubling between April 1979 and April 1980. The National Government's response was to invest in Think Big large-scale industrial projects, mainly based around energy projects, in order to reduce New Zealand's dependence on foreign energy sources. An alternative short-term response was the introduction of carless days for motor vehicles, introduced in July 1979; even so, there was little reduction in petrol consumption, and the scheme was abandoned in May 1980.

The 1978 general election, conducted under the first-past-the-post system, saw the National Party returned with a reduced majority (down from 55 seats to 51 — securing 39.82 per cent of the total votes). The Muldoon administration had failed to reduce either overseas borrowing or the government's internal deficit; there was double-figure inflation, low economic growth and high unemployment. The Labour Party had gained increased representation (from 32 to 40 seats — securing 40.41 per cent of total votes), and the Social Credit Political League secured one seat, with Bruce Beetham becoming the party's second MP (they had secured 16 per cent of the total votes).

In 1981, the election saw the return of the National Party Government with a further-reduced majority of two over all of the other parties. National won 47 seats (34.3 per cent), Labour 43 (34.5 per cent), and Social Credit (18.3 per cent) 2 seats. In spite of the government's unpopularity, the opposition had failed to gain sufficient voter confidence.

Another notable political event during this period was the launch of the Mana Motuhake party by Matiu Rata, a former Labour Cabinet minister. Rata had tuned into the rising dissatisfaction with mainstream political responses to concerns held by Māori, and the Mana Motuhake party was launched at an Easter hui in 1980 at Tira Hou Marae in Auckland. Rata was of the view that Māori would always be marginalised if they remained inside the main political parties; key aspirations of the party included Māori autonomy and a vision of cultural unity.

The key legislative changes during this period revealed a focus on biculturalism, family relationships and civic rights. Biculturalism was evident in the establishment of the Waitangi Tribunal by the Treaty of Waitangi Act 1975. The Tribunal is a permanent commission of inquiry charged with making recommendations on claims brought by Māori relating to actions or omissions of the Crown that potentially breach the promises made in the Treaty of Waitangi. The Tribunal was initially mandated to review claims made from 1975. It was not until 1985 that the remit was extended to claims from 1840. Upon the recommendation of the Tribunal, the Crown makes settlements through the Office of Treaty Settlements.

During this period the emphasis on family relationships was apparent in three Acts that marked changes regarding the relative power differential between women and men, including a focus on domestic violence. The first of these was the Matrimonial Property Act 1976 (which also recognised de facto relationships), which represented a further recognition of the need to redress gender inequality. The Act recognised the equal contributions of both partners to a relationship, and provided for a just division of property, in particular noting the interests of children. There was a general presumption that property would be divided equally between a couple. This Act was intended to work in association with the Domestic Purposes Benefit 1973, which aimed to help women with a dependent child, or children, who had either lost the support of a husband, or who were inadequately supported by him. The Domestic Purposes Benefit set the benefit at a level that would enable sole parents to care for their children without needing to find paid employment, thus enabling many women and children to leave violent family situations. Together these two Acts removed another impediment to women who were trapped in unhealthy relationships and often subjected to family violence — financial dependence.

The Family Proceedings Act 1980 was the second Act. This Act established a single ground for divorce (dissolution of marriage or civil union); namely, irreconcilable differences proved by two years' living apart. Counselling was to be made available to assist couples regarding disputes concerning the care of children; provision was also made for a mediation conference chaired by a Family Court judge. The Act was empowering, too, in that it encouraged couples to assume responsibility to resolve disputes.

The third Act was the Domestic Protection Act 1982 (which came into force in 1983). This was the first piece of legislation in New Zealand to respond directly to domestic violence, introducing non-violence and non-molestation orders. Historical responses to domestic violence had reflected societal attitudes that considered domestic violence to be 'a private affair', and police intervention had primarily been in the role of mediator, with few cases resulting in prosecution. The women's movement of the 1960s and 1970s increased public awareness of domestic violence, and the first women's refuges were established in 1974 and 1975.

Changes in court structures also had implications for family relationships. The Family Court was established in New Zealand by the Family Courts Act 1980, and began operating on 1 October 1981. Although it is a division of the District Court, the Family Court has its own identity, with a Principal Family Court Judge and judges who are permanently appointed by the Governor-General. The Family Courts Act requires Family Court proceedings to avoid unnecessary formality.

The period was marked by three developments regarding civic rights. First — a reflection of the increasing centralisation of information held by the government — was the establishment of the National Law Enforcement System, also known as the Wanganui Computer, in 1976. This database held information accessible to the Police, Department of Justice and Land Transport Safety Authority. It recorded details regarding motor vehicle registration, driver's and firearms licences, and traffic and criminal convictions. While the Police minister hailed it as a 'most significant crime-fighting weapon', the database was controversial, and many questioned the State's right to gather information on its citizens.

Second, the Human Rights Commission was established by the Human Rights Commission Act 1977. The Commission was given a range of functions and powers to protect rights under United Nations covenants and conventions. The Human Rights Commission Act outlawed discrimination on the basis of sex, marital status and ethical or religious belief.

The third development was the Official Information Act 1982, which sought to balance the public's right of access to official information against the government's need to withhold information. The Act set out the principle of availability: that the public should have the right to access official information unless there is good reason for withholding it. Further, making information publicly available was considered to be consistent with the promotion of good government, enhancing respect for the law by enabling more effective public participation in the making and administration of laws and policies, and increasing the accountability of ministers and officials.

The mid-1970s witnessed events that were an expression of Māori self-determination, and that also presented a challenge to the perception that race relations in Aotearoa New Zealand were an example to the world. Rapid urbanisation and assimilation practices had led to Māori being over-represented in negative health and wellbeing statistics. There were renewed calls for the Treaty of Waitangi to be adhered to by the Crown, particularly as these matters pertained to Māori land that had been taken by the government.

In 1975, there was a Māori Land March in the form of a hīkoi from Te Hāpua in the far north to the steps of Parliament in Wellington. This hīkoi was led by Hokianga community leader Dame Whina Cooper, who became known as Te Whāea of Te Motu (Mother of the Nation). Thousands of Māori and Pākehā joined the initial small group of 50 marchers as they completed the 1000-kilometre walk to protest. Their intent was encapsulated by her statement 'not one more acre'. The march was an expression of Māori determination to halt the further transfer of Māori land to both Pākehā and the Crown, and was influential in politicising many Māori (King, 2004).

The occupation of Takaparawhā (Bastion Point) is another seminal marker of Māori concern regarding land issues. Takaparawhā is a promontory above Tāmaki Drive overlooking the Waitematā Harbour in Auckland, and was gifted to the Crown by Ngāti Whātua, the local iwi, as a defence site in 1885; subsequently, the land surrounding the point was appropriated for housing. In late 1976, Muldoon announced plans for a housing development at Takaparawhā. On 5 January 1977, the Ōrākei Māori Action Committee, led by Joe Hawke, occupied Takaparawhā in opposition to the Crown's intention to dispose of the land. The dispute was subsequently taken to the Waitangi Tribunal, and in July 1988 the government agreed to the Tribunal's recommendation that the land be returned to Ngāti Whātua.

In 1982, Hiwi Tauroa, the Race Relations Conciliator, released a report, *Race against time*. This report was based on a public survey, and argued that the state of race relations in New Zealand required urgent action. He asserted that biculturalism must be the first step towards multiculturalism since Māori and Pākehā represent 'the two cultural foundations of New Zealand society'.

The establishment of Te Kōhanga Reo (Language Nest) by the Department of Māori Affairs was to have a seminal contribution in the regeneration of te reo in Aotearoa New Zealand. The total-immersion Māori-language programme targeted children from birth to the age of six, and aimed to promote language and support whānau in the principles of Māori child-rearing practices. The first kōhanga reo opened in April 1982; by the end of the year, 100 had been established. By 2016, there were 460 kōhanga reo throughout Aotearoa New Zealand, and kōhanga have also been established in Australia and the United Kingdom. Following this total-immersion initiative for younger children, primary schools (kura kaupapa) and high schools (whare kura) were established from 1985. Wānanga (universities) were set up from 1981.

Race relations with Pasifika people also assumed prominence during this period. In 1976, the government's intolerance towards Pasifika migrants found expression in the intensification of 'dawn raids' on Pasifika over-stayers (first introduced by the Labour Government in 1974). The background to this situation traced back to the 1950s, when the New Zealand government had encouraged emigration from Pasifika countries to provide labour to meet shortages caused by post-war economic expansion. However, as the result of economic recession and increasing unemployment in the 1970s, attention was now focused on immigrants whose temporary visas had expired. These migrants were disproportionately represented in unemployment and crime figures, and there was a perception that they were placing pressure on the welfare system. The raid tactics were accompanied by accusations of racism, and damaged relations with Pasifika countries like Samoa and Tonga.

A further expression of government exercise of power occurred in 1982. In 1962, Western Samoa was the first Pasifika nation to regain its independence, and a Treaty of Friendship was signed with New Zealand.

However, the citizenship status of Western Samoans was uncertain, and a case was taken to the Privy Council, which ruled that Western Samoans born since 1924 and their descendants were entitled to New Zealand citizenship. Concerned about increased migration to New Zealand, the government challenged the ruling and was accused of a breach of faith and racism.

The 1981 South African rugby tour was one of the watershed events in the development of public opinion regarding racism. Prior to the 1981 Springbok tour, the issue of racial discrimination in South Africa had sparked significant debate in Aotearoa New Zealand. A number of organisations emerged in the 1960s in opposition to the tours, including Halt All Racist Tours (HART), Citizens' Association for Racial Equality (CARE) and National Anti-Apartheid Council (NAAC). There was also active support for the tour promoted by Society for the Protection of Individual Rights (SPIR). In 1960, 150,000 New Zealanders signed a petition against sending a race-based rugby team to tour the Republic of South Africa. However, the call for 'No Maoris — No Tour' was ignored by the New Zealand Rugby Union, and the tour proceeded. In 1970, the All Blacks toured the Republic with a multiracial team, although this did not reflect a change in the attitude of the South African government — Māori were allowed to enter the Republic only as 'honorary whites'.

In 1981, public opposition to the race-based policies of the South African government resulted in protests aimed at halting the Springbok tour of Aotearoa New Zealand. Over 200 demonstrations were held, with more than 150,000 protesters taking part, of which 1500 faced prosecution. The focus of the anti-tour protest was racism, and many Māori participated. One of the consequences of the protest against the tour was to heighten public consciousness regarding race relations in Aotearoa New Zealand.

Feminism was also gaining momentum as an international social and political movement. The United Nations (UN) marked 1975 as International Women's Year, and organised the first World Conference on Women in Mexico. Since 1976, 8 March has been celebrated as International Women's Day, and the United Nations Decade for Women (1976–1985) was established. The UN organisation dedicated to gender equality and the empowerment of women, UN Women, was established, with five priority areas for intervention: increasing women's leadership and participation; ending violence against women; engaging women in all aspects of peace and security processes; enhancing women's economic empowerment; and making gender equality central to national development planning and budgeting. In Aotearoa New Zealand, a national committee continues to be responsible for coordinating activities.

The contentious public issue of abortion, reflected in the debate between pro-choice and pro-life lobby groups, was addressed in the Contraception, Sterilisation, and Abortion Act 1977. This Act specified 'the circumstances in which contraceptives and information relating to contraception may be supplied and given to young persons, to define the circumstances under which sterilisations may be undertaken, and to provide for the circumstances and procedures under which abortions may be authorised after having full regard to the rights of the unborn child'. The Abortion Supervisory Committee was established, and reports annually to the New Zealand Parliament. The committee's key functions are to maintain the list of certifying consultants and to monitor the quality of abortion services.

The International Year of the Child in 1979 was a United Nations initiative which marked the twentieth anniversary of the Declaration of the Rights of the Child. In New Zealand, various events, such as a fundraising Telethon, conferences and exhibitions were held. While the International Year of Disabled Persons (IYDP) was marked in 1981, it had been proclaimed in 1976 by the United Nations General Assembly, which had called for action aimed at equalising opportunity, and promoting rehabilitation and the prevention of disabilities. The following year the World Programme of Action concerning Disabled Persons was adopted, and this thrust was continued during the United Nations Decade of Disabled Persons (1983–1992).

The above review highlights the political dominance of the National Party, characterised by interventionist economic policy. However, in spite of low economic growth and rising unemployment, opposition parties had been unable to gain sufficient support to form an alternative government. The establishment of Mana Motuhake was to foreshadow later developments in Māori political consciousness and organisation. Key legislative changes engaged biculturalism, family relationships and civic rights. Significant bicultural developments reflected increasing Māori self-determination, a focus on race relations, and the significance of te reo. Finally, concern with issues affecting race relations (particularly the 'dawn raids' and the South African rugby tour), women, and the needs of children and disabled persons were all harbingers of a developing social consciousness.

The development of social work

The social work profession was emerging within the above social and political context. The New Zealand Association of Social Workers, formed in 1964, was now over 10 years old, and the Department of Social Welfare Act 1971 acknowledged social workers in law for the first time in New Zealand. Concern with establishing the professional identity and credibility of social work as a profession was evident when, in 1975, the New Zealand Social Work Training Council (NZSWTC) introduced measures aimed at raising standards in social work training. These included instituting basic minimum standards, a system of accreditation, and, in 1980, a Certificate of Qualification in Social Work (CQSW).

Formal social work education during this period consisted of the Diploma in Social Science through Victoria University. In 1976, the University of Canterbury started offering an MA in Sociology with an option in Social Work. The University of Auckland offered an MA in Sociology in Social Welfare and Development (with financial support from Mobil Oil); however, this offering was subsequently removed in 1980. In 1982, the Auckland College of Education established a Diploma in Social Work.

During this period, the issue of the registration of social workers was a contentious issue among members of the NZASW. While the advantages of registration were identified (protection for clients and employers, professional development, training, skills development and protection for social workers), there was concern that the proposed eligibility criteria for registration (the holding of a professional qualification) would exclude the vast majority of those then practising as social workers. The debate regarding registration and the professionalisation of social work has continued across the decades to the present day.

Further concern regarding the construction of social work as a professional enterprise was evident in the 1981 report *People in the social services*, which was commissioned by the NZSWTC. It was found that 78 per cent of paid social service workers held no social service qualification, while the figure was 85 per cent for the unpaid worker group. The authors drew attention to the importance of social workers receiving appropriate training in light of the complexity of practice and the fact that social work intervention could have a long-term impact on clients.

In 1980, the NZASW membership was also engaged in a debate over professionalism and social work. A proposal to restrict membership to those who had completed training, which would lead to the NZSWTC CQSW, was resoundingly defeated. This reflected concern for the position of unqualified but experienced practitioners who would be excluded from membership. This concern with training and competence to practise is a theme that has continued to influence the development of policy and legislation to the present time.

Concern with broader social issues was also evident. The theme of the 1982 NZASW Biennial Conference, held in Auckland, was 'Social justice — a social work concern for the '80s', and conference speakers included Alf Kirk, a Federation of Labour economist. Lecturer Ian Shirley called for social workers to link the private troubles of their clients to the social structures and systems of privilege and power which made them poor. Sister Pauline O'Connor, a staunch and well-known community worker from Christchurch, gave a practical example of working with the powerless to bring about change. It was noted that Māori input to the conference was welcomed (Nash, 1998a).

Throughout this decade, the NZASW was divided over professionalisation, the desire to prevent the social work/welfare split that had become established in Australia, and the twin issues of criteria for membership of the Association and the introduction of a system of registration. The decade ended with attention becoming focused on equality issues, including feminism, racism, Te Tiriti o Waitangi, and social work delivery within Department of Social Welfare institutions. An illustration of public interest and concern with the broader social work sector was evident in the inquiry of the Auckland Committee on Racism and Discrimination (ACORD) into allegations of the ill-treatment of residents in Auckland Social Welfare homes. This led to an inquiry and report by the Human Rights Commission that made public its investigation into practices, in particular responses to 'the racial, ethnic and cultural identity of children and young people who were placed in the Homes' (Human Rights Commission, 1982, p. 41).

During this period, a focus on professional identity, credibility, registration and training was evident in the work of the NZSWTC and the NZASW. While the number of social work training providers was limited (Victoria University, University of Auckland, Auckland College of

Education, University of Canterbury and Massey University), there was clear emphasis on expanding the academic and professional foundations of social work practice.

During the 1975–1982 period, broader societal and political influences provided a context characterised by changes in public consciousness (in particular regarding bicultural development, race relations, and concern for specific populations) that would require a response from both social work education programmes and the broader social work profession. With this in mind, attention now moves to the establishment and early development of the Massey University social work programme.

The development of the Massey University social work programme began in 1975 with the appointment of Merv Hancock and Ephra Garrett. Merv Hancock was determined to establish a university degree programme that would include both theory and practice, and have strong links to the profession and social services sector. It was also considered important that the degree be connected to the other programmes offered in the Bachelor of Arts, such as education, psychology and sociology, as this would ensure that social work students were being taught by subject specialists as well as achieving a foundational understanding of these social sciences. Further, the degree was to be accredited internationally, and it was this requirement that was part of the process of constructing a curriculum with a distribution of theory and practice across four years. International colleagues monitored the programme and ensured that graduates could be employed overseas.

Merv had been one of the first cohort of 15 students to complete the highly respected Diploma in Social Sciences at Victoria University. In the 1960s and 1970s, the social work occupation in Aotearoa New Zealand was largely driven by people who had the Victoria University diploma.

Ephra (Te Ātiawa and Ngāti Mutunga, as well as Irish and English descent) had been a Māori Welfare Officer, was the first Māori woman to receive a Diploma of Social Science, and worked as a child psychologist in the mid-1960s. She was appointed as a lecturer in the Education Department at Massey in 1968, and over time had built a Māori dimension into teaching and research in the Departments of Social Work and Psychology. In 1978, Ephra established and ran the university's first Women's Studies paper.

Merv had a clear vision, and wanted to develop a relevant and cutting-edge programme that responded to the needs of practice, but also had the potential to lead and influence practice. This included having a programme that both met international standards and also responded to the unique context of Aotearoa New Zealand. Merv believed that it was important to maintain strong connections with the social work sector, and that staff were encouraged to engage in research, thus contributing to an indigenous construction of practice.

He recognised the importance of having Māori and Pasifika students in the programme, and of respecting their voices within the profession of social work. Together with Ephra Garrett, he was very clear that it was a bicultural programme, and Māori development was integrated from the beginning of the degree. This included critical analysis of how practitioners could embrace and sustain effective ways of working with both tangata whenua and tauiwi. As the years progressed, the curriculum was cemented from a cultural and indigenous perspective, with Ephra playing a central role.

Drawing on Merv Hancock's vast practice experience, a consultative process involving those in the social work occupation was implemented, with meetings held at Massey, and Massey staff attending local fora. There was a significant challenge to develop the programme by early 1975 in order to be submitted for approval at the outset of the university quinquennium plan for the University Grants Committee. Regular meetings were held involving staff members Graeme Fraser (the Professor of Sociology, who originally approached Merv to undertake the development of the social work programme), Merv Hancock, Ephra Garrett and Tom Curran (Department of Psychology). The location of the Social Work Unit within the sociology department was important, as this afforded social work staff the opportunity to work alongside other academics.

The Bachelor of Social Work (BSW) was to have an applied professional focus that would offer opportunities for students to both understand theory and apply knowledge and skills in practice. Massey had a long tradition of providing applied education, and the Bachelor of Technology provided a model upon which the BSW was developed; the four-year degree from the University of Sydney was also considered. The curriculum was broad-based and offered a liberal arts component alongside social work and the social sciences. There was a strong connection between theory and practice, and a connection between social work and social policy. Graeme Fraser noted that this also contributed to the decision to opt for a four-year Bachelor degree when he said:

> We opted for a four-year degree because we really wanted to see partnership between theory and practice, and they were to be contrapuntal themes throughout the four years.

In order to support students undertaking the applied part of the degree, it was recognised that a network of qualified supervisors would be required. This was to involve both the provision of training at Massey University and the establishment of a qualification to recognise the status of these supervisors. Graeme Fraser notes that there were challenges associated with establishing the academic credibility of the social work programme that reflected the experiences of other applied professions. However, the focus of social work (with a broad concern for the provision of support for people with a diverse range of needs) did not fit as easily into the paradigm that existed for other professions, such as nursing (care of unwell people) or teaching (educating children). The successful establishment and expansion of the programme was dependent upon student enrolments, which was the basis for determining the appointment of additional staff.

Merv Hancock recruited staff from around the globe — from England, South Africa and the United States — those he considered could best contribute to the development of the programme; and their different perspectives on social work practice and theory created a dynamic mix. This overseas recruitment continued until Aotearoa New Zealand personnel had acquired the relevant qualifications for teaching social work to take on lecturing positions.

It was acknowledged that it was important for staff to develop not only teaching but also research skills. However, opportunities for staff to undertake research were extremely limited, due to the demands of developing courses, writing study guides, teaching internally, teaching during the vacation period, and supporting colleagues to complete their higher research degrees.

Merv Hancock and Ephra Garrett had a strong sense of aligning social work learning to the community. The university connection to community and to the issues of the community was considered to be critical. There was a significant focus on community development and social justice, and a concern about poverty and the impact of this on the marginalised populations. The teaching of community development approaches in the curriculum remains an important influence to the present day, and emerging perspectives, such as community-led development, are a core component of the teaching and practice of social work.

Wheturangi Walsh-Tapiata, a student of both Merv and Ephra, emphasised the importance of their leadership, passion and contribution when she said:

> Both Merv and Ephra, as the leads in our programme at that time, there was never ever any doubt about their passion and their commitment and their connection with community . . . We were

incredibly lucky to have Merv and Ephra as our original guides, as our original kaitiaki.

Initially, the programme was provided only on campus, with students placed for one day each week with local agencies in Palmerston North; placements were also held over the summer vacation. In 1976, the first students enrolled in the BSW, and second-year papers were taught to students with practice experience and those who had already commenced study towards a Bachelor of Arts. Field placements were completed in years three and four, with concurrent placements (three days each week) during the academic year and 'block' placements (12 weeks) held over the summer vacation. Following a visit from the NZSWTC in May 1979, the BSW was accredited from January 1980.

The provision of an extramural study option was developed in response to a more diverse group of students, including those in rural areas and mature students who were unable to study full-time at the university; this has been a distinguishing characteristic of the Massey programme. Furthermore, the inclusion of a more diverse range of students also enriches the degree, as they bring with them many different perspectives. Many distance students were already employed or working voluntarily in the broader social services, and these students were able to remain in their own communities and apply the different perspectives gained through the social work programme.

Graeme Fraser observed that in the initial years of the degree there was a great deal of diffidence within the wider university community about whether or not extramural study was really university education; the only papers offered by distance were at the 100 and 200 levels. However by 1977/78 the 300-level course was also made available. A feature of the distance programme is attendance in person at contact courses held on the Manawatū campus, based on the importance of face-to-face contact between students and the academic staff.

A feature of the field education experience for students was the establishment of specialist student units that were overseen by supervisors who were also appointed as associate lecturers. The units were located in the Department of Social Welfare, Palmerston North Hospital, Community Health (Palmerston North), and the Department of Justice (Probation).

The broader programme expanded quickly. In 1977, Master of Social Work (MSW) papers were first offered, and in 1980 Roy Bowden became the first MSW graduate; his study examined the position of senior social workers from the Department of Social Welfare. A key finding was that while the participants experienced satisfaction in task performance, they also experienced difficulty in balancing agency requirements with those of their supervisees. In 1979, the Certificate in Social Service Supervision papers were first offered. In 1980, the task-centred approach was adopted as the practice model used for the application of theory to practice, drawing on the work of William Reid and Laura Epstein, whose research suggested that, in a majority of cases, durable change in a client's situation took place in the early stages of a relationship. The system's emphasis on time-limited intervention aimed at alleviating target problems identified by the client was designed to increase the efficacy of social work practice, and to enable clients to exercise a degree of control over the helping process (Reid & Epstein, 1992).

In 1982, Professor Bradford Sheafor, Fulbright Scholar from Colorado State University, was asked to review the social work programme for the Social Work Unit, with particular reference to the relationship between academic requirements and the actual practice of social work in New Zealand (see Chapter 2 for Professor Sheafor's observations). The ongoing success of the Massey social work programme owes much to the work completed in the early years, during which a number of principles were

NEWS RELEASE

Massey University establishes a new Social Work Unit

From the beginning of 1977, Massey University will have a Social Work Unit. Professor G.S. Fraser explained that the Social Work Unit will be an integral part of the Department of Sociology but will function independently for purposes of contact with social work agencies throughout the community and in the general relationship of the University to community welfare programmes.

Mr M.W. Hancock is Senior Lecturer in charge of the Social Work Unit. Mrs Ephra Garrett and another staff member, to be appointed early in 1977, complete the Unit staff.

Since the establishment of the Bachelor of Social Work degree at Massey University introduced in 1976, there has been very considerable student interest. Enrolments in Part I of the degree for 1976 were more in number than had been anticipated. A transitional course was also offered for a group of people to commence Part II of the degree. In 1977 Part III of the degree will be offered.

The first significant steps in offering the Bachelor of Social Work degree on an extramural basis will be taken in 1977 when the first professional paper from Part I of the degree will also be offered. In 1978 it is anticipated that the Part II professional papers will be added to the extramural programme. The majority of papers from the other contributing academic disciplines are already offered by the University on an extramural basis.

The establishment of the Social Work Unit will not only facilitate the development of the new Bachelor of Social Work degree but will permit the development of social welfare research and facilitate the securing of funds for that purpose from the community.

Social work practitioners in the community will be encouraged to take a close interest in the operation of the Social Work Unit and make use of it in support of their interests.

This news release (1976) highlights the success of the programme and intention to create a Social Work Unit. SCHOOL OF SOCIAL WORK

established that are now hallmarks of the programme:
- the relationship between theory and practice
- the linkage between social work and social policy
- a commitment to bicultural practice and Māori development
- a strong connection between the programme and the community
- a commitment to student access to the programme via distance learning.

In addition to establishing the first four-year BSW in Aotearoa New Zealand, postgraduate opportunity was available through the MSW, while the Certificate in Social Service Supervision provided a significant opportunity for professional development for those already in practice. A foundation had been established that would enable the social work programme to engage effectively: within the university system, with the professional development of social work (both locally and internationally), and with the changing requirements of individuals, families and communities.

During the establishment period of the programme, staff were heavily involved in developing and teaching the core curriculum. Notwithstanding the pressures associated with the founding of the Social Work Unit, a number of salient points can be made regarding the contribution of the programme.

The BSW programme addressed the significant need for social work education and training. In 1974, the majority of social workers in Aotearoa New Zealand (405 staff) were employed by the Department of Social Welfare. The hospital boards employed 186 staff, the Department of Justice employed 167 staff, and the Department of Māori Affairs employed 99. Only 17 per cent of the combined staff had a recognised qualification in social work. In 1976, Massey University launched the first four-year social work degree in Aotearoa New Zealand. The first 10 BSW graduates were capped in 1979, followed by 28 in 1980, the numbers of graduates

Academic staff appointments and changes, 1975–1982

- 1975: Merv Hancock and Ephra Garrett appointed to Department of Sociology.
- 1976: The Social Work Unit established; Merv Hancock is appointed as Director.
- 1977: Ian Shirley appointed as a lecturer.
- 1978: Mary Ann Baskerville and Eve Hessey appointed.
  - Associate lecturers and student unit supervisors appointed:
    - Department of Social Welfare — G. Stenton.
    - Palmerston North Hospital — Anne Thompson.
    - Palmerston North Student Unit Community Health — R. A. Clement.
    - Department of Justice (Probation) Student Unit — Murray Short.
- 1979: Rajen Prasad and Randy Herman appointed.
- 1980: Jenny Pilalis appointed.
  - Ian Shirley promoted to senior lecturer.
  - Mike O'Brien appointed.
- 1981: Fiona Fordham and Angie Herman employed as demonstrators.
- 1982: Merv Hancock resigns as Head of Social Work Unit to return to private practice.
  - Mary Nash and Bruce Asher employed as demonstrators.

continued to grow to the extent that the graduate destination survey undertaken from 1979–1983 in 1984 identified 150 graduates.

The 1978 NZASW Biennial Conference was held at Massey University, Palmerston North, on the theme of 'The Disabling Professions'. The keynote speaker was Ivan Illich, an Austrian philosopher and the author of *Deschooling society* and *Medical nemesis*. He argued that powerful professional groups tended to disable the non-professional's ability to think and act for themselves. Illich's address to the conference was considered influential in encouraging an emerging focus on social justice (Nash, 1998a, p. 265). Eve Hessey, along with Professor Graeme Fraser, presented at the conference on 'Small-scale research for practising social workers'.

During the initial years of the degree, staff worked under considerable pressure developing and teaching the programme, and, as noted above, consequently had limited time to conduct research. However, the Department of Social Work staff published articles on a range of themes, with Ian Shirley leading the way with notable contributions on community development. In 1979, his *Planning for community: The mythology of community development and social planning* was published by the Dunmore Press. This was followed in 1982 by *Development tracks: The theory and practice of community development*, which he both contributed to and edited. The significance of the contribution of *Development tracks* was noted by Gavin Rennie in 2006:

> Little of the standing of this work had been written either before
> or since on the theory and practice of community development
> in New Zealand. Twenty-three years on, this book is still read by
> students and teachers of community development.

Ian Shirley also engaged with social policy issues, and along with Paul Spoonley and David Pearson edited *New Zealand: Sociological perspectives*. A focus on the family was maintained by Jenny Pilalis,

This photograph is of the first Bachelor of Social Work graduates and staff outside Wharerata, on Massey's Manawatū campus, April 1979. *Back row, from left:* Robyn Munford, Penny Wood, Louise Auret, Angela Gilbert, Mike Behrens, Ian Shirley, Merv Hancock, Tim McBride, Graeme Fraser, Ephra Garrett. *Middle row:* Eve Hessey, Bruce Asher, Robert Asplin. *Front row:* Keith (Jacko) Jackson, Richard Tocker, Russell Taylor (in absentia Sonya Hunt). **MASSEY UNIVERSITY ARCHIVES**

including commentary on challenges for social workers with family groups, and consumer feedback from short courses in family therapy. Mike O'Brien provided commentary on social values, while Eve Hessey discussed group supervision for social workers.

During the period 1975 to 1982, the social work programme was established at Massey University against a broader political context driven by the shift from rights-based social policy — characterised by the emergence of feminist discourse and growing demands from Māori for both rights and self-determination — to the emergence of neoliberalism — characterised by economic deregulation and the diminution of the welfare state (Stanley-Clarke, 2016). These movements were responding to the paternalism, patriarchy and monoculturalism in society that reflected in Muldoon's dominance and in New Zealand being one of the most regulated societies in the world. Concern about social justice is a hallmark of the social work mandate, and this was reflected in the core characteristics of the social work programme team's engagement with the need for political analysis, recognition of the role of social policy, and a commitment to bicultural practice. As noted previously, concern with establishing the professional and academic foundations of social work practice was evident amongst the limited number of social work providers in Aotearoa New Zealand. The NZASW and the NZSWTC also played influential roles within this development (as ANZASW and subsequent regulatory bodies have continued to do).

At Massey University, much of the focus of the early period concerned the development and accreditation of the social work programme within the university and academia, and in particular the vision of social work as a graduate discipline. A strong connection was established with the social work practice community, where students were able to consolidate theoretical knowledge and develop skills while completing placements.

Ivan Illich, with Graeme Fraser to his right, in 1978. **MASSEY UNIVERSITY ARCHIVES**

The stewardship exercised by the foundation staff set a benchmark against which subsequent programme development and achievement can be considered. The legacy of Merv Hancock, Ephra Garrett and Graeme Fraser continues to influence the current School of Social Work at Massey.

Chapter Two
Consolidating through a period of social and economic transformation, 1983–1992

The period from 1983 to 1992 was marked by the gathering pace of neoliberalism that was to redefine the role of the State, and in particular challenge the welfare approach to social policy. This period was one of social and economic transformation, which began with the decline of the Muldoon years of significant government borrowing to maintain the standard of living within a highly regulated, State-controlled protectionist economy, and ended with an economic and social transformation to a market-led neoliberal country.

A foreshadowing of the transformation to come was Aotearoa New Zealand's first trade agreement, the Closer Economic Relations agreement with Australia, signed in 1983. This agreement was intended to open up market opportunities, streamline processes, reduce costs, and create more certainty and security for companies doing business in both countries. In short, it aimed to create a free market between Australia and Aotearoa New Zealand.

The policies of the Fourth Labour Government, which held office from 1984 until 1990, drove this sea change, breaking with previous Labour ideology regarding the management of the economy and the role of the State. The final years of this period saw the return of a National administration determined to drive home the neoliberal agenda.

The political climate

In 1984, the David Lange-led Labour Party was elected to government, and, on reaching power, was presented by Treasury officials with a financial crisis, and a plan for dealing with it in which the Treasury recommended a radical review of the welfare approach to social policy. The new ideological approach placed responsibility for welfare squarely back with the family and the local community, and was fuelled by the State's need to respond to economic difficulties. The policies of Minister of Finance Roger Douglas (termed 'Rogernomics' by the media) were characterised by market-led restructuring, deregulation and the control of inflation through tight monetary policy, accompanied by a floating exchange rate and reductions in the fiscal deficit.

The Labour Government also pursued an independent foreign policy, which included an anti-nuclear position. This position was strengthened in 1985 when it announced its decision to ban ships that were either nuclear-powered or nuclear-armed. Washington responded by severing intelligence and military ties with New Zealand, and downgraded its political and diplomatic exchanges. Prime Minister David Lange appeared in the widely televised Oxford Union debate, arguing the proposition that 'nuclear weapons are morally indefensible', receiving applause with his reply to an American student: 'Hold your breath just for a moment — I can smell the uranium on it as you lean toward me!'

Then on the evening of 10 July, two explosions ripped through the hull of the Greenpeace flagship *Rainbow Warrior*, which was moored at Marsden Wharf in Auckland, killing a crew member. The ship was preparing to protest against a planned French nuclear test in Mururoa, and the sinking was carried out by members of the French foreign intelligence service. This event engendered a public outcry, and cemented support for the anti-nuclear stance of the government.

In August 1987, the Labour Government was re-elected, following a campaign that emphasised the country had been through economic reform, and that the next three years would focus on social policy. However, disharmony was evident within the Labour caucus, between the Lange and Douglas factions, as a result of Lange wanting to slow down the roll-out of Rogernomics. Roger Douglas resigned from Cabinet in 1988, but was re-elected by the Labour caucus. David Lange viewed this as a lack of confidence in his leadership, and resigned as prime minister (remaining in Parliament until retiring prior to the 1996 general election).

Further evidence of dissent within the Labour Party was evident when Jim Anderton formed the breakaway New Labour Party. Leadership change continued, with Geoffrey Palmer being followed by Mike Moore prior to the 1990 election, which saw the return of a National Party administration.

Jim Bolger became prime minister (a position he held until 1997), and, with Ruth Richardson as finance minister, National announced $1.275 billion worth of social welfare cuts in December 1990. Most benefits were reduced, including the domestic purposes benefit (DPB). The 1991 'Mother of all Budgets' reduced government spending further, and the focus was clearly on individual and family responsibility rather than State responsibility. Other changes in the political landscape were evident in the formation of the Green Party in 1990, and then the Alliance Party in 1991 (comprising New Labour, the Green Party, Mana Motuhake and the Democratic Party — previously Social Credit). Dame Cath Tizard became the first woman governor-general, in December 1990.

The legislative changes between 1983 and 1992 reflected the social transformation of this period within a diverse range of fields, including health, criminal justice, homosexual law reform, public sector restructuring, children, youth and families, and employment relations.

The Area Health Boards Act 1983 resulted in the country's 25 hospital boards eventually being replaced by 14 area health boards with locally elected and appointed board members. Key changes included: population-based funding; decentralisation of the Department of Health's responsibilities to the boards; a move from curative to preventive health services; and emphasis on management and accountability structures for the boards.

Concern at rising imprisonment rates, the perception that the approaches to crime reduction were not working, and the requirement for a more efficient use of resources, together with a desire for greater community involvement in the rehabilitation of offenders, were evident in the findings in the *Report of the Penal Policy Review Committee* of 1981. The quest for effective criminal justice policy was influenced by the 'what works' debate that had been initiated by the work of Martinson (1974) in the United States.

The penal policy review led to the 1985 Criminal Justice Act. This Act gave new directions to courts on sentencing practice, and the scope of community alternatives to imprisonment were broadened; courts were instructed to make use of these provisions for property and other non-serious offences. The Act also provided direction regarding the use of imprisonment for serious violent offending, making this almost mandatory for violent offences punishable by at least five years' imprisonment.

There was at times bitter public and political debate in the mid-1980s during the homosexual law reform campaign. Labour MP Fran Wilde introduced a private member's Bill, the Homosexual Law Reform Bill, with the aim of decriminalising sexual relations between men aged 16 and over. The resultant New Zealand Homosexual Law Reform Act 1986 legalised consensual sex between men aged 16 and older, removing the provisions of the Crimes Act 1961 that criminalised this behaviour.

Significant change to the administration of the state sector were evidenced in, first, the State-Owned Enterprises Act, which resulted in a number of government departments becoming commercially oriented organisations with a stronger emphasis on efficiency and profitability. For example, the Post Office Department was replaced by three state-owned enterprises — New Zealand Post, Telecom and Postbank — with Telecom and Postbank being eventually privatised. The impact of rationalisation in services was felt in many communities where post offices were closed in a drive for efficiency.

The second key piece of legislation was the State Sector Act 1988. This introduced private sector models: notably, chief executives employed on fixed-term contracts replaced permanent heads of departments; compulsory industrial arbitration in the state sector was abolished; and private sector labour relations law was introduced.

Finally, the Public Finance Act 1989 introduced statutory reporting requirements that included both financial and non-financial measures. This reflected a growing interest in the measurement of social performance within the public sector, with an emphasis being placed upon efficiency, effectiveness and accountability in government agencies.

The most influential legislative change of the period for social work was the ground-breaking Children, Young Persons, and Their Families Act 1989, which was introduced to reform the law relating to children and young persons who were in need of care or protection or who offend against the law. There was a particular focus on the wellbeing of children and young persons in relation to their membership of families, whānau, hapū, iwi and family groups. The Act introduced the family group conference as a means of making decisions about a child or young person that did not involve a court hearing. The Act set out procedures for the removal of abused children from their parents' care, making the best interests of the child the first consideration. It also set out procedures for dealing with youth offenders, making arrest and imprisonment interventions a last resort.

In the field of industrial relations, the Employment Contracts Act 1991 aimed to reduce the influence of trade unions by introducing the option of employment negotiations directly between employer and employee via individual agreements rather than collective bargaining. In the same year, the number of unemployed exceeded 200,000 for the first time (up to 11 per cent of the workforce, compared with 4 per cent in 1986).

Concern for individual rights was reflected in the introduction of the Mental Health (Compulsory Assessment and Treatment) Act 1992. The Act established a range of rights that applied as soon as a person became a patient or a proposed patient under the Act. These were the right to: information; respect for cultural identity; an interpreter; treatment; information about treatment; refuse video recording; independent psychiatric advice; legal advice; company; have visitors and to make telephone calls.

There was also a significant change in race relations within Aotearoa New Zealand in this period, with a focus on racism, biculturalism and redress through Te Tiriti o Waitangi. In March 1984, the song 'Poi e' featured for 22 weeks on the bestsellers' chart, four of them at number one. In 1982, Ngoi Pēwhairangi and Dalvanius Prime had written 'Poi e' and two other songs in a single day, but the record companies weren't interested. So Prime decided to form his own label, Maui Records, and recorded 'Poi e' in late 1983. The Pātea Māori Club provided the vocals above a funky rhythm that featured bass, Linn drums and a synthesiser. Commercial radio barely played the song until a story on TVNZ's *Eyewitness News* gave it its big break. This is an example of attitudes at the time, and the resilience of Māori to challenge these. In 1985, The Treaty of Waitangi Act was amended to enable the Waitangi Tribunal to hear claims that went back to 1840. This period also saw the recognition of te reo Māori, and the establishment of the Treaty of Waitangi Policy Unit.

Youth detention centres came under question in the 1980s, with borstals closing in 1981. The education approach in these centres was mostly unsuccessful, and could not replace families as caregivers; recidivism was high, and abuse by staff an issue. Māori children were often placed in State care for minor wrongdoings.

Concern with racism was evident in the report *Institutional racism in the Department of Social Welfare*, which was published in 1985 by the Women Against Racism Action Group, a group of nine women employed by the Department of Social Welfare in Auckland (Berridge et al., 1985). The report concluded that the ethnic composition of staff was dominated by Pākehā; that the recruitment, selection and promotion of staff was culturally biased in favour of Pākehā applicants; that staff training was monocultural, and ignored the issue of personal and institutional racism; and that the physical environment of the department was monocultural and alienating to Māori consumers.

This growing awareness of institutional racism within the then Department of Social Welfare culminated in *Pūao-te-Āta-tū — The daybreak report*, which was written in 1988 by the Ministerial Advisory Committee on a Māori Perspective, chaired by John Rangihau, for the Department of Social Welfare. This report provided a commentary and enquiry into racism within New Zealand society, and in particular within the Department of Social Welfare. It contained a detailed account of New Zealand's history, focusing on the interactions between the indigenous Māori people and the British settlers. The report detailed the harm done to the Māori people and culture, and the effects that this had on the wellbeing and socioeconomic status of Māori. Recommendations were given with regard to Aotearoa New Zealand becoming an anti-racist society and achieving social equality for Māori. The report was influential in the drafting of the Children, Young Persons, and Their Families Act 1989.

In 1988, Moana Jackson published *He whaipaanga hou, The Māori and the criminal justice system: A new perspective*. In it, he suggested that the process of colonisation had contributed to widening the socioeconomic disparities between Māori and non-Māori, and was directly associated with the denigration of Māori culture. The consequences of colonisation were shown to be associated with an increase in Māori vulnerability towards crime. Māori were also more likely to enter the criminal justice system due to systemic racism (i.e. policing bias and sentencing) (Maynard, Coebergh, Anstiss, Bakker, & Huriwai, 1999).

The Māori Language Act, which came into force on 1 August 1987, made te reo Māori an official language of New Zealand. Te Komihana Mo Te Reo Māori — the Māori Language Commission — was established to promote the use of Māori as a living language and an ordinary means of communication.

In 1988, the Treaty of Waitangi Policy Unit was formed within the Department of Justice. Its role was to advise on policy, and assist in any negotiations and litigation involving Māori claims through the courts and to the Waitangi Tribunal. Major Treaty settlements with Māori claimants were reached from 1992. In that year, a settlement on commercial fisheries was signed, vesting $170 million with the Waitangi Fisheries Commission to enable it to buy 50 per cent of Sealord Products Ltd, a large Nelson-based fishing company.

Later in this period, several noteworthy events reflected both the influence of neoliberalism policy and a growing social consciousness regarding individual rights. The first occurred in June 1987, when *Metro* magazine published an article by Sandra Coney and Phillida Bunkle entitled 'An unfortunate experiment'. This article raised serious questions about the treatment of cervical cancer patients at National Women's Hospital, Auckland. Silvia Cartwright, an Auckland District Court judge, was appointed to conduct an inquiry into the allegations. The subsequent Cartwright Report was released on 5 August 1988, and the recommendations led to the establishment of a national, centrally coordinated cervical cancer screening programme and to major improvements to the process for securing the informed consent of patients.

The stockmarket crash on 20 October 1987 was another significant event, which resulted in the value of New Zealand shares being reduced by billions within weeks. Companies that had over-extended themselves became insolvent, affecting many investors.

In 1988, three influential reports — focusing on social policy, health and education, respectively — were released. The first of these was by the Royal Commission on Social Policy, whose five-volume report, among other things, expressed a bicultural vision for the public services in New Zealand. The Commission had been established to undertake a nationwide inquiry in order to set social policy goals and to recommend what action was required to make New Zealand a more fair and just society. The report was received unevenly. For example, there was criticism of a failure to recognise poverty as a deciding theme of social policy, and also that the report failed to provide a coherent framework for addressing social issues. In contrast, it was thought that the report had identified core values held by New Zealanders, and extended the boundaries regarding which policy areas should be considered when making social policy (Barnes & Harris, 2011).

The second report was the 'Gibbs Report', *Unshackling the hospitals,* on 'options for the reorganisation of the public hospital system' (Gibbs, 1988). The focus of this report was on how to improve equity, access, responsiveness and efficiency in New Zealand public hospitals. The report formed the basis for the health reforms initiated by the National Government in the 1990s.

The third report, the 'Picot Report', *Administering for excellence: Effective administration in education,* on the Department of Education, described the department as 'inefficient and unresponsive'. It was recommended that it be replaced by a Ministry of Education, and that regional education boards be abolished. It was proposed that schools become self-managing, controlled by locally elected boards of trustees, which would be responsible for learning outcomes, budgeting and the employment of teachers. The government's response, *Tomorrow's schools*, in the main accepted the recommendations of the Picot Report. There was a mixed response to the reforms, however. On the one hand were those who argued that the reforms were largely driven by neoliberal ideology, while on the other hand there were those who accepted the assertion that the old education structures were both outdated and inflexible.

The United Nations Convention on the Rights of Children (UNCROC), a comprehensive human rights treaty that enshrined specific children's rights in international law, was signed in 1990 and ratified in 1993. Adopted by the United Nations in 1989, UNCROC defined universal principles and standards for the status and treatment of children worldwide. The rights included civil, political, economic, social and cultural rights, and the convention set out in detail what every child needed to have a safe, happy and fulfilled childhood. As a signatory, the Aotearoa New Zealand government was required to report every five years to United Nations on its progress in relation to the rights of children.

A further example of the influence of neoliberalism was the intro-duction of the Student Loan Scheme Act 1992. This replaced the previous system of governmental bursaries and grants that did not require repayment. The change was attributed to a combination of increased demand and the growth of the tertiary education sector, which made the previous approach no longer feasible.

This review highlights the role of the Labour Party in promoting: economic policy characterised by market-led restructuring and deregulation; a change in the structure and role of the State, with an emphasis on cost, efficiency and effectiveness; and a reduction in the role of the State regarding public welfare. The tensions generated by this shift from the previous core ideology of Labour eventually resulted in a fractured party, and the return of a National administration that was to build on the foundations that had been established by Labour. Labour's nuclear-free stance established a government position that has continued to be endorsed by the electorate. Legislative and policy changes in health, education, criminal justice and social welfare continued to reflect a drive to improve effectiveness, responsiveness and efficiency in the delivery of State-funded services. A willingness to address concerns regarding racism within government organisations was evident in *Pūao-te-Āta-tū — The daybreak report*, and the subsequent changes embraced within the Children, Young Persons, and Their Families Act 1989 were seen to provide the opportunity for a service that would be more responsive to Māori. From this broad contextual overview, we now turn to the development of social work.

The development of social work

A focus on professionalism and biculturalism in social work can be seen in a range of developments between 1983 and 1992.

At the start of this period, there was government interest through a ministerial request in 1983 for a report on the training needs of community workers, and in 1984 the establishment of a ministerial committee to review the New Zealand Social Work Training Council (NZSWTC). The subsequent review report, released in 1986 and authored by Merv Hancock, resulted in the disestablishment of the NZSWTC and the establishment of the New Zealand Council for Education and Training in the Social Services (NZCETSS) (Nash, 1998a).

NZCETSS was chaired by Professor Ian Shirley, and the initial Director was Dr Robyn Munford. NZCETSS issued the National Guideline for Accreditation and Course Approval for Social Service Courses in 1991 (NZCETSS, 1991), and *Kahukura*, a vision for a bicultural curriculum

(Benton, Benton, Croft, & Waaka, 1991). In 1984, arguments were advanced in *New Zealand social work* for indigenous models, biculturalism, Māori rights and confronting racism, and NZASW formed a working party on racism. In the same year the Auckland Hospital Board adopted the stance of not hiring social workers without professional qualifications (this included graduates of the Auckland College of Education, as this programme was not recognised as meeting the required competency standards) (Nash, 1998a).

The 1986 NZASW Biennial Conference at Tūrangawaewae Marae, Ngāruawāhia, was a watershed conference for the association. The conference theme was 'Social work in a changing world'. Race Relations Conciliator Wally Hirsh was the opening speaker. The future structure of the association was then discussed, and a proposal that there be a Māori and Pākehā (later, Manuhiri; then Tauiwi) caucus was eventually carried. Sarah Fraser became President of the Pākehā caucus, and Rahera Ohia became President of the Māori caucus; both were graduates of the BSW programme at Massey University. In 1988, the NZASW reaffirmed a commitment to the Treaty of Waitangi by resolving to include the Treaty in its constitution, and work commenced on a Bicultural Code of Practice to be part of the association's Code of Ethics (Nash, 1998a).

A growing division between social work and community work was also becoming apparent, with the first hui of the Aotearoa Community Workers Association being held in Nelson in 1988, with Massey University graduate and staff member Wendy Craig involved in the hui and subsequent developments.

Other developments within the local profession included the commencement of a competency assessment process for full membership of the NZASW in 1990; publication of accreditation guidelines for social work courses by the NZCETSS in 1991; and the launching of a competency programme by the New Zealand Children and Young Persons Service (NZCYPS). A critical note regarding the professionalism of social work was sounded in the report of the Ministerial Review Team to the Minister of Social Welfare, regarding the Children, Young Persons, and Their Families Act 1989. The review was chaired by retired High Court Justice Ken Mason, and noted the low level of qualified social workers in the then Department of Social Welfare. Another recommendation was a call for mandatory reporting of incidents involving child abuse. The mandatory reporting recommendation was the subject of much debate within the profession in the early 1990s.

In 1992, in line with the overarching reorganisation of state sector organisations, the Department of Social Welfare was restructured into business units: New Zealand Income Support Service; New Zealand Children and Young Persons Service; New Zealand Community Funding Agency; the Social Policy Agency; and the Corporate Office.

Another feature of the broader social work context in Aotearoa New Zealand during this period was the ongoing debate regarding the construction of social work as a profession. This was evidenced in concern with curriculum, training, qualifications and accountability. During this period, formal social work education was mostly provided by the Auckland College of Education, Massey University, the University of Canterbury, the University of Otago and Victoria University of Wellington.

Internationally, social work continued to be influenced by the empirical practice movement, the development of the ecological-systems perspective, and critiques from empowerment theories. The influence of positivism was evident in the emergence of the empirical practice movement, which sought to build a scientific, credible and politically acceptable knowledge base for the social work profession. In this tradition, the primary purpose of social work knowledge is to provide guidance for accurate assessment, diagnosis and problem-solving activities (Payne, 1991; Scott, 1990; Trotter, 1999).

Schön (1995) identifies 'technical-rationality' as a dominant epistemology for professional practice that is reliant on the scientific paradigm. In this model, the professional practitioner should first acquire practice knowledge that is scientifically derived before developing skills of knowledge application. The application of practice skills involves instrumental problem-solving techniques that have been validated through scientific theory and research (Schön, 1995). This approach can be seen to be congruent with the neoliberal emphasis on validity and cost-effectiveness that was evident in contemporary government policies in health, care and protection, and corrections.

The ecological-systems perspective, which retains currency today, presents a framework that enables practitioners and clients to think about the reciprocal relationships between people and their environment. Concepts taken from ecological and systems theories act as a metaphor that assists social workers to conceptualise the transactions between person and environment. The developing person is seen as an active participant who changes, restructures and finds a mutual accommodation with their environment (O'Donoghue & Maidment, 2005).

The critique from empowerment theories was derived from the significant strides being made in identifying, naming and trying to mitigate oppression, and considerable efforts were also being made in the empowerment of people from marginalised groups. In this period, there was a convergence of social, political and economic movements, such as indigenous people's rights, the women's movement, the black power movement and the gay rights movement. Liberation theories from theology, political science, psychology and economics contributed to the synthesis that became the social work empowerment approach. Lee (1996) also attributes the integration of Paulo Freire's critical approach into social work theory as key to the development of the social work empowerment approach.

Massey Social Work Unit Newsletter

First Edition   *March 1983*

We will be sending you our Newsletter three times in 1983 - please post it where all staff can see it. Invitations to Supervisors Seminars and Administrators Conferences will be included.

MERVYN HANCOCK, MA, Dip.Soc.Sci. resigned as Director of our Social Work Unit at the end of 1982. He set up the BSW and MSW degrees which are unique in New Zealand and meet international standards. The BSW programme which he set up, addresses itself to all forms of social work, including not only case work and family work but also social policy, social work management and adminis- tration, community work and cross-cultural issues in social work policy and practice.

Perhaps one of the most forward thinking parts of the programme has been the emphasis on research on both the part of staff and students. This research emphasis is vital to making practice relevant to the needs of the community. The curriculum of the BSW programme demonstrates Merv's imagination and drive and his capacity to be an innovator and a pioneer.

Merv came to Massey with a wealth of experience as a social worker both in his years in the Child Welfare Division and his six years in private practice as a human relationships counsellor and a welfare consultant. He was in the first group of social workers to receive a professional training in N.Z. in 1951/52 at Victoria University, and he helped write the constitution of the N.Z. Association of Social Workers nearly twenty years ago.

The staff of the Social Work Unit wish him well and admire his initiative in going back into private practice.

So, Merv, your Social Work Unit colleagues say 'thank you' for your inspiration and hard work, and 'thank you' for the contribution you are making to social work practice in N.Z. by having set up a unit which is graduating imaginative, pioneering and well-educated social workers, well-educated for the 1980's and beyond and not just for to-day.

> The Social Work Unit Staff are holding a special function in honour of Merv on the 30th of March - an invitation to all friends and colleagues on page 3.

The *Massey Social Work Unit Newsletter* (first edition, March 1983), highlighting Merv Hancock's resignation. **SCHOOL OF SOCIAL WORK**

Merv Hancock resigned from Massey University at the end of 1982 in order to return to private practice, and Ian Shirley was appointed as Director of the Social Work Unit from January 1983. The platform that had been established by Merv and his colleagues — with an emphasis on the integration of theory and practice, the role of social policy, and a commitment to biculturalism — continued to influence the development of the social work programme, and this period was clearly one in which the academic portfolio and programme was consolidated within the university. The university itself was in transition, with the Vice-Chancellor Sir Alan Stewart retiring and Dr Neil Waters taking over from February 1983.

As noted in Chapter 1, in 1982 Fulbright Scholar Professor Bradford Sheafor was asked to review the university's social work programme, in particular the relationship between academic requirements and the actual practice of social work in New Zealand. Professor Sheafor's resultant report rated Massey University's social work programme among the finest he had reviewed.

A primary purpose of the review was to guide decisions on curriculum development for the BSW. The content validation method used examined curriculum, while also assessing the relevance of that curriculum to social work practice in various job settings. The results showed a very strong correlation between curriculum content and the content of social work jobs. One area for improvement, however, related to fieldwork placements, which were reduced from four to three. The first block placement at the end of part two was retained, and, while the concurrent year-three placement was deleted, the year-three block placement was retained. The fourth-year placement extended to an in-depth concurrent placement of 52 days (up 22 days from the previous 30 days). The advantage of the changes was a clear developmental focus for each placement, and greater depth and articulation of the curriculum. These changes included the integrated practice approach being introduced in 1984 into the third year of the BSW.

The commitment to providing the opportunity for ongoing professional development to practitioners in the field saw the Certificate in Social Service Supervision being offered extramurally in 1984, with 57 students enrolled. The course consisted of papers on social and community work practice, management in social welfare services, social welfare research, learning issues in social service development, and theory and process in supervision, including a practicum. A Diploma in Welfare Administration was also offered, with 12 enrolments. In 1986, a Diploma in Social Sciences (Welfare, Development and Social Work) commenced, with 45 students enrolled extramurally.

The integrated framework for practice developed by Dr Rajen Prasad (1986) quickly became a hallmark of the Massey University social work programme. The framework emerged from Dr Prasad's research and training of social workers as a heuristic device to assist practitioners to think critically about the knowledge that informs their knowing, decision-making and action in social and community work practice. It promoted informed and intentional social work practice, and was a means through which the practitioner could describe, explain, scrutinise, evaluate and justify their assessment of, and intervention with, clients.

The framework orientated practitioners to critically reflect on themselves as social workers whose vision and imagination was influenced by the set of lenses they used to make sense of the situation, the problems presented and the social work task. It is through this set of lenses that they developed the interpretive understanding that influences how they perceived and related both to and with the client in the reality of social work practice. In other words, integrated practice provided a frame for organising and conceptualising social work practice events, as well as inviting the practitioner to engage in an ongoing process of critical action-reflection through which they evaluated what informed and influenced them as a social worker engaged in practice.

In addition, the framework required the practitioner to address conditions that disenfranchised people, as well as personal troubles and public issues. It recognised that there was no standard approach to social work practice, and avoided imposing one by accepting that different practitioners began from varying philosophical positions and, likewise, would choose to emphasise particular theoretical orientations and models (Prasad, 1993).

The programme's strength was emphasised in a graduate destination survey of BSW graduates from 1979 to 1983. This survey of 150 graduates had a 70 per cent response rate, with 105 respondents. The majority of graduates had secured a social work position of their preference, with over 50 per cent completing only one job application. The graduates were employed as follows: hospital boards 42 per cent; voluntary or religious agencies 20 per cent; Department of Social Welfare 14 per cent; Probation 4 per cent; with 6 per cent in social work overseas. Eleven per cent were not employed in social work, with 11 graduates not in paid employment (7 of this 11 were involved in voluntary social work activities). Fifteen graduates were in non-social work positions by choice, while three were enrolled in a graduate social work programme.

Over this period, the staff were making both an international and a local impact. Ian Shirley, for example, was overseas for most of 1984, attached to the Faculty of Social Sciences at the University of Kent and working in areas of social policy, social planning and community development. From August to November, he was at the Ecumenical Institute for Development of Peoples in Paris, and was invited to write a publication on the theory and practice of community development with particular reference to New Zealand. That same year, Roy Bowden was accepted as a member of the New Zealand Association of Psychotherapists and Counsellors. Rajen Prasad had a sabbatical in the United States in 1986, and contributed to training American foster care workers.

It was also a period in which the qualification base of the staff was strengthened, with Ian Shirley and Rajen Prasad both completing their

PhDs in 1986. Ian Shirley was appointed to the foundation Chair in Social Policy and Social Work at Massey University in the same year. Other staff who completed doctoral degrees in this period were Angie Barretta-Herman, Wendy Craig and Michael O'Brien.

Massey University is arguably a forerunner of Māori social work policy and practice. The Māori Renaissance movement of the early to mid-1980s had a pronounced impact on social work practice and education. Māori students became aware of what was missing from the curriculum, and were active in expressing the need to replace imported practice models with those developed in Aotearoa New Zealand. Leland Ruwhiu acknowledged the legitimacy provided by the programme to explore the tenets of indigenous social work, both in his time as a student and later when he joined the staff in 1991. For Leland, the watershed moment for the Aotearoa New Zealand Association of Social Workers was the meeting at Ngāruawāhia in 1986 which resulted in the formation of a Māori caucus.

In 1988, the Social Work and Social Policy Unit became the Department of Social Policy and Social Work (separate from Sociology), with Professor Ian Shirley as Head of Department. The academic portfolio of this new department was comprehensive and included:

- Certificate in Social and Community Work
- Certificate in Social Service Supervision
- Bachelor of Social Work
- Diploma in Social Science (Social Policy and Social Work)
- Master of Social Work or Master of Philosophy
- Doctor of Philosophy.

This academic portfolio provided pathways for students to gain qualifications at different levels. For example, the Certificate in Social and Community Work enabled adult-entry students who had never undertaken university study, but who worked in the field, to obtain a foundation certificate. Many of these students would later go on, having developed their competence, to complete the Bachelor of Social Work. The Diploma in Social Science (Social Policy and Social Work) provided a professional social work qualification for the practising social worker who had a degree in another field. The advanced research degrees provided the basis by which staff and practitioners could add and further develop knowledge in policy and practice.

In June 1989, a reunion was held to celebrate the 10-year anniversary of the first graduates, with 80 attending an afternoon tea followed by a formal dinner. Special guests were the Kai Iwi people, who had hosted students on their marae noho. By 1989, the programme had produced 300 graduates. Later that year, Ephra Garrett, the only remaining foundation staff member, retired from the department. Ephra was aptly described as the social work midwife. She had contributed 14 years to the social work programme. Ephra Garrett was awarded an Honorary Doctorate, DLitt (Hons Causa) on 2 December 1993.

Overall, this period resulted in the further development and consolidation of the programme, with the Sheafor Report reflecting positively on the work of the foundation staff. Programme offerings were extended, and now ranged from certificate courses to the PhD. A number of staff completed their PhDs, reflecting a commitment to academic excellence and research. The programme was well established in its own department, with a well-respected foundation professor in Ian Shirley.

From 1983 to 1992, staff, students and alumni made increasing contributions to the broader development of social work practice in Aotearoa New Zealand, via research, publications, and participation in projects and associations (for example, NZASW and NZCETSS).

Nga wawata o te iwi Maori
— A MAORI PERSPECTIVE

Students on marae

Mr Garry Christensen (right) gives a hongi of greeting to Massey University lecturer Mr Merv. Hancock to welcome him to the Kai Iwi marae.

Behind them Mrs Agnes Bennett gives a similar greeting to Massey University's Ms Ephra Garrett (left).

The lecturers brought 47 second-year students to the marae for four days to learn something of the history and customs of the Ngarauru and experience marae life at first hand as part of their studies toward a Bachelor of Social Work degree.

The visitors also learned elementary flaxcraft and Maori language basics. Field trips were taken to the Wanganui Regional Museum, Bushy Park and Anzac remembrance services in Moutoa Gardens before the students returned to Palmerston North yesterday.

Merv Hancock and Ephra Garrett lead students on a visit to Kai Iwi Marae (date unknown). They are being welcomed by Garry Christensen and Agnes Bennett.

SCHOOL OF SOCIAL WORK

Academic staff appointments and changes, 1983–1992

- 1983: Ian Shirley appointed Director of the Social Work Unit.
  - Roy Bowden appointed as a lecturer.
  - Angie Barretta-Herman appointed as a junior lecturer.
- 1984: Ephra Garrett was Acting Director of the Social Work Unit.
  - Randy and Angie Barretta-Herman were in the United States from July.
  - Mary Nash resigned tutor position.
  - Jane Brook appointed as a tutor.
  - Kuresa Faleseuga appointed Student Unit supervisor, Kohitere.
  - Carol Travers appointed Student Unit supervisor Palmerston North Hospital.
  - Murray Cree appointed Student Unit supervisor Palmerston North Hospital.
- 1985: Bruce Asher and Angie Barretta-Herman both enrolled in PhDs.
  - Associate lecturers Les Atkins, Mike Behrens (lawyers), Gary Cockburn (Department of Social Welfare), Angela Gilbert (Palmerston North Hospital) and Bernie Marra (Probation).
- 1986: Jane Brook left as a tutor.
  - Mary Nash rejoined as a tutor.
  - Bruce Asher left to take up a position as a research officer in the Department of Justice.
  - Dave Robinson replaced Bernie Marra as Student Unit supervisor at Probation.

- Jackie Sayers took over as supervisor in the Community Health Student Unit from Murray Cree, who departed for a teaching position in social policy in Tasmania.
- Wendy Craig commenced work in the Student Unit.
- 1987: John Pratt and Vapi Kupenga appointed.
- 1988: Angie Barretta-Herman and Celia Briar appointed lecturers.
- 1989: Paul Close and Mark Tisdall joined the department.
  - Ephra Garrett retired from the department.
- 1990: Christine Cheyne started in the department.
- 1991: Robyn Munford appointed as a lecturer.
  - Associate Professor Andrew Trlin, Kuresa Tiumalu-Faleseuga and Leland Ruwhiu joined the department.
- 1992: Lareen Cooper, Wheturangi Walsh-Tapiata, Gwen Ellis and Richard Shaw joined the department.

In 1985, Roy Bowden and Mary Ann Baskerville contributed to the development of the NZSWTC Supervision resource package. As mentioned in Chapter 1, in 1986 Sarah Fraser became President of the NZASW Pākehā caucus and Rahera Ohia became President of the Māori caucus; they were both graduates of the BSW programme. Jenny Blagdon (Mental Health Social Worker) served as the President of the NZASW from 1990 to 1991, and Robyn Munford served as Director of the NZCETSS from 1988 to 1991. A Massey University editorial collective and members of the Manawatū Branch of ANZASW assumed responsibility for editing *Social Work Review* in 1991. This group included Carole Adamson, Lareen Cooper, Gwen Ellis, Robyn Munford, Mary Nash, Mike O'Brien, Rajen Prasad, Lesley Reid, Jackie Sayers, Richard Shaw and Mark Tisdall.

Department of Social Work staff publications and theses during this period covered a range of themes. In 1983, Randy Herman submitted a Master of Social Work (MSW) thesis on 'Formal and informal support systems in a rural town and county report of the research on mental health in Dannevirke borough and county'. In the same year, Wendy Craig published *A community work perspective*. In 1985, while completing her PhD, Robyn Munford commenced her significant contribution to the disability field of practice with a publication in *New Zealand Social Work*. Robyn's doctoral dissertation was completed in 1989: 'The hidden costs of caring women who care for people with intellectual disabilities'. Rajen Prasad's focus on foster care resulted in his 1986 doctoral dissertation: 'Transitions in foster care: The development of training programmes for foster care workers'. This thesis provided the foundation for a series of publications with American Foster Care Resources Inc. These publications addressed theoretical frameworks, practice principles and foster care training.

The programme's strong emphasis on social policy continued to be reflected in publications by Ian Shirley, Mike O'Brien and Christine Cheyne. In 1986, Ian Shirley completed his doctoral dissertation 'Social practice within a capitalist state'. This thesis set aside conventional occupational distinctions between scientists, administrators and managers, in an examination of social practice within a capitalist state.

The establishment of the social work programme within the Department of Sociology continued to be reflected in a range of publications, including: *Alternatives: Socialist essays for the 1980s* (1986) edited by Steve Maharey and Mike O'Brien; and *New Zealand society: A sociological introduction* (1990) edited by Paul Spoonley, David Pearson and Ian Shirley.

In 1987, Mary Nash completed her MSW thesis on 'Women and social work: A study of feminist social work student placements'. In 1990, Angie Barretta-Herman's doctoral dissertation addressed 'The restructuring of the Department of Social Welfare and implications for social work

Helen Simmons (past student and staff member), husband Mike Delany and children at her Bachelor of Social Work graduation in 1992. Helen's picture and story were published in the *Manawatu Standard* because she completed the BSW over 16 years part-time. She has since gone on to complete a Master of Philosophy (Social Work), focusing on the role of spirituality in supervision.

MANAWATU STANDARD

practice, 1986–1988' (1990b). This exploratory study analysed changes in the practice of social work in the Department of Social Welfare which occurred as a consequence of the department's restructuring in 1986. The thesis found that the department's role became increasingly concerned with funding, monitoring and evaluating services.

Biculturalism and the needs of Māori were shown to be critical factors in these shifts. The practice of social work within the Department of Social Welfare also became more limited and more specialised, and its professional identity was altered by the changed organisational emphasis and the requirements of the department.

Wendy Craig submitted her doctoral dissertation in 1991: 'From rocking the cradle to rocking the system: Women, community work and social change in Aotearoa'. The dissertation explored women's involvement in community work in Aotearoa and argued that women's significant contributions to community work have been hidden, devalued or ignored in mainstream writing and teaching. This research was seen as a celebration of women's experiences and knowledge of community work in Aotearoa, and enabled other women community workers to use the research to reflect on their own work.

Michael O'Brien's doctoral thesis (1991), entitled 'The problem of poverty ideology, the state and the 1972 Royal Commission on Social Security', was an important social policy thesis. In this study he critically examined and reviewed the Royal Commission report and the ideological perspective of poverty within it. This thesis still has direct relevance for the current debates about poverty in Aotearoa New Zealand.

A range of other professional issues were engaged that provided a focus on the development of social work:

- Angie Barretta-Herman offered commentary on issues concerning management and administration, including: practising within a bureaucracy (1983); women social work managers (Barretta-Herman & Cruse, 1989); and the effective staff meeting (1990a).

- Ian Shirley maintained a focus on employment/unemployment, contributing in journals and edited books, and in 1990 co-authoring the text *Unemployment in New Zealand* (Shirley, Easton, Briar, & Chatterjee, 1990).
- In 1992, Andrew Trlin and Paul Spoonley edited and contributed in *New Zealand and international migration: A digest and bibliography*. This was the second in a series of five publications between 1986 and 2010.

Staff supervised two Master in Social Policy theses and nine Master of Social Work/Master of Philosophy theses to completion during this period. The policy theses engaged employment issues concerning equal employment opportunities and job creation schemes.

The Master of Social Work/Master of Philosophy theses included an interest in professional development touching on the demise of the New Zealand Social Work Training Council, a model of social work practice, and in-service social work education. Other topics included a study of discrimination and equal employment opportunities policy in the state sector, women survivors of sexual abuse identification and disclosure, social work supervision as a political function, and New Zealand Labour Party 1987 social policy debate.

Both alumni and students contributed to the development of social work discourse in Aotearoa New Zealand by publishing in the NZASW journal. A diverse range of topics was engaged, including supervision in social work; a Māori perspective on social work training in Aotearoa; violence as an occupational hazard for social workers; and social work practice with gay men with HIV/Aids. Special mention can be made of contributions by Ken McMaster in the field of working with angry and aggressive men. In 1984, he co-published a journal article on an anger management course for aggressive men, followed by two texts: *A private affair? Stopping men's violence to women* (McMaster & Swain, 1989), and *Feeling angry, playing fair: A guide to change* (McMaster, 1992).

The broader political and social context from 1983 to 1992 was shaped by the emergence and dominance of the neoliberal ideology and policy that was unleashed by the Labour Party. Ultimately the Labour administration was to fall apart due to the tensions generated by this shift in position. The drive to improve the effectiveness, responsiveness and efficiency of state services, including those concerned with social welfare, heralded an era where evidence-based policy and interventions would have a significant impact on social work practice.

Discontent with racism in the social services led to reports such as *Pūao-te-Āta-tū — The daybreak report*, which provided the impetus to review core government services that could offer the prospect of greater responsiveness to Māori. The challenge, as with all policy change, would rest in how the new perspectives would be implemented in practice. Social work programmes were also challenged to respond to the needs of Māori students, and to support the development of indigenous approaches to social work.

Concern with the professionalisation of social work continued, with debate continuing regarding curriculum, training, qualifications and accountability. The social work programme both grew and was consolidated within Massey University, with the establishment of its own department and foundation Professor in Social Policy and Social Work, an increased academic portfolio, and a stronger impact by way of research and publications. This included contributions from students, alumni and staff.

Chapter Three
Expansion and development in a period of reform, 1993–2000

The period from 1993 to 2000 was characterised by the continuation of the scaling back of the State and the application of managerialism in the social services. Concern with the status of social work as a profession remained a dominant discourse, and the Massey University social work programme expanded its offerings in three locations. In this section, changes in government, legislation and policy, bicultural development and social issues are explored.

The political climate

There were important changes both in how the country was governed and in its political parties during this period. In 1993, Winston Peters, the MP for Tauranga and former Minister of Māori Affairs, left the National Party, arguing that National had broken election promises about the economy and an extra tax on the elderly. He won the Tauranga by-election as an independent MP, and then founded the New Zealand First party, which contested New Zealand's last first-past-the-post general election in 1993, holding the Tauranga seat and also winning the Northern Māori seat. Also in 1993, a referendum was held on the preferred method of voting, with a 53.9 per cent majority voting to change to the mixed member proportional (MMP) voting system, which was introduced at the 1996 general election.

The first MMP election was held in 1996, with the National Party returning to government in coalition with New Zealand First. MMP was to result in increased Māori and minority group representation, which opened up new opportunities for marginalised populations to have a voice in the political system. It also created a new political dynamic: coalition, which differed markedly from the previously longstanding model of single-party government. In 1997, Jim Bolger resigned as prime minister after losing the support of the National Party caucus, and was replaced by New Zealand's first woman prime minister, Jenny Shipley. The following year saw the dissolution of the National–New Zealand First Coalition Government, leaving the Jenny Shipley-led National Party as a minority government.

In 1999, Helen Clark's Fifth Labour Government was sworn in without a clear parliamentary majority — a situation that would exist over its following three terms in office. This required Labour to govern with support from one or more minor parties, resulting in policy concessions; for example, the establishing of Kiwibank was promoted by the Alliance Party. Significantly, the Labour Government lacked both the ability and the political will to redress the previous changes made under the name of 'Rogernomics'.

Legislative changes for the further restructuring of the public service were accompanied by Acts which embraced a range of issues, including human rights, health and disability, government responsibility, domestic violence, early childhood education, child welfare and employment relations.

The ongoing restructuring and reform of public services began in health, with the area health boards becoming 23 Crown Health Enterprises (CHEs), which were structured as for-profit organisations subject to company law in July 1993. They were later reconfigured in 1997 as Hospital and Health Services and became not-for-profit Crown-owned companies.

A similar restructuring occurred in the area of welfare, with the

Department of Work and Income (branded as 'Work and Income New Zealand' or 'WINZ') being established by the merger of Income Support with the New Zealand Employment Service, Community Employment Group and Local Employment Co-ordination. At the same time, the housing policy function of the Ministry of Housing was transferred to the Social Policy Agency of the Department of Social Welfare. By 1996, 'new managerialism' was at its height in the public sector, and was clearly exposed and critiqued in the book *Public management: The New Zealand model* by Jonathan Boston, John Martin, June Pallot and Pat Walsh.

The Human Rights Act 1993 deals mainly with the right to be free from discrimination and to be treated fairly and equally. It also sets out the role of the Human Rights Commission, which has the power to resolve disputes relating to unlawful discrimination.

The Privacy Act 1993 was enacted to promote and protect individual privacy. The Act had principles on the collection, use and disclosure of information relating to individuals, and access by individuals to information held about them.

The following year saw the passing of the Health and Disability Commissioner Act 1994, whose purpose was set out in Section 6: '*to promote and protect the rights of health consumers and disability services consumers, and, to that end, to facilitate the fair, simple, speedy, and efficient resolution of complaints relating to infringements of those rights*'. The Code of Health and Disability Services Consumers' Rights was a regulation under this Act. The Code granted a number of rights to all consumers of health and disability services in New Zealand, and placed corresponding obligations on the providers of those services.

Concern with responsible government was the focus of the Fiscal Responsibility Act 1994, which aimed to improve fiscal policy by specifying principles of responsible fiscal management and strengthening reporting requirements. Governments were required to follow a legislated set of principles and publicly assess their fiscal policies against these principles.

In particular, the Act required the government to reduce total Crown debt to prudent levels.

The Domestic Violence Act 1995 recognised that domestic violence in all its forms was unacceptable behaviour, and was passed with the aim of reducing and preventing violence in domestic relationships. Protection of victims was strengthened through the introduction of protection orders and the police safety order.

In 1996, *Te whāriki he whāriki mātauranga mō ngā mokopuna o Aotearoa Early childhood curriculum* was released by the Ministry of Education. *Te whāriki* ('the woven mat') incorporated four strands to support learning: empowerment of children to learn and grow; emphasis on the holistic development of children; the integral role of the family and the wider community; and the significance of responsive and reciprocal relationships.

The historically vexed issue of the role of the State regarding the welfare of children and young people was re-articulated with the creation of the Department of Child, Youth and Family in 1999, with a focus on supporting families to achieve wellbeing for their children and young people. The status of the department was to be subsequently reviewed in 2006 when it became a service delivery arm of the Ministry of Social Development (see Chapter 4).

Employment relations were also under review with the passing of the Employment Relations Act 2000. The Act provided a structure for employers and unions to negotiate and enter into collective agreements, and for employers and employees to negotiate and enter into individual agreements. The Act also provided processes for resolving employment problems.

The issue of land continued to influence the construction of biculturalism in Aotearoa New Zealand; two events are noted as examples of how the past continued to influence the present. The fiscal envelope policy was set in 1994. It created a 'fiscal envelope' of $1 billion for the settlement of all historical Treaty claims, which represented an effective limit on the amount the Crown would pay out in settlements. At a number of consultation hui, Māori opposed such a limitation in advance of the extent of the claims being fully known. The concept of the fiscal envelope was subsequently dropped after the 1996 general election.

In the same year, the Waitangi Tribunal recommended a generous settlement of Taranaki land claims, a $40 million Whakatōhea settlement was announced, and a $170 million Ngāi Tahu settlement was proposed. Continuing concern regarding land found expression in the 1995 occupation of Pākaitore (Moutoa Gardens) in Whanganui. Māori claimed that this was the site of a pā and a traditional place for trade, and that it had been set aside from the purchase of Whanganui. Pākaitore was occupied for 79 days, until eventually the dispute was resolved with an agreement being signed between the Whanganui iwi, the government and local government. The essence of this protest lies in the Whanganui iwi claim to the river, considered to be an ancestor and of continuing spiritual significance.

A number of other issues reflected the broader social fabric of Aotearoa New Zealand. The centennial of women's suffrage was celebrated in 1993. A Suffrage Centennial Year Trust had been established in 1991 to promote the centennial throughout the country. The Trust was also responsible for allocating funding to projects that promoted women's social, political, economic and cultural development. The government instituted the New Zealand Suffrage Centennial Medal, which was awarded to 500 women and men who had made a contribution to the rights of women or to women's issues in Aotearoa New Zealand.

In 1997, in a postal referendum, a compulsory contributory superannuation scheme was rejected by a margin of more than nine to one. The substantive issue underlying the referendum was the ageing population, and how the public sector could make provision for the projected increased health and pension costs without creating an excessive tax burden on the future workforce. The result of the referendum resulted in the removal of superannuation from the policy agenda.

The National Government distributed a copy of a publication called *Towards a code of social and family responsibility* to every household in New Zealand in February and March 1998 (Department of Social Welfare, 1998). The code, focusing on responsibilities within households, included best practices for childcare, health, money management and employment. A questionnaire was included and generated 94,303 responses. However, the replies received did not enable the government to make any clear decisions, and the code was eventually abandoned.

The proposed code represented an attempt to generate a post-welfare state consensus around social issues. An underlying premise of the code was a shift towards family and community responsibility for collective wellbeing. Further, the code advanced the notion of 'active citizenship' in which participation in paid work, for both men and women, was considered the key to social inclusion.

On 1 October 1998, the 'Hīkoi of Hope' converged in Wellington to protest against the government's policies towards the poor. There was a call for income and benefit levels sufficient to move people out of poverty. The hīkoi had commenced on 1 September from Spirits Bay in the North Island, and from Stewart Island to the south, and around 40,000 New Zealanders participated during the course of the march.

Support for vulnerable children and families were the focus of two initiatives in 1999. First, the Strengthening Families initiative involved collaboration between government agencies and community groups. With the aim of providing assistance before intensive or statutory intervention is required, Strengthening Families was conceived to be a way for families to receive coordinated access to services to meet the unique needs of each family and whānau.

The second initiative was Family Start, which was a support programme delivered by contracted providers with the aim of ensuring services are provided in a manner that is responsive to each community. It is based on international evidence regarding the efficacy of home-based early-intervention programmes. Family Start workers made regular home visits a focus for addressing issues such as parenting skills, children's health and education, and were able to facilitate referrals for other concerns, such as substance abuse, mental health and family violence.

The defining characteristic of the social and political context during the period 1993 to 2000 reflects a continuing scaling-back of the State, and the emergence of the 'third way', with its focus on civic responsibility, earned rights and individual autonomy. Within this framework the foundations were laid for a social development approach to welfare that balanced market-driven policy with a commitment to support those in need (Stanley-Clarke, 2016).

The new MMP voting system ushered in a new era of political compromise that was to afford voice to previously marginalised populations. Public sector restructuring continued apace, with particular emphasis placed on efficiency and effectiveness. Of particular import to social work was the emerging focus on social inclusion, reflected in responses to education, domestic violence and families. The performance of the premiere State welfare agency was under continued scrutiny, and, notwithstanding the pertinent observations made regarding broader community responsibility, the responses were driven by managerialist imperatives characterised by organisational restructuring. This raised the question of how well did developments in social work reflect and respond to this broader social environment.

The development of social work

A focus on professionalism and biculturalism in social work can be seen in a range of developments between 1993 and 2000. The demonstration of expertise that is based on specialist education, training and skills presents as a core characteristic of a profession. This expertise is applied in a reflexive manner that enables professionals to continuously develop their knowledge and skills, and to complete work tasks that require judgement and creativity. The professional usually demonstrates commitment to a profession through membership of a formal association that sets and enforces standards of accreditation, training and conduct through registration procedures and a code of ethics. NZASW had adopted an Interim Code of Ethics at its inception in 1964, followed by the adoption of the International Federation of Social Workers' Code in 1976. Following the formation of an ethics committee in 1993, the first ANZASW Code of Ethics and Bicultural Code of Practice was adopted, which would guide decision-making regarding complaints of ethical breaches made against ANZASW members.

Also in 1993, evidence of the impact of 'new public management' was apparent in the disestablishment of the social work student units located in the welfare, probation and health sectors. At this time, the student units were seen by government as expensive and unnecessary. The units had been established in 1977 and, within the units, dedicated Student Unit Supervisors fieldwork educators supported, supervised and educated students, and provided excellent learning opportunities. The supervisors were also associate lecturers who contributed to the Massey social work programme.

In 1994, a radical reorganisation of The Children and Young Persons Service followed the release of *A study of financial management practices in the Children and Young Persons Service*, known as the 'Weeks Report'. An entirely new national office structure was introduced, with executive responsibilities aligned to output classes; a new purchase agreement was constructed and implemented, including key performance indicators; and the computerised social work information system was redesigned.

Four regions and 36 branches were disestablished, replaced by 14 area offices, each being responsible for a number of local site offices. The changes were similar to those in other government agencies; for example, the Department of Justice was restructured into the Ministry of Justice, Department for Courts and the Department of Corrections, and then each of these new entities were re-engineered and restructured further.

Equally significant were observations made in the Weeks Report regarding social work practice. Following the establishment of the Department of Social Welfare (DSW) (via the consolidation of several government entities), it was noted that '. . . very few staff with a Social Work background secured senior management positions, most of which were filled by staff from the Social Security Department' (Weeks, 1994, p. 50). In response to rising unemployment in the 1980s, the DSW had become more focused on staffing the growth in the DPB and the unemployment benefit area. Social work was likened to a 'second-class citizen', with insufficient focus being directed to the development of social work practice, or staff training.

A number of events can be seen as responses to this criticism. The Department of Social Welfare published *Te punga: Our bicultural strategy for the nineties*, its response to *Pūao-te-Āta-tū*. Key result areas were identified, including developing a bicultural workplace and working with iwi. *Te punga* was described as 'our anchor', and it stated that the department was determined to overcome a history of monocultural biases. The metaphor of an anchor has been open to interpretation, with Cram (2012) asserting that, for sceptical Māori, *Te punga* symbolised an anchor and the probability that the canoe of *Pūao-te-Āta-tū* would not be allowed to move anywhere.

At this time, CYPS began to develop a practice journal — with a board appointed in December 1994, and the first issue published in July 1995 — in which the importance of promoting reflective and innovative social work practice was noted. Other notable events from 1994 included the appointment of Mike Doolan as Chief Social Worker, and the commencement of Polytechnic Diploma in Social Work courses at Waikato, Christchurch and Manukau.

In June 1995, the NZCETSS was formally disestablished and was replaced by Te Kaiāwhina Ahumahi Industry Training Organisation for the Social Services. The organisation issued guidelines for education providers in 1997, which led to the National Diploma in Social Services and a proliferation of polytechnic courses; for example, the Eastern Institute of Technology in Hawke's Bay, the Western Institute of Technology in Taranaki, the Nelson and Marlborough Institute of Technology in Nelson, and various private training establishments. Also in this period there were changes in the university sector, with the University of Canterbury starting to offer a four-year BSW from 1998. It is notable that, up until this point, Massey University had been the only tertiary provider offering a BSW degree, and it had been doing this for 22 years.

The work of the statutory child and family welfare agency continued to experience scrutiny. In 1995, the NZ Children and Young Persons Service was renamed Children, Young Persons and their Families Service (CYPFS). Then, on 1 October 1999, the Department of Child, Youth and Family was created, as an amalgamation of CYPFS and the Community Funding Agency (thereafter referred to as CYF). A national call centre was established to provide a full 'front-of-house' service for the new department, including social work intake services.

The Social Workers in Schools (SWiS) programme was developed in 1999, with Child Youth and Family Services funding 12 pilot school social work projects. The SWiS initiative provided school-based social services that sought to enhance the social, educational and health outcomes of students. This service has expanded significantly over the years.

The Ministerial Review of the Department of Child, Youth and Family Services: Report to the Minister of Social Services and Employment Hon. Steve Maharey by Michael J. A. Brown was released in December 2000.

Judge Brown expressed concern at the capacity of the nation to deal with the issues surrounding child and adolescent mental health, and further issued a challenge that neglect and abuse of children should not be accepted as a 'natural phenomenon'. The report offered 57 recommendations overall, and suggested that the changes would require, first, increased resources from the government, and, second, changes to the culture and operation of the department. In the same year Mike Doolan retired as Chief Social Worker and Shannon Pakura was appointed to the position.

ANZASW maintained an active presence in the social work landscape. In 1995, the first issue of *Te Kōmako*, focusing on tangata whenua social work, was published, and the ANZASW competency recertification programme was also rolled out. Ongoing concern about professional practice was evident in the ANZASW supervision policy issued in 1998. At the 1998 ANZASW conference at Kirikiriroa Marae in Hamilton, Kieran O'Donoghue, who attended the conference, recalled that:

> Life memberships were awarded to John Bradley and Turoa
> Haronga. We had political speakers: Bob Simcock from the
> National Government, Minister of Social Services; Steve Maharey,
> Labour; and James Ritchie from Waikato University. It was also
> the moment when the registration debate took impetus. From my
> perspective, it reflected an impetus for biculturalism and Māori
> development within the association, and professional regulation.
> It should also be noted that when Merv Hancock gave his paper on
> the social work profession in the next 10 years, the wharenui was
> packed, with people standing outside.

In 1999, members of ANZASW voted in favour of introducing a system of registration, although exactly what form members wished to see introduced was unclear. The campaign was taken up by the Ministry of Social Policy and supported by the Minister for Social Welfare. A discussion paper released by the Ministry of Social Policy noted concern about the lack of credibility of social work as a profession, and identified the expectation that those in the profession be more accountable and their work be more transparent. Further, it was observed that vulnerable clients of social work services should be protected from any harm associated with poor social work practice.

The first Aotearoa New Zealand supervision conference, 'From rhetoric to reality', was held in 2000 at the Auckland College of Education. Attended by 175 people, the conference afforded the opportunity for new ways of thinking about supervision to be heard that reflected the culturally diverse nature of Aotearoa New Zealand. Also in 2000, the International Federation of Social Work issued a revised definition of social work (replacing the 1982 definition), which aimed to both reflect the state of the art of social work practice and be a guiding principle for professional activity:

> The social work profession promotes social change, problem
> solving in human relationships and the empowerment and
> liberation of people to enhance well-being. Utilising theories of
> human behaviour and social systems, social work intervenes at the
> points where people interact with their environments. Principles
> of human rights and social justice are fundamental to social work.

This definition was published in the *Social Work Review 12*(2), p. 2.

The challenge to enhance the professional credibility of the social work profession emerges as a key issue during the period 1993 to 2000. There were external drivers (such as critical reviews of DSW) that contributed to responses by both social work agencies and ANZASW. Te Kaiāwhina Ahumahi Industry Training Organisation for the Social

Services responded to the call for a better-qualified workforce, and the establishment of the National Diploma in Social Services resulted in an increased number of polytechnic social work programmes. The debate regarding the registration of social workers also gained momentum, and the Social Workers in Schools initiative marked a significant milestone in providing access to social work services. Judge Brown's report on the Department of Child, Youth and Family Services provides a transition point from which to consider the subsequent period 2001 to 2009. Among the many recommendations made, two key messages were given: the need for additional resources from the government; and the need to change the culture and operations of the department.

M assey University's Albany campus opened in 1993, with business and social sciences being the first programmes offered. In 1995, the Head of the Department (HOD), Professor Ian Shirley, transferred to the Albany campus. There was major development at the Albany campus within a short period of time: the opening of the study centre (1995), the Quadrangle A building (1999), and the Atrium building (2000). Professor Shirley was the first HOD based at Albany.

Vice-Chancellor Sir Neil Walters retired on 31 December 1995, and was succeeded by Professor James McWha. The new Vice-Chancellor embarked on an agenda of expansion and change. This included the university merging with the College of Education (located at the Hokowhitu campus in Palmerston North) and the Māori Studies Building Te-Pūtahi-a-Toi being opened at the Turitea campus in 1997.

Organisational change saw the establishment of colleges; the College of Humanities and Social Sciences was established in 1998, with Professor Barrie Macdonald as Pro Vice-Chancellor. The Department of Social Policy and Social Work became the School of Social Policy and Social Work, with Robyn Munford as head of school. In 1999, Massey University merged with the Wellington Polytechnic, leading to the establishment of the College of Design, Fine Arts and Music, and giving Massey a presence in Wellington. The Bachelor of Social Work was offered from Wellington in 2000. This restructuring also resulted in the formation of the School of Social and Cultural Studies in Albany, which included the social work programme, with Associate Professor Michael O'Brien as head of school. Also in 2000, the School of Social Policy and Social Work merged with the School of Sociology and Women's Studies to become the School of Sociology, Social Policy and Social Work, with Professor Robyn Munford as head of school. At this time the social work programme was offered by two schools and from three campuses.

During the period 1993 to 2000, changes occurred to the social work academic programme:

- The Bachelor of Arts (Social Policy) was offered in 1993.
- Outreach developments resulted in joint first-year offerings being trialled by Massey University at Hawke's Bay, Taranaki and Tairāwhiti polytechnics.
- In 1995, work started on the Master of Social Work (Applied), and was offered from 1997.
- The Diploma in Social Science (Social Policy and Social Work) was closed to new enrolments, and in 1998 the Post Graduate Diploma in Social Service Supervision was first offered.

The MSW (Applied) provided an opportunity for graduates in related social sciences (such as psychology and sociology) to complete an intensive two-year programme set at Master's level. The degree included two supervised placements, and there was also a requirement to undertake supervised research. The availability of the programme via distance, either full- or part-time, made it particularly attractive to in-post workers seeking a recognised professional qualification.

Dr Mike O'Brien, Dr Andrew Trlin, Gwen Ellis, Rachael Selby and Dr Rajen Prasad at Massey's Albany campus (exact date unknown). **SCHOOL OF SOCIAL WORK**

Professor Ian Shirley presents Dr Rajen Prasad with a gift on Dr Prasad's appointment as director of the social work programme at the Albany campus. **SCHOOL OF SOCIAL WORK**

Academic staff appointments and changes, 1993–2000

- 1993: Associate Professor Rajen Prasad, Michael Belgrave, Grant Duncan, Michael O'Brien, Okustino Mahina, Carole Adamson and Mereana Taki were the staff at Albany.
  - Ruth Anderson, Rachael Selby and Martin Sullivan appointed at Palmerston North.
  - A notable associate lecturer was Judge Anand Satyanand.
- 1995: John Bradley, Mike Garland, Wendy Parker and Mervyl McPherson appointed at Palmerston North.
  - Marilyn Waring, Judith Morris, Jill Worrall, Cindy Kiro, Tafa Mulitalo-Lauta and Jocelyn Quinnell appointed at Albany.
- 1996: William Low, Neil Lunt and Peter Mataira appointed at Albany.
- 1997: Chris Eichbaum appointed Director of Labour Studies.
- 1998: John Bradley, a loved and respected member of staff and a Life Member of ANZASW, died.
- 1999: Kathryn Hay and Christine Thomas joined the school as tutors.
  - Jenny Jakobs joined the school in Wellington.
- 2000: Restructuring resulted in two staff taking voluntary redundancy, and three staff reducing their hours of work.
  - Tracie Mafile'o joined the school as an assistant lecturer.

Master of Social Work (Applied) year one cohort and teaching staff outside Wharerata, 1997. *Back row, from left*: Mike Garland, Natasha Cromarty, Rachael Selby. *Fourth row*: Stacey Gasson, Vivienne Smith, David Younger, Michael Deegan, Mary Farrelly. *Third row*: Judy Wivell, Lois Carter, Wendy Parker, Sue Martin, Anna Fenwick. *Second row*: Paul Watkin, Jeanette McLaughlin, Tania Rajcic, Sarah McDonald, Sue Nathan. *Front row*: Marije van Epenhuijsen, Kirsten Andrews, Ella James, Andrea Potts. **MASSEY UNIVERSITY ARCHIVES**

The launch of the new Post Graduate Diploma in Social Service Supervision (DSSS) and the book *Supervising social workers*, which was used as an initial text for the course, 1998. Merv Hancock, Kieran O'Donoghue, Mary Ann Baskerville, Kieran's wife Rosemary O'Donoghue, and Robyn Munford stand with the DSSS students. **SCHOOL OF SOCIAL WORK**

This period marked further significant contribution of the Massey University programme to the development of social work in Aotearoa New Zealand; with new academic offerings and with a presence at additional campuses, the reach of the programme was increasing.

In 1993, Massey offered the only university social work programme in Auckland, and there were outreach developments with joint first-year offerings being trialled by Massey University at Hawke's Bay, Taranaki and Tairāwhiti polytechnics.

Robyn Munford and Jackie Sanders (Barnardos) were awarded a major research grant from the Foundation for Research, Science and Technology (FRST) in 1994 to investigate the nature of effective support work with families. The project findings were reported in three stages — in 1996, 1998 and 1999 — with emphasis placed on utilising a strengths-based perspective to work with clients to overcome challenges. Robyn Munford and Jackie Sanders published an influential text, *Supporting families*, in 1999. The success of the Working Successfully with Families research project led to the signing of a memorandum of understanding in 1999 between the School of Social Policy and Social Work and Barnardos — Child and Family Research Centre.

John Bradley, Wheturangi Walsh-Tapiata, Rachael Selby and Leland Ruwhiu were members of the Tangata Whenua Editorial Board of the inaugural issue of *Te Kōmako* (1995). They were later joined by Cindy Kiro and Peter Mataira for the ensuing issues.

In 1996, Associate Professor Rajen Prasad was appointed Race Relations Conciliator. The Race Relations Office was established with the introduction of Aotearoa New Zealand's first human rights legislation, the Race Relations Act 1971, which came into force in April 1972. The office was later merged with the Human Rights Commission. The key focus of the Race Relations Conciliator was responding to complaints and providing advocacy and education, with a broad goal of fostering fair treatment, freedom of expression, and participation in society for all New

Zealanders. When Rajen ended his five-year term, he expressed optimism regarding the future of race relations in Aotearoa New Zealand, believing that there was a deeper understanding of race relations, and a wider appreciation of our society and its peoples. He observed that:

> People are also more aware of the havoc that negative race relations has visited on a growing number of countries around the world and thus are more determined to ensure that such incidents do not come to pass in New Zealand.

Rajen nevertheless cautioned that the ongoing challenge remained to achieve a deeper level of comfortable relationships amongst members of the various ethnic and cultural groups that live in New Zealand.

In 1998, Professor Ian Shirley was awarded almost a million dollars from a Public Good Science Fund grant for a study on the interface between individuals in households and paid employment in both regional and national areas.

Andrew Trlin's New Settlers research programme (1998–2006) was funded by the New Zealand Foundation for Research, Science and Technology (FRST) and the Public Good Science Fund (PGSF). This multi-disciplinary research programme focused on immigrant settlement in New Zealand, and aimed to contribute to the attainment of three broad, interrelated outcomes: (1) the development of a balanced, well-integrated institutional structure of immigration, consisting of an immigration policy regulating entry, an effective post-arrival immigrant policy geared to the economic, social and cultural needs of migrants (assisting them to adjust and integrate), and an ethnic relations policy appropriate to a situation of emerging multiculturalism; (2) a reduction in the difficulties experienced by immigrants in the process of settlement; and (3) an increase in the benefits accruing to New Zealand from its targeted immigration programme.

John Bradley, a highly respected member of staff and an important contributor and leader within the social work profession, was awarded life membership of ANZASW at the November 1998 conference for his outstanding contribution to tangata whenua social work. His friend Turoa Haronga, who was also award life membership at the same time, took the certificate directly from the conference to John. John died in late December 1998.

Dr Martin Sullivan was made a Winston Churchill Fellow in 2000 for his work on the development of disability studies and the disability movement in the United Kingdom. Martin's doctoral research was on the sociology of the body, specifically the paraplegic body and the ways traumatic paraplegics reintegrated body, self and society, and how this affected life changes and subjectivity.

In 2000, Massey University, in partnership with the Auckland College of Education, was contracted by CYF for delivery of the clinical supervision training for CYF supervisors, with the first course taking place at Rotorua. This programme continued successfully until 2009.

This period was marked by ongoing contributions by staff. The strong thread of focusing on social policy continued, with Grant Duncan offering commentary on the ACC in the areas of reform and rehabilitation, the trend towards privatisation, and its labour relations in 1993. Mike O'Brien focused on income, social security and 'The tragedy of the market'. Professor Ian Shirley considered 'Social and economic trends in New Zealand' when addressing social service personnel attending a seminar organised by the Justice, Peace and Development Commission of the combined churches. Christine Cheyne, Mike O'Brien and Michael Belgrave published *Social policy in Aotearoa New Zealand: A critical introduction* in 1997, which was the first social policy textbook. Later, in 2000, Christine explored 'Fin de siècle neo-liberalism: Governmentality and post-social politics', while Richard Shaw considered public choice and bureaucratic reform (Shaw, 2000, 2001a).

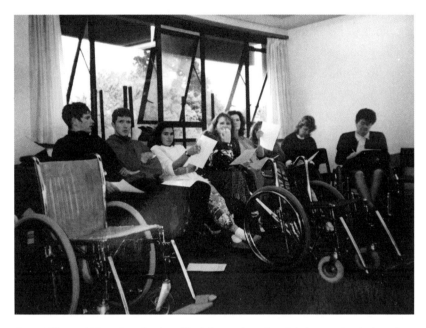

Gwen Ellis and Mary Ann Baskerville (pictured on the right) run a Bachelor of Social Work skills lab (date unknown). **SCHOOL OF SOCIAL WORK**

Social work in action, the first New Zealand social work text, edited by Robyn Munford and Mary Nash, was published in 1994 (Munford & Nash, 1994b). In addition to editing the book, Munford and Nash wrote a joint chapter on the feminist contribution to social work (Munford & Nash, 1994a). They also contributed to other chapters, with Nash writing about social work education, and Munford, Sara Georgeson and Janice Gordon providing a chapter on social work with people with disabilities and their families (Munford, Georgeson, & Gordon, 1994). This text also included many contributions from Massey University staff and alumni. Notable examples include Mike O'Brien (1994), who wrote about the case of the neglected triplets — policy, class, poverty; Leland Ruwhiu, who discussed Māori development and social work (Ruwhiu, 1994); John Bradley, who reviewed Maatua Whangai (Bradley, 1994); and Rachael Selby, who wrote about her whanau (Selby, 1994); while Richard Shaw contributed a chapter on radical social work (Shaw, 1994).

The period between 1993 and 2000 was marked by significant Māori contribution within the social work profession, which included critique regarding the profession (drawing mainly on North American and European influences) as a coloniser of Māori. Also a key focus for NZCETSS was on expanding access to education by developing a national framework for social service education, and importantly a focus on bicultural education and practice. Massey Māori academics were at the forefront of this discourse. John Bradley's 'Before you tango with our whanau, you better know what makes us tick: An indigenous approach to social work' (Bradley, 1995a) challenged non-Māori to gain an understanding of te ao Māori as an essential foundation for bicultural practice. He also raised the issue of the devolution of social service provision to Māori (Bradley, 1995b). John was both a highly respected member of staff and an important contributor and leader within the social work profession.

Rachael Selby, Wheturangi Walsh-Tapiata and Leland Ruwhiu also contributed to *Te Kōmako* in 1995, and in 1996 Rachael and Wheturangi published *Māori and the social services: An annotated bibliography* (Selby & Walsh-Tapiata, 1996). Other contributors included Peter Mataira and Cindy Kiro (Kiro, 2000).

Robyn Munford and Martin Sullivan continued their contribution to the development of theory and knowledge in the field of disability, and Robyn Munford and Wheturangi Walsh-Tapiata published *Strategies for change: Community development in Aotearoa New Zealand* in 1999. Andrew Trlin and Paul Spoonley maintained their focus on migration in the third edition of *New Zealand and international migration: A digest and bibliography* (1997).

Social work in schools was an emerging field of practice, with Rachael Selby and Moya Field writing in *Te Kōmako* in 1999 about a new professional presence in schools. In 2000, the *Evaluation of the Social Workers in Schools pilot programme: Final report* was authored by Michael Belgrave, with a number of staff and students from the school.

In 1997, field education was engaged by Jill Worrall and Liz Beddoe, who commented on the challenges and changes in a market economy, and Gwen Ellis posed the question 'Have you supervised a student lately? (And if not, why not?)'. Concern with social work practice in health was addressed in *Social dimensions of health and disease: New Zealand perspective* edited by J. Spicer, Andrew Trlin and J. Walton (1994), while Robyn Munford and Anne Opie explored social workers' contributions working in multi-disciplinary teams (1996).

A focus on women's issues was continued by Christine Cheyne (1993a and 1993b), who wrote about the history of women's organisations in New Zealand. Commentary regarding social policy and women's experience was provided in a text edited by Celia Briar, Robyn Munford and Mary Nash (1992).

In 1996, Celia Briar's text *Working for women? Gendered work and welfare policies in twentieth-century Britain* was published, and, in 2000,

Robyn Munford and Sylvia Rumball considered women in university power structures (Munford & Rumball, 2000). The professional issues in social work addressed by staff included mandatory reporting (Cooper, 1993), cross-cultural awareness, (Nash, 1993), private practice (Baskerville & Durrant, 1996), the provision of care (Munford, 1999), the education and training need of workers in the voluntary sector (Ellis, Nixon, & Sayers, 1996) and the therapeutic process (Anderson, 1997).

S taff supervised 33 Master's-level Social Policy theses to completion during this period. Among these, there was an emphasis on Māori issues, including: land and resource consent; personal identity; and perceptions of Te Tiriti o Waitangi. Another area to receive attention was employment, where the following topics were engaged: experiences of women in casual work; employment equity; equal employment opportunities; job creation policy; and the Employment Contracts Act 1991. A focus on income and women was central to three theses, which engaged: income support policy for solo mothers; mid-life women and retirement income planning; and lone mothers and paid work.

Nine doctorates were awarded in Social Policy. The first of these was Mulengu (1994), whose thesis, *From job creation to training, 1840–1990: A descriptive analysis of the development and demise of job creation policy as the mainstay of state responses to unemployment in New Zealand,* provided a historical analysis of job creation for the unemployed, and examined the competing ideas and interests which conditioned the adoption, growth, fluctuations and the eventual demise of job creation as the mainstay of the New Zealand State's responses to unemployment. A history of the reinforcing of ancient divisions of labour along lines of gender and ethnicity, and of the relative privileging of 'Pākehā' men in terms of their access to paid work provided by the State, were key findings from this thesis.

School of Social Policy and Social Work staff, circa 1993: *Back row, from left*: Richard Shaw, Andrew Trlin, Mark Tisdall. *Third row*: Janet Milne, Mary Nash, Gwen Ellis, Keri Rauhihi, Leland Ruwhiu. *Second row*: Ian Shirley, Rachael Selby, Ruth Anderson, Sharon Brook, Mary Ann Baskerville, Evelyn Mills. *Front row*: Martin Sullivan, Lareen Cooper, Wheturangi Walsh-Tapiata, Mereana Taki, Celia Briar, Christine Cheyne. **SCHOOL OF SOCIAL WORK**

Robyn Munford and Celia Briar (Mary Nash absent) with their edited text *Superwoman: Where are you?*, December 1992.
MASSEY UNIVERSITY CAMPUS NEWS

The next thesis was *Male breadwinner households and work: Alterations in the transition to a liberal welfare regime* (Barrett, 1997). This thesis examined how the nexus between households and work in New Zealand has been altered by the transition from a wage-earner-cum-social-expenditure welfare regime to a liberal welfare regime.

A disability focus was apparent in the next two theses, with Michelle Lunn (1997) undertaking a feminist postmodern analysis of the lives of women with physical disabilities. In contrast, Pauline Boyles' thesis was an example of emancipatory research used within the field of disability studies, and was focused on enabling participation through partnership to enhance the potential for change for disabled people (Boyles, 1998). The thesis described how a group of 12 disabled students formed the Disability Action Research Group (DARG), identified some goals for change in their immediate environment, and subsequently developed a disability equity training package to be delivered to the staff of Victoria University. The key theme of partnership represented the potential for alliances between disabled people as well as with their nondisabled allies. 'Enabling participation through partnership' underpinned every aspect of this thesis and reflected its fundamental principles.

Sharon Milne's (1998) thesis examined the housing issues experienced by women who parent alone. She found a significant level of hidden homelessness, and the higher level of mobility experienced by women in rental homes was a result of those women's efforts to avoid homelessness. Milne argued for changes in housing policy that increased the choices and opportunities for women, and enabled them to participate more fully as citizens in economic, social and political life by accessing housing of their choice.

Leland Ruwhiu completed his thesis, *Te puawaitanga o te ihi me te wehi: The politics of Māori social policy development*, in 1999. The thesis presented a framework for developing Māori social policy which met the welfare needs of all Māori, and argued that Māori social policy was about

Māori wellbeing, and that Māori wellbeing drew strength from the past, present and future — Te puawaitanga o te ihi me te wehi.

In 2000, three doctorates were completed. The first of these was Cindy Kiro's *Kimihia mo te hauora Māori: Māori health policy and practice*, which examined the effects of health reforms announced in 1991 in respect of Māori health policy and Māori health services within the Auckland region. It found that there was considerable innovation by Māori policy-makers and purchasers in order to shift resources to Māori communities to provide services for themselves. However, it was also found that improvement in Māori health status also required a shift in macro-environments, such as labour market participation and greater egalitarianism.

Peter Mataira's thesis, *Nga kai arahi tuitui Māori: Māori entrepreneurship: The articulation of leadership and the dual constituency arrangements associated with Māori enterprise in a capitalist economy*, examined the significance of entrepreneurship as a level of leadership required to assist Māori, in particular tribal iwi, to move into what is widely described as the era of 'neo-tribal' postmodernism. Mataira found that Māori entrepreneurs provided the necessary tier of business leadership, complementary to that of tribal political leadership, required to make economic development and commercial investments viable options.

The third thesis was that of Mervyl McPherson (2000), who surveyed *The nature and role of the extended family in New Zealand, and its relationship with the State*. She found that the predominantly European/ Pākehā society of New Zealand did have extended family, in the modified sense, with extended families based on egalitarianism and choice rather than power and control, and which were characterised by a loose, informal set of kin relationships involving an interlocking set of nuclear families which may be geographically dispersed and economically independent, but were bound by a sense of obligation based on affective relationships and the exchange of mutual aid services. The thesis also found that, while people generally believed in helping family members, they also believed this help should be given by choice, not obligation, and that nuclear family and labour force commitments took priority over commitments to the extended family.

Child welfare provided a focus for eight Master's theses that addressed a diverse range of topics, including attachment, funding contracts, dangerous dynamics, kaupapa Māori and responsiveness, kinship care, staff welfare, and the experience of women child protection social workers.

Five theses were concerned with criminal justice, including how the Department of Corrections related to voluntary sector agencies; case management intervention with violent offenders; driver offenders; the imprisonment of women in New Zealand; and the social support and monitoring of men who had completed therapy for sexual offending.

The field of disability was engaged by five theses, including: *The Disabled Persons Assembly 1983–1999: Successes, challenges and lessons for the disability movement in New Zealand*; an evaluation of the implementation and outcomes of the Health and Disability Commissioner Act 1994; the development of social policy in New Zealand for people with learning disabilities; the experience and viewpoints of people with intellectual services regarding services; and stories from parents of children with visual and other disabilities.

Increasing awareness of the issue of domestic violence was reflected in three theses that considered women's attendance at protected persons programmes; identifying and assessing risk in men who had a history of violence towards their female partners; and the social and cultural context of domestic violence in Papua New Guinea.

A high level of interest in health was demonstrated in six theses that focused on the experience of multiple sclerosis through the eyes of women; the voices and standpoint of 12 Plunket nurses; caregiving and bereavement; the prevention of severe behaviour problems; dementia care; and caring for a family member diagnosed with schizophrenia. Pamela Highet, whose MSW thesis was concerned with the experience of multiple sclerosis through the eyes of women, was also honoured in the 1999 New Year's Honours list with an MNZM for services to people experiencing disabilities.

Māori issues were addressed in three theses that explored personal and political issues of identity for white Māori women — *Whakatoro te torangapu me te ake o nga kaupapa tuakiri mo nga wahine Māori ma; He tapu te whare tangata*; support for young Māori mothers during pregnancy, birth and motherhood; and management responsiveness to Māori health issues in the reformed health service of the 1990s. Wheturangi Walsh-Tapiata completed her thesis in 1997 on *Raukawa Social Services: Origins and future directions.*

There were also theses that focused on older persons: the life stories of older disabled women; community care service provision for older people; and the implications of the caregiving role.

In 1998, Gwen Ellis completed a thesis on fieldwork supervisors' perceptions of their role, support needs and education and training. Issues pertaining to new managerialism and contracting resulting from the purchaser–provider split were explored by Kieran O'Donoghue (1999) and Kathryn Hay (2000) in their respective theses.

Six social work doctoral theses were completed between 1995 and 1998. Jean Hera's (1995) thesis was an ecofeminist analysis of women's roles in after-death work and ritual in Aotearoa/New Zealand. Her study contributed a process that demystified death and assisted women and the wider community to reclaim control over the last rites (rights).

Garth Bennie (1996) examined the development and current status of supported employment, a relatively recent concept that held much promise for improving the employment prospects of disabled people.

His findings revealed a great deal of concern about the effectiveness of employment support services. In particular, participants identified disabled people's lack of power in the development and use of services. Bennie proposed an emancipatory model of supported employment in which disabled people were empowered to reveal the contradictions and power imbalances of conventional approaches to vocational rehabilitation and job placement. This, in turn, meant that employment support services and related policies were challenged to shift from a focus on assimilation in the workplace to the transformation of workplaces and employment support services in disabled people's interests.

Leigh Richards-Ward's (1996) thesis explored the characteristics and complexities of the informal care provided within a family to a member diagnosed with schizophrenia, in New Zealand. The main finding from the study was that the dominant understandings of care should be extended in order to reflect the informal care provided to a family member diagnosed with schizophrenia.

Cognitive rehabilitation for people with traumatic brain injury was the focus of Deborah Sutherland's thesis. Her findings suggest adaptations to both settings and relationships might be necessary for a successful recovery after brain injury. The importance of providing the scaffolding of the meaning-negotiating process during a liminal period of recovery was noted, and suggestions were offered on interactive strategies which fostered adaptive, purposeful and independent lifestyles. The thesis concluded that, because realities were created through interaction, the principles of symbolic interactionism should become more central in the design of rehabilitation programmes (Sutherland, 1996).

The two doctoral theses completed in 1998 were focused on social work education. Ksenija Napan's thesis examined the importance of integrating theory, practice and experience through the contact-challenge method. She proposed an integrative approach to teaching and learning social work, where theory, practice and experience are integrated in order to produce change in knowledge, skills, values and attitudes. According to Napan (1998a), the contact-challenge method provides a context where students' individual learning outcomes could be achieved and the quality of life of social work clients could be improved. The last of the doctorates awarded in this period was to Mary Nash for her thesis on the history of social work education, entitled *People, policies and practice: Social work education in Aotearoa/New Zealand from 1949 to 1995*. The thesis was a case study of the history of social work education in Aotearoa/New Zealand between 1949, when the first professional course for social work was established, and 1995, when the social services Industry Training Organisation was formed. It traced influences responsible for shaping social work education.

Alumni and students made important contributions during this period, which reflected concern with the key issues and debates in social work at the time. The most notable award was to former foundation staff member Ephra Garrett, who was awarded an honorary Doctorate in Literature (DLitt) in 1993 in recognition of her contribution to social work, Māori and women's studies, and a QSM for services to community and Māori in 1997. Several alumni made important contributions by way of publications on the care and protection field of practice, through articles published in the *Social Work Review* that covered: experiences of social workers, risk assessment, loss and grief in adoption. Gary Cockburn (1994) also provided significant coverage of 'The Children, Young Persons and Their Families Act 1989: Past, present, future', in his chapter in *Social Work in Action*. In 1995, John McCarthy and Ian Lambie addressed issues in the assessment, interviewing and treating of adolescent sexual offenders, in two articles in the *Social Work Review*, while Jane Brook (1997) wrote about sexual abuse with people with disabilities. A focus on the perennial issue of registration was maintained by Jenny Blagdon, Madeline Taylor and Bev Keall (1994), and David McNabb in 1997. David also served as president of ANZASW from 1996 to 1998.

Interest in the foundational process of social work supervision was engaged both in *Social Work Review* articles and in two monographs published by the school; namely, Garth Bennie's (1995) *Social work supervision: An annotated bibliography,* and Kieran O'Donoghue's (1998) influential *Supervising social workers: A practical handbook.* Gary Cockburn (1994) provided a 'brief statement of the essentials of supervision in social work', and Garth Young (1994) identified 'Critical components in the supervision of child protection social workers in a statutory agency'. Kieran O'Donoghue, Mary Ann Baskerville and Andrew Trlin (1999) wrote about 'Professional supervision in the new managerial climate of the Department of Corrections', while Emma Webber-Dreadon (1999) presented an indigenous approach to social work supervision, and John Bradley, Ema Jacob and Richard Bradley (1999) shared important reflections on culturally safe supervision.

In summary, the contribution of the social work academic staff and students was characterised by both scope and scholarship. The emergent career of Professor Robyn Munford (one of the foundation social work students) was a highlight from this period. Significant research was completed in diverse areas, from supporting families and migration to disability. The publication of *Social work in action* was a milestone for staff and alumni contributors. The depth of Māori scholarship over this period was impressive, with Leland Ruwhiu, Peter Mataira and Cindy Kiro completing doctorates. Postgraduate research was prolific and diverse, with 33 Social Policy and seven Social Work Master's degrees awarded, and nine Social Policy and six Social Work doctorates completed. The growth and consolidation of the Massey programme placed it in an excellent position to embrace the forthcoming challenges of the twenty-first century.

During the period between 1993 and 2000, the Aotearoa New Zealand political landscape was altered by the introduction of MMP, which was to challenge the previous status quo by introducing a new politics of compromise. The scaling-back of the State continued, and by 2000 the emergence of 'third way' policies laid the foundations for a social development approach to welfare. Particular concern continued to be exhibited regarding the performance of the statutory State agency responsible for the care and protection of children and young persons; with the need for additional resources from the government, and the need to change the culture and operations of the department, being key recommendations made by Judge Brown.

The issues of curriculum, training, qualifications and accountability remained on the broader social work agenda. ANZASW remained active in leading and contributing to the debate. The question of the status of social work as a profession was attracting attention, and the question of registration was now clearly on the horizon.

At Massey University, the social work programme had expanded and consolidated. Social work courses were available at three campuses and via distance-learning and new postgraduate options had been introduced. The depth and breadth of scholarship from academic staff, students and alumni was having an impact, as was the contribution of graduates who were occupying a range of social work roles nationally and internationally.

Chapter Four
Riding the waves of change: Reform, regulation and repositioning, 2001–2009

The period from 2001 to 2009 was characterised by the social reforms of the Fifth Labour Government; the rise of the Māori Party; the regulation of social work and tertiary education; and repositioning in the form of organisational change and in response to the Global Financial Crisis.

The government successfully pursued significant legislative and policy changes, and there were challenges to the country's bicultural development, particularly through the middle of the decade, which was dominated by the foreshore and seabed controversy. Social issues reflected the government's progressive reformist agenda in the areas of sexuality, child discipline, public health, welfare and family support.

The political climate

The Fifth Labour-led Government held office until the end of 2008. There is clear evidence of the 'third way' shift towards a social development approach to welfare over this period, one example being the establishment in 2001 of the Ministry of Social Development, following an amalgamation of the Ministry of Social Policy and the Department of Work and Income. The new ministry was charged with advising the government on social policy, and providing social services.

Labour had been returned to government for a second term following the election in July 2002, allowing a continuation and development of the policy platform established in 1999. This policy platform resulted in interest accrual being removed from student loans while students were studying, the consolidation of welfare benefits, and the development of the Working for Families tax-credit scheme.

But a change in the political balance occurred with the formation of the Māori Party. The foreshore and seabed controversy highlighted tensions regarding indigenous rights, and was the catalyst for Tariana Turia's resignation from Labour in May 2004 to form the Māori Party. In a by-election two months later, Turia retained her Te Tai Hauāuru electorate, marking the beginning of the political presence of the Māori Party that has continued. The dynamics of the MMP electoral system were evident following a close general election in October 2005 that resulted in Helen Clark's formation of a Labour-led Coalition Government with the Progressive Party. Both New Zealand First and United Future supported the government, resulting in each party receiving ministerial positions outside Cabinet. The following year, the government announced an $11.5 billion surplus, the largest in the country's history.

Other political changes occurred in 2006, with Anand Satyanand becoming the nineteenth governor-general of New Zealand, succeeding Dame Silvia Cartwright. In the same year John Key became leader of the National Party, and at the 2008 election Labour was defeated. The minority National-led Government, with Key as prime minister, had confidence-and-supply support from the ACT, United Future and Māori parties. Tariana Turia and Pita Sharples became ministers outside Cabinet, reflecting the determination of the Māori Party to form alliances that would advance the interests of Māori.

The legislative changes between 2001 and 2009 included social work registration, regulation of health professionals, a smoke-free environment, reform in the areas of prostitution, criminal records, civil unions, welfare payments, and the use of force in disciplining children.

In March 2002, Kieran O'Donoghue and Professor Robyn Munford appeared before the Social Services Select Committee in support of the Social Workers Registration Bill as part of the Aotearoa New Zealand Association of Social Work Educators submission. After decades of debate regarding the registration of social workers, the Social Workers Registration Act was passed in 2003. The Act provided the framework for the voluntary registration of social workers, and enabled the establishment of the Social Workers Registration Board (SWRB). The SWRB is a Crown entity that provides the public with an assurance that registered social workers (RSWs) are qualified, competent and fit to practise. It also holds RSWs accountable for their conduct, and requires them to undertake ongoing professional development.

Further interest in the competence of professionals was evident in the introduction of the Health Practitioners Competence Assurance Act 2003, which provided a framework for the regulation of health practitioners in order to protect the public where there was a risk of harm from professional practice. The principal purpose of protecting the health and safety of the public was emphasised, and the Act included mechanisms to ensure that practitioners were competent and fit to practise their professions for the duration of their professional lives.

Concern about public health was evident in the passing of the Smoke-free Environments Amendment Act 2003. Smoking was banned in workplaces and licensed premises, and all indoor workplaces became 100 per cent smoke-free. Another occupational health and safety initiative was the Prostitution Reform Act 2003, which aimed to safeguard the human rights of sex workers and protect them from exploitation, and to promote the welfare and occupational health and safety of sex workers (Sheehan, 2015).

A human rights focus was apparent in the Civil Unions Act 2004 and the Relationships (Statutory References) Act 2005, which removed discrimination on the basis of relationship status, and resulted in couples (same-sex, heterosexual and de facto) having the same legal rights as heterosexual married couples.

The rights, welfare, best interests and development of children through guardianship and care arrangements were the focus of the Care of Children Act 2004. Another piece of legislation pertaining to the care of children was the Crimes (Substituted Section 59) Amendment Act 2007, which was introduced as a private member's Bill by Sue Bradford, a Green Party MP. This Act removed the legal defence of 'reasonable force' for parents prosecuted for assault on their children, and was subject to considerable public debate, to the extent that a non-binding citizens-initiated referendum was held in 2009 in relation to whether the smacking of children should become a criminal offence. There was no change to the law as a result of this referendum.

The de-stigmatisation and rehabilitation of minor offenders was the aim of the Criminal Records (Clean Slate) Act 2004. This Act allowed people who had not reoffended for seven years to not have to declare minor criminal convictions in most circumstances. It was recognised that the majority of people affected by this change had committed a minor offence in their youth. However, many professions, including social work, continued to require disclosure of a full criminal record for persons seeking admission into the profession.

Significant change in government policy regarding welfare payments was evident when in 2005 the Social Development minister Steve Maharey announced that seven benefits would be merged into one, with supplements available for accommodation, disability and childcare. The benefits replaced included unemployment, sickness, disability and the domestic purposes benefit. The new benefit regime was applied from 2007, and involved three tiers of assistance. The first tier referred to benefits such as the domestic purposes benefit and the unemployment benefit, which were expected to meet basic living costs and were subject to income tax. Additional assistance to meet particular circumstances and alleviate hardship was available. These payments constituted the second and third tiers, and were not taxed. Eligibility for second-tier assistance was mostly income-tested, and might be cash-/asset-tested. Third-tier assistance was tightly income- and asset-tested, and was provided generally in relation to hardship that was established by a formula-based assessment where essential costs could not be met within the applicant's current income and assets. These changes reflected the aims of the social assistance system of emphasising sustainable employment and providing social and financial support to people for whom work was not appropriate, or who for some reason were not able to work for a time.

B icultural relations remained an area of contention as different points of view continued to be articulated. Controversy erupted following the 'Nationhood' speech by National Party leader Don Brash, delivered to the Orewa Rotary Club on 27 January 2004. Brash was critical of the government's policy towards Māori, and in particular the special status of Māori people. He advocated 'one rule for all' and the ending of what he saw as special privileges for Māori. Despite being criticised by many as racist, the speech (dubbed 'the Orewa speech') resulted in a major surge of support for the National Party. From 28 per cent in the polls a month before the speech, the National Party jumped to 45 per cent two weeks after it — 10 points ahead of the Labour Party. This contributed to Labour reviewing its policies to ensure that they were based on need, not race.

A few months later, the government became embroiled in the foreshore and seabed controversy. The background to this controversy was a Court of Appeal decision in respect of *Ngāti Apa v Attorney General* in June 2003, which determined that the Māori Land Court had jurisdiction to determine whether the foreshore and seabed had the status of Māori customary land. In response to public concern about this situation, the government decided that it would bring legislation in the form of the

Foreshore and Seabed Act 2004, which in essence would put all public foreshore and seabed in Crown ownership. The government's foreshore and seabed legislation resulted in the resignation of Cabinet minister Tariana Turia, who then formed the Māori Party. On 5 May 2005, a hīkoi arrived in Wellington in protest against the proposed legislation to vest ownership of New Zealand's foreshore and seabed to the Crown.

In 2009, the National-led Government, as part of a November 2008 confidence-and-supply agreement with the Māori Party, undertook a review of the Foreshore and Seabed Act 2004. In response to the review, the Marine and Coastal Area (Takutai Moana) Act 2011 was passed, repealing the 2004 Act. The new law replaced Crown ownership of the foreshore and seabed with a 'no ownership' regime, and restored the right of iwi to seek customary rights and title in court. This change in policy illustrated the political pragmatism associated with the MMP political environment.

On 15 August 2006, Māori Queen Dame Te Atairangikaahu died after a long illness. She was the first woman, also known as 'The Lady', to lead the Kīngitanga, and the first Māori queen. Te Atairangikaahu had endeared herself to her people, and assumed the Māori title Te Arikinui. One of the most important achievements during her reign was Tainui–Waikato's 1995 settlement with the government over land confiscations. Te Atairangikaahu was inducted into the Order of New Zealand in 1987, and was made an honorary doctor of laws by Victoria University of Wellington in 1999. Tuheitia Paki, the eldest son of Dame Te Atairangikaahu, was selected as the new Māori King.

Between 2001 and 2009, there were several social issues of public interest. The first was concern about the power of the international banking sector, and found expression in the launch of the New Zealand-owned Kiwibank in 2002; the bank originated from Alliance Party policy during the 1999–2002 term of the Labour-led Coalition Government. The bank sought to provide competitive services, products and interest rates. The Kiwibank Board was accountable to New Zealand Post and its shareholding ministers (the Minister of Finance and the Minister of State-Owned Enterprises).

The next issue concerned the lives of children, and saw the Agenda for Children launched by the Ministry of Social Development, in June 2002, as a strategy aimed at improving the lives of children. In particular, the agenda articulated principles to guide government policies and services affecting children that included a 'whole child' approach to child policy and service development. There was also a commitment to end child poverty; this goal has proved difficult to achieve, however, with child poverty rising from 15 per cent in 1984 to 29 per cent in 2015 (Simpson, Duncanson, Oben, Wicken, & Pierson, 2015).

Reaction to the 9/11 attacks in the United States could be seen in the role of the Security Intelligence Service. The case of Ahmed Zaoui, an Algerian member of the Islamic Salvation Front who arrived in New Zealand in December 2002 seeking, and achieving, refugee status, attracted considerable media and political attention and divided the public. The government overrode the decision to grant status, maintaining it had information that Zaoui was a credible security risk. In December 2005, the Supreme Court granted Ahmed Zaoui bail, and objections from the Security Intelligence Service were finally withdrawn in September 2007, allowing him to remain in New Zealand. Ahmed Zaoui was granted New Zealand citizenship in 2014.

The forces of religious conservatism were evident in August 2004, when the Destiny Church led the 'Enough is enough' march to Parliament in protest at the Labour Government's policy changes to the drinking age, the legalising of prostitution, and the introduction of the Civil Union Bill. In particular, the church was concerned at the official recognition of same-sex relationships, which was thought to undermine traditional marriage.

The march attracted around 7500 members of the fundamentalist church.

The issue of student loans and associated debt had attracted public interest since the introduction of the loan scheme in 1992. In 2006, the Labour Government enacted an election promise to remove interest on loans to students living in New Zealand. Average student loan balances had increased substantially over time; a 2007 survey by the New Zealand Union of Students' Associations found that the average student debt was over $28,000, up 54 per cent from 2004. The impact of debt on students was significant, affecting their ability to pursue further study, purchase housing and save for retirement. This issue remains contentious. For example, between 2008 and 2016 tertiary providers have experienced a 9 per cent rise in costs, whereas government funding has risen 3.5 per cent, resulting in increased student fees, and consequentially, student debt.

The New Zealand economy entered recession in early 2008, before the effects of the Global Financial Crisis set in later in the year. Domestic activity had slowed due to the high fuel and food prices that reduced domestic consumption. At the same time, high interest rates and falling house prices resulted in a rapid decline in residential investment. The impact on the unemployment rate was marked, rising from 4.2 per cent in 2008 to 6.9 per cent in 2012.

Following a positive response to a pilot in 30 decile-one schools in 2008, the KickStart Breakfast programme was launched by the government, in a partnership with dairy giant Fonterra and Weet Bix producer Sanitarium. The programme represented an attempt to reduce inequities, and improve the health, and social and academic outcomes for vulnerable children. Advocates fighting child poverty hailed the move as long overdue, but also argued that the programme did not address society's fundamental problems. A contrary view held that the programme absolved parents of their responsibilities and added to a culture of dependency. The programme continues, and in 2015 was providing breakfasts of milk and

Weet-Bix twice a week to children in more than 500 lower-decile schools two days a week (48,000 breakfasts a week).

The MMP environment continued, with coalition and minority-led governments, and this offered further evidence of the influence of the minor parties, and their ability to exert leverage. The case of Ahmed Zaoui highlighted government concern with political risk following 9/11, but also brought into sharp relief societal attitudes towards refugees and migrants; working to support new arrivals' settlement into Aotearoa New Zealand was an emerging area of social work practice.

For social work, the formation of the SWRB heralded a new era in both regulation of the profession and monitoring of education providers. As the construction of social welfare moved towards a focus on social development, the influence of neoliberal thought regarding self-responsibility remained evident in the issue of student loans, which continues to have implications for the training of social workers and other lower-paid social service professions.

While apparent national concern for the welfare of children was seen (in the 'anti-smacking' Bill, the Agenda for Children, and the breakfast-in-schools programme), the debate regarding the role of the State was contested, with the question of who was responsible for advocating for children unable to act on their own behalf remaining unclear.

The development of social work

ANZASW remained active throughout this period, being involved in competence assessment, programme approval, and the promotion of social work education and practice. The Niho Taniwha, the Māori competency approach for Māori social workers, was launched in 2001. This kaupapa Māori process was developed by the association's Māori caucus, Tangata Whenua Takawaenga o Aotearoa. This was led out by Massey University graduate Turoa Haronga.

In 2002, ANZASW established a course approval board and conducted the first course approval at the University of Otago, followed by the Unitec Institute of Technology (2004) and the University of Auckland (2004). It was hoped that the ANZASW course-approval system could be linked with the SWRB; however, the prospect of a joint approach did not eventuate (McNabb, 2014). In the end, this programme was discontinued, and the SWRB now has responsibility for the recognition of social work qualifications in Aotearoa New Zealand.

The association continued to hold regular conferences. The 2002 Christchurch conference theme was 'Local and global visions for social work practice in Aotearoa New Zealand'. In 2004, the ANZASW's fortieth-anniversary conference was held in Auckland. In celebrating this anniversary, ANZASW established National Social Workers Day, to be held annually on the third Wednesday of September. This day promotes social work, and acknowledges the contribution of social workers to the fabric of Aotearoa New Zealand society, as well as aiming to raise the professional profile of social work. Palmerston North was the venue of the 2006 conference, which had the theme of 'Keeping your balance', with keynote speakers being Toni Hocquard, Dr Tracie Mafile'o, Rawinia Hape and Diana Crosson (the then Retirement Commissioner).

In keeping with the bicultural focus of ANZASW, the Tangata Whenua Takawaenga Māori caucus also ran its own annual hui. ANZASW changed its structure and constitution in 2007, replacing the national executive and national council with a governance board. The same year, the title of its journal *Social Work Review* was changed to *Aotearoa New Zealand Social Work Review* from 19(2) issue onwards, continuing to offer *Review*, *Te Kōmako* and *Tu Mau* issues. Ksenija Napan and Gavin Rennie resigned as editors, with Kieran O'Donoghue and Mary Nash from Massey University editing the journal from issue 19(3) through to issue 27(3) in 2015.

A national congress was held in 2008, with Children's Commissioner Dr Cindy Kiro delivering the inaugural Merv Hancock Address. ANZASW also launched its continuing professional development service, and a new bilingual version of the code of ethics. The next year marked the first national fono of the Pasifika Social Workers Interest Group (PSWIG), held in Wellington on 16 April 2009. Later that year, Dr Mary Nash was invited to give the Merv Hancock Address: 'Imagination, hope and steady nerves: A tried and true ANZASW recipe for success' at the ANZASW Congress in September.

As noted above, the SWRB was established in 2003, with the nine members of the inaugural board announced by Minister Steve Maharey on 5 November 2003. Two of the inaugural board members, Sonya Hunt and Yvonne Crichton-Hill, were Massey University social work alumni. In 2004, Sean McKinley was appointed as registrar, and the board produced a range of position papers and policy statements, including: a discussion paper on recognised qualifications; *Entitlement to registration*; *Fit and proper*; *Enough experience and competency*. A policy was also released on recognised qualifications, raising the foundation qualification to a minimum of a three-year Bachelor's degree. The Massey social work programme made submissions on all of the SWRB discussion and position papers in 2004.

Shannon Pakura became the first registered social worker, on 9 December 2004, and in April 2005 members were appointed to the Complaints and Disciplinary Tribunal. The SWRB Code of Conduct was issued in May 2005, and an education advisory group was established to develop a process for the recognition of social work qualifications, with the first recognition being completed at the University of Otago in 2006. Also introduced in 2005 was Te Ara Aromatawai — Te Kaiawhina Ahumahi competence assessment process as an alternative to the ANZASW process. By 2006, more than 1000 social workers had registered with the SWRB (SWRB, 2006). Other developments included the new Graduate Competence Policy in 2008, and the introduction of the SWRB's own competence accreditation service in 2009.

The Child, Youth and Family service (CYF) was to continue to undergo change which reflected the ongoing challenge of working in the field of child protection. On 23 October 2003, the CYF baseline review was released. The review was conducted by Treasury, the Ministry of Social Development, the State Services Commission, and Child, Youth and Family. Child, Youth and Family Minister Ruth Dyson stated:

> The review has revealed systemic problems with Child, Youth and Family, unclear outcome priorities and variability in the quality of service. Our goal now is to help the department stabilise its operations, learn more about what works, and improve its performance. (Dyson, 2003)

The five key recommendations of the review were to clarify the expectations, outcomes, roles and functions of CYF; address the demand for CYF services; improve CYF's interface with other agencies and sectors; adopt a whole-of-organisation approach to service delivery; and build corporate and business systems, information and workforce capability. It is apposite to note that the issues and challenges identified in 2003 would be revisited in 2015. Dr Marie Connolly, appointed Chief Social Worker of CYF in 2005, became the driving force behind the development of an integrated set of practice frameworks, designed to establish the foundations for effective practice in the agency. The frameworks were described as follows:

> Practice Frameworks articulate ethically-informed practice that supports strong engagement with families, harnesses the strengths of the child's extended family system, reinforces longer term safety and belonging for the child or young person and ensures a justice accountability within youth justice. It sets a standard for service delivery providing a high level vision of

practice that the organisation wants to see across Child, Youth and Family. (Child, Youth and Family Practice Centre, 2016)

A summary of Marie Connolly's work can be found in 'Practice frameworks: Conceptual maps to guide interventions in child welfare' in the *British Journal of Social Work* (Connolly, 2007).

In July 2006, Child, Youth and Family merged with the Ministry of Social Development (MSD) as a service line of the ministry. It was argued that the merger would allow closer working with partners in the social sector to improve services to vulnerable children and young people and their families. Further, the merger would strengthen CYF's whole-of-government approach to helping children and young people in need.

This period was also one of significant professional development activity. In 2004, there were two conferences for social workers. The first was the supervision conference, 'Weaving together the strands of supervision', in Auckland, convened by the Auckland College of Education, which had recently been incorporated into the University of Auckland from being a standalone college. Dr Leland Ruwhiu presented a keynote address about Tangata Whenua Supervision; another keynote was that of Allyson Davys, who had recently completed her Master of Social Work thesis entitled *Perceptions through a prism: Three accounts of good social work supervision* (Davys, 2002). Several Massey University staff (Kieran O'Donoghue, Chris Thomas and Helen Simmons) presented, along with graduates from the Post Graduate Diploma in Social Service Supervision.

The second conference, the 'Global Social Work Congress 2004: Reclaiming civil society', was held in Adelaide, South Australia. A significant contingent of the Massey University social work programme staff attended and presented at the conference. Wheturangi Walsh-

Tapiata gave a keynote speech on 'The past, the present and future: The New Zealand indigenous experience'.

In November 2009, the 20th Asia Pacific Social Work Conference was held in Auckland, and was attended by almost 400 delegates from around the Asia Pacific region. The conference with a theme of 'Many voices, many communities, social justice for all' was a joint venture hosted by ANZASW and the Asia Pacific Association of Social Work Educators (APASWE) on behalf of the International Federation of Social Workers, and APASWE.

In 2006, the Non-Government Organisation Study Awards were established by the Ministry of Social Development. The purpose of the awards was to build the capability of people working in community-based social services, by assisting non-government organisation (NGO) employees to undertake part-time study for a degree-level qualification in social work. Funding could assist the student with course fees, and the employer with study-related expenses, including backfilling the employee's position while they were studying or on placement. In 2015, the ministry reported that 432 students had successfully gained a recognised qualification since the inception of the awards, and that 31 per cent of recipients had attended Massey University. Regrettably, the awards have now been disestablished for new applicants.

In 2009, about 100 of the country's 1000 tangata whenua social workers gathered at Pūkaki Marae in Mangere to launch the Tangata Whenua Social Workers Association. The group's aim was to support Māori working for mainstream and iwi providers, and help train new kaimahi to operate effectively with Māori whānau. The development of 'by Māori for Māori' services has grown progressively over the past 20 years. The association asserted:

Rangatiratanga has always been the aspiration of New Zealand's indigenous social workers . . . Māori practice models, Māori frameworks, Māori fields of practice and iwi/Māori social services are all assertions of rangatiratanga. (Tangata Whenua Social Workers Association, 2009)

The development of social work in Aotearoa New Zealand during this period continued to be influenced by the ongoing commitment of ANZASW to professionalism. However, following the establishment of the SWRB, this began to change as the regulatory authority became more prominent in its recognition of social work qualifications, competence assessment and ethical conduct.

The development of the Tangata Whenua Social Workers Association at the end of the period was important, and as an exercise of rangatiratanga paralleled to some extent the development of the Māori Party. The performance of the State agency responsible for the care and protection of children was again in the spotlight particularly with regard to unallocated cases. That said, with the development of the CYF practice framework and online practice centre there were clear signs of a stronger practice focus. With regard to children's issues, the definition of child poverty (and the responsibility to respond) remained a contentious issue. The merger of CYF into the MSD reflected the dominance of the social development discourse.

For the tertiary education sector and Massey University, this was a period of significant change and competition. The establishment of the Tertiary Education Commission (TEC) in 2002 as the sole body responsible for administering all post-compulsory education funding was the first significant change. At that time, the tertiary education sector encompassed eight universities, 20 polytechnics, four colleges of education, three wānanga, over 500 registered private training establishments, 46 industry training organisations, nine government training establishments and 17 other tertiary education providers. In 2001/02, the government budget for tertiary education was $3.3 billion, which was 1 per cent of gross domestic product (GDP), and 5 per cent of government spending.

The TEC introduced the fees maxima limit in 2004, to provide a ceiling beyond which fees and course costs could rise. The TEC also introduced and administered a new system for funding research and for research degree completions in the form of the Performance Based Research Fund (PBRF). The fund was introduced to ensure that excellent research in the tertiary education sector was encouraged and rewarded. The tertiary education organisations (TEOs) are assessed and then funded on the basis of their performance. There are three components to the fund: research degree completions; external research income; and the quality evaluation, which is an assessment by expert peer-review panels of the research performance of staff whose research is presented in an evidence portfolio. In this period, there was a baseline round in 2002, followed by a second round in 2006, which encompassed research completed up until 31 December 2005.

For the Massey social work programme there was increased competition within the university sector, with the University of Canterbury offering an MSW (Applied) in 2003, and the Auckland College of Education being merged with the University of Auckland in 2004 and offering a four-year BSW from 2006. Then, in 2009, the University of Waikato applied to offer a Bachelor of Social Work from its Tauranga campus. The SWRB recognition of New Zealand social work qualifications policy in 2005 shifted the foundation qualification to a Bachelor's degree, with the result that the polytechnic and institute of technology sector upgraded diploma programmes to three-year (360-credit) degrees. Also in this period, Te Wānanga o Aotearoa developed its social work and social service offerings, with a Bachelor in Bicultural Social Work available from 2004.

There were also significant changes and developments, the first being a change in senior leadership in 2002 with the resignation of Vice-Chancellor Professor James McWha, who was subsequently replaced by

Professor Judith Kinnear in early 2003. That same year, Professor Mason Durie was appointed Assistant Vice-Chancellor Māori.

On the campuses there was also further development. At Albany, the building programme continued with the library building being occupied in February 2003, with an extension to the library completed in 2009. The Recreation Centre was opened in August 2004, and the Sir Neil Waters Lecture Theatre in February 2006. In Palmerston North, the Social Science Tower was refurbished at the end of 2001; in Wellington, the College of Humanities and Social Sciences established its presence in Block 7.

The Massey University Foundation was established in 2004, the university's registered charity to foster philanthropy at Massey. The foundation's vision is to create an endowment fund that will exist in perpetuity to ensure that Massey University continues to define New Zealand by contributing to its life and economy through excellent teaching, research and invention.

By 2006, the university's student numbers had grown to a total of 35,213; including 18,462 internal students (7772 in Palmerston North, 6606 in Auckland and 4084 in Wellington) and 16,751 extramural students. In 2009, the university celebrated having a thousand concurrently enrolled PhD students.

Within the College of Humanities and Social Sciences there was organisational repositioning of programmes in 2006, which occurred shortly after Professor Munford stepped down as the Head of the School of Sociology, Social Policy and Social Work. The sociology programme moved to the School of People, Environment and Planning from the start of 2007. Professor John Overton became Head of School Social Work and Social Policy for six weeks, before Professor Paul Spoonley assumed the role for most of 2007 in Palmerston North. In November 2007, Associate Professor Mike O'Brien was appointed Director of Social Work and Social Policy, effective from 1 January 2008.

The Social Work and Social Policy programme then merged with Health Sciences to become the School of Health and Social Services. This decision also meant that the social work and social policy staff from the School of Social and Cultural Studies at Albany transferred from that school into the new School of Health and Social Services.

In 2009, the head of school, Professor Carol McVeigh, resigned, and Emeritus Professor Warwick Slinn was appointed acting head of school until Professor Steve LaGrow took up the position from 1 November 2009. Another change in senior leadership occurred when Vice-Chancellor Professor Judith Kinnear retired in February 2008, and the Honourable Steve Maharey, former Minister of Education, was designated as the new Vice-Chancellor, taking up the position in October 2008. Other changes in senior leadership saw Pro Vice-Chancellor of the College of Humanities and Social Sciences Professor Barrie Macdonald farewelled after 37 years' service, with confirmation that he would be a professor emeritus of the university, an honour awarded by the University Council. Professor Macdonald was succeeded by the internationally recognised historian Professor Susan Mumm.

Massey's social work programme continued its development in response to academic requirements and expectations from the social work sector. The twenty-fifth anniversary of the BSW at Massey was celebrated at the Turitea campus with the 'New initiatives' conference on 29–30 November 2001, with the conference keynote speaker being Professor Robyn Munford. The conference was followed by a 25-year reunion of BSW alumni organised by Mary Ann Baskerville. Merv Hancock and Ephra Garrett were in attendance as honoured guests.

The following year, the Merv Hancock and Ephra Garrett Awards were established at the Turitea campus in recognition of Merv and Ephra's contribution to the social work programme. The Merv Hancock Award is for the outstanding tauiwi student, while the Ephra Garrett Award is for the outstanding Māori student. Sadly, Ephra passed away on 3 April 2008; since her passing, her whānau have attended the award ceremony each year, and the recipient of the Ephra Garrett Award has the honour of wearing Ephra's korowai.

Other programme developments that occurred through this period included:

- In 2001, a specialist programme PG Dip Arts (Disability Studies) was offered with a focus on autism.
- The first social work courses commenced using WebCT (the forerunner to Moodle) support in the MSW (Applied) in 2002. Stream (the Moodle platform) was introduced in 2009, with the BSW being one of the pilot degrees.
- Offerings for the Master of Social Work were enhanced with specialist papers added in mental health (2002), spirituality in social work (2003), and child welfare (2004), which was developed in conjunction with Child, Youth and Family's Chief Social Worker's Office.
- The MSW (Applied) was amended to increase the credit value of placement papers from 15 credits to 30 credits, while the Management and Applied research methods papers were reduced to 15 credits.
- In 2005, police checks were introduced for placement papers in both the BSW and MSW (Applied).
- In 2006, a project to develop core social work skills DVDs was undertaken by Mary Nash, Kieran O'Donoghue, Carole Adamson and Tracie Mafile'o, with Maria Rivera-Scotter as project coordinator. This was supported by the Fund for Innovation and Excellence in Teaching, and the project materials were incorporated into teaching in a range of papers in all years of the BSW programme.
- The Certificate in Pacific Development was first offered in 2009 to assist students and workers from a range of professions to better understand Pacific cultures.

- The PG Certificate and the Diploma in Whānau Development were offered from the Albany campus in 2009.

In 2006, an internal qualification review of the social work programmes was completed. Qualification reviews are considered to be a key element of the university's quality assurance and enhancement framework. The 2006 review commended the staff and the university on the quality of the programme and its fitness for purpose. The report made some other significant recommendations related to marketing the programme, advancing whakawhānaungatanga throughout the programme, establishing an external advisory group, and making the Master of Applied Social Work a separate degree rather than an option within the MSW regulations. The report concluded by highlighting the risks of too much organisational change on the programme, and suggested a risk-management approach towards future change.

With a focus of enhancing the programme, the Pro Vice-Chancellor convened a working party on social policy and social work, to provide advice regarding the academic portfolio and the staffing profile for an integrated social work programme within the college. The working party comprised Professor Warwick Slinn, Dr Julie Bunnell, Dr Mark Henrickson, Associate Professor Peter Lineham, Professor Robyn Munford and Professor Paul Spoonley. Recommendations to be subsequently adopted by the Pro Vice-Chancellor included:

- An integrated social policy and social work programme across both Albany and Palmerston North campuses
- No new BSW students internally on the Wellington campus from 2008
- A transition plan from 2008 to 2010 for students in the BSW in Wellington to complete their studies
- The development of a fully extramural BSW in years three and four — prior to this students had studied internally from the third year.

At the 2001 anniversary conference. *From left*: Professor Robyn Munford, Mary Ann Baskerville, Alison Hancock, Merv Hancock, Ephra Garrett, Dr Mike O'Brien and Dr Mary Nash. **DR MARY NASH COLLECTION**

Ephra Garrett's son, Lyn Garrett, explains the significance of Ephra's korowai to fourth-year social work students in 2016. To his left is Merv's daughter, Mary, and Professor Robyn Munford, holding a picture of Ephra. **SCHOOL OF SOCIAL WORK**

Formal external accreditation of the BSW and MSW (Applied) degrees under the Social Workers Registration Act 2003 occurred through a programme recognition visit in 2008 by an SWRB panel to both campuses. This resulted in both the BSW and MSW (Applied) being recognised for five years through to 31 December 2013. One of the recommendations from this review was the re-establishment of the role of Director of Field Education, which Kathryn Hay assumed in 2009.

Two long-serving staff members who had been with the programme since its earliest years retired in 2007. The first of these was Mary Ann Baskerville, who had been with the programme since 1978, and had made an outstanding contribution to field education and supervision. In 2008, the Mary Ann Baskerville Field Educator Award was established to recognise Mary Ann's work in this area. This award is made annually to an outstanding field educator of a student completing placement in a social work degree.

The second retirement was Janet Milne, who was the school administrator at the beginning of the programme. Janet had supported Merv Hancock, Graeme Fraser, Ian Shirley and Robyn Munford in their time as leaders. She trained the administration staff, set up the school systems, and supported staff through all of the mergers and the development of the programme at Albany and Wellington. At her farewell, the administration team formed a guard of honour and saluted Janet for her leadership and support.

During the period reviewed, the Massey social work programme remained responsive to both the university and the external social work environment. In the face of increasing competition, organisational change was implemented. This focused on achieving greater synergies between the academic programme, research and business efficiency. Also of significance were the demands of the PBRF programme, the development of new offerings, and the continued development of the profile of staff within the social work arena.

Professor Robyn Munford farewells longstanding staff member Janet Milne, in 2007. Janet's husband Professor Ken Milne enjoys the speech. **SCHOOL OF SOCIAL WORK**

Academic staff appointments and changes, 2001–2009

- 2001: Gwen Ellis, Director of Field Education, resigned and returned to practice.
  - Jane Brook started as a tutor at Wellington.
  - Maureen Arathoon employed as a tutor.
- 2002: Associate Professor Rajen Prasad returned to Massey University after being Race Relations Conciliator.
  - Kieran O'Donoghue employed as a lecturer in social work at Palmerston North.
  - Justina Webster employed as a tutor.
- 2003: Helen Simmons employed as a tutor at Palmerston North.
  - Gail Bosmann employed as an assistant lecturer at Palmerston North.
  - Jenny Blagdon employed as a tutor at Wellington.
  - Christa Fouché employed at Albany as an associate professor.
  - Mark Henrickson employed at Albany as a senior lecturer.
  - Fiona Te Momo employed at Albany as a lecturer.
- 2004: Hayley Bell appointed as an assistant lecturer at Palmerston North.
  - Barbara Staniforth employed at Albany as a lecturer.
  - Karen Shepherd appointed as a tutor in Palmerston North.
  - Carmen Payne appointed as a tutor at Wellington.
- 2005: Associate Professor Andrew Trlin retired.

- Associate Professor Robin Peace appointed to teach social policy and develop the Social Sector Evaluation Diploma.
- Simon Nash employed at Palmerston North as a lecturer.
- Dr Jacqueline Sanders employed as a research officer.
- 2006: Dr Richard Shaw, Dr Christine Cheyne and Associate Professor Robin Peace transferred to the School of People, Environment and Planning.
  - Dr Celia Briar resigned.
  - Hanny Naus employed at Wellington campus.
- 2007: Jan Rimmer started at Albany as a field education coordinator.
  - Associate Professor Mike O'Brien appointed Director of Social Work and Social Policy.
  - Mary Ann Baskerville retired.
  - Janet Milne, School Administrative Services Manager, retired.
- 2008: Associate Professor Mike O'Brien stood down as director.
  - Rachael Selby appointed as acting director.
  - Dr Sue Hanna employed as a senior lecturer at Palmerston North.
  - Dr Tony Stanley appointed at Albany as a senior lecturer.
  - Drs Tracie Mafile'o, Carole Adamson and Tony Stanley resigned and left the university for overseas positions.
  - Pa'u Tafaogalupe II Mulitalo-Lauta resigned from Massey University.
- 2009: Litea Meo-Sewabu started as an assistant lecturer.

The period 2001 to 2009 was marked by Massey's continued contribution to the development of social work in Aotearoa New Zealand by Massey's social work programme. This was particularly evident in the increased numbers of staff publications, theses completed, and recognition gained by both staff and alumni.

A number of Massey social work staff received recognition in the form of awards and appointments:

- In 2002, Professor Robyn Munford was made an Officer of the New Zealand Order of Merit for services to social work education and policy.
- In 2003, Mary Nash was awarded life membership of ANZASW.
- In November 2004, Kieran O'Donoghue was awarded the Certificate of Commendation: He Koha Tohu Aroha Na Tumuaki by ANZASW, in recognition of his outstanding contribution to ANZASW in relation to the preparation of the association's professional standards, course approval standards and audit tools.
- In June 2004, Dr Rajen Prasad was appointed as the first Chief Commissioner of the newly established Families Commission, serving until 2008.
- In 2006, Professor Robyn Munford was awarded the Massey University Research Supervisor Medal.

The contribution of staff to indigenous practice issues was significant. Wheturangi Walsh-Tapiata was seconded from 2004 to 2006 to an HRC/FRST research project entitled 'Whaia te hauora o nga rangatahi', which investigated the health and wellbeing of rangatahi Māori. The project was under the umbrella of Te Runanga o Raukawa Inc.

Tu Mau, the first Pasifika peoples issue of *Aotearoa New Zealand Social Work Review* (formerly, *Social Work Review*), was edited by Tracie Mafile'o and Christine Newport. *Te Kōmako* 2003 was edited by Rachael Selby, Wheturangi Walsh-Tapiata, Gail Bosmann-Watene and Justina Webster.

Massey University was contracted by the University of Melbourne to train the staff of Fiji's Department of Social Welfare from 2002 to 2006, under AusAid. The team, supported by Professor Munford, comprised Rachael Selby, Wheturangi Walsh-Tapiata, Tracie Mafile'o, Gail Bosmann and Helen Simmons. The team was supported by BSW graduate and Department of Social Welfare consultant Emele Duituturaga. The work undertaken by the staff in Fiji led to the Fijian Association of Social Workers joining the International Federation of Social Workers in 2008.

A focus on research was maintained, with Massey staff securing a number of prestigious grants.

- Professor Robyn Munford (with Jackie Sanders) received a grant for the period 2002 to 2008 from the Foundation for Research, Science and Technology for a project entitled 'Family and community well-being: Managing changes'.
- Dr Martin Sullivan was awarded a research grant from the Health Research Council for the period 2007 to 2012. The grant was to complete 'A longitudinal study of the life histories of people with spinal cord injury'.
- Professors Robyn Munford and Jackie Sanders were awarded a grant from the Ministry of Business, Innovation and Employment (MBIE) to undertake a national mixed-methods investigation of troubled children's and young people's pathways to resilience, in the Pathways to Resilience Project (PtRP), over the period 2008–2016.
- Professors Robyn Munford and Jackie Sanders were awarded a further grant from MBIE to the following project from 2009 to 2019: 'Long-term successful youth transitions — a national, longitudinal mixed-methods investigation'.

Following the withdrawal of the Auckland College of Education in 2002 from a CYF professional supervision contract, the Massey University social work team, through the Practice Research and Development Hub under Professor Munford's leadership, undertook to deliver the course on their own through to the end of 2009. The hub also provided a developing advanced practice programme for senior practitioners.

Three Master's theses were completed by staff during this period. Jenny Jakobs focused on how messy teenage bedrooms affected parents (Jakobs, 2005). Christine Thomas and Helen Simmons completed theses concerned with supervision. Chris's thesis was focused on the implementation of strengths-based supervision, while Helen's explored the expression and experience of spirituality with supervision (Thomas, 2005; Simmons, 2006).

Five staff completed doctorates. The first of these was Richard Shaw, whose thesis explored the motive of senior politicians and officials involved in the decision-making on the government's employment strategy, and the influence individual actors and institutional arrangements had on the development of the employment strategy (Shaw, 2001b).

Jackie Sanders' (2004) doctoral thesis was an ethnographic account of everyday life for 18 healthy and safe children aged between 10 and 11 years from small-town Aotearoa New Zealand, and provided the foundation for the funded research she undertook later in this period.

In 2005, Carole Adamson completed a thesis concerned with staff support systems in mental health after critical incidents and traumatic events (Adamson, 2005b).

Tongan metaphors of social work practice were the focus of Tracie Mafile'o's thesis, which demonstrated that a Tongan worldview provides a relevant framework for social and community work practice amongst Tongans in the diaspora (Mafile'o, 2005b).

Lastly, Simon Nash's social policy thesis was concerned with local government environmental planning and decision-making (Nash, 2007).

The influence of PBRF became evident during the period 2001 to 2009, with staff contributing in both Aotearoa New Zealand and international journals and publications. A brief commentary follows on themes that emerged in these publications.

A range of Māori and indigenous development issues were explored by several staff. For example, Michael Belgrave co-edited *Waitangi revisited: Perspectives on the Treaty of Waitangi* (2005), while Peter Mataira built on his PhD study through discussing partnership, indigenous entrepreneurship, and the politics of cross-cultural research in the social sciences. Leland Ruwhiu examined bicultural issues in social work, and Māori tools of engagement in both policy and practice. Fiona Te Momo addressed Māori volunteerism, work–life balance for Māori academic women, and whānau development. The focus for Wheturangi Walsh-Tapiata was rangatahi, and issues surrounding identity, leadership and health. Wheturangi also contributed to discourse surrounding the indigenous experience of social work, and Māori and Pasifika indigenous connections. Wheturangi proposed a model for Māori research, and reflected upon what social services can learn from the practice of research in an iwi setting. The scope of Rachael Selby's scholarship was extensive. In particular, Rachael's expertise regarding oral history was evident, and in 2005 she co-edited *Māori and oral history: A collection* (Selby & Laurie, 2005). Rachael also engaged in environmental issues, the Treaty and Māori research, and contributed a chapter in *Social work theories in action* (2005a).

Child wellbeing was the focus of work by Robyn Munford, Jackie Sanders and Jill Worrall. Robyn Munford and Jackie Sanders wrote on a range of topics, including responsive service provision, children's narratives (along with Andrew Trlin), authentic relationships with children and young people, and the potential of multi-layered interventions. Jill Worrall wrote on the Aotearoa New Zealand experience of kinship care of the abused child, and published *Grandparents raising grandchildren: A handbook for grandparents and other kin caregivers* (2001b, 2003).

Working effectively with families provided the focus for collaboration between Massey and Te Aroha Noa (an innovative NGO in Palmerston North). Bruce Maden (CEO of Te Aroha Noa), Jackie Sanders and Robyn

Munford published on the successful community development approach that focuses upon family and whānau (Munford et al., 2007).

Robyn Munford and Jackie Sanders edited *Making a difference in families: Research that creates change* (2003), to which they also contributed, along with Celia Briar, Mike O'Brien and Leland Ruwhiu. In 2005, Jackie and Robyn wrote on strengths-based approaches to working with families in *Social work theories in action,* and *Strengths-based social work with families* in 2006.

Community development was a further theme to emerge from the work of Massey academics. Jackie Sanders and Robyn Munford published on issues traversing action research in community settings, evaluation of family support in New Zealand, community centre practice, and the possibilities for change for marginalised young women. Robyn Munford and Wheturangi Walsh-Tapiata considered working in the bicultural context of Aotearoa New Zealand, and contributed a chapter 'Community development: Principles into practice' in *Social work theories in action* (2005).

Martin Sullivan and Robyn Munford maintained a focus on disability, traversing a range of issues. Robyn Munford and Garth Bennie contributed the chapter 'Social work and disability' in Marie Connolly's *New Zealand social work: Contexts and practice* (2001), and with Jackie Sanders commented on creating research encounters with parents with an intellectual disability.

Martin co-edited and contributed to *Allies in emancipation: Shifting from providing service to being of support* (2005), and with Robyn considered the question of disability and support. Martin also commented on: philosophy, ethics and the disability community; the emancipatory research paradigm; and a liberation theology of disability.

Celia Briar's emphasis on women's issues included gendering of inequalities in work; family policy; and lone mothers. Feminism, disability and research practice was the subject of an article by M. Lunn and Robyn

Wheturangi Walsh-Tapiata acknowledges Ephra Garrett on her birthday in 2003.
Looking on is Robyn Munford and Wharerata staff member Shirley Crothers.
SCHOOL OF SOCIAL WORK

Editors Kieran O'Donoghue, Professor Robyn Munford and Dr Mary Nash at the
launch of *Social work theories in action*, 2005. **SCHOOL OF SOCIAL WORK**

Munford published in the *Scandinavian Journal of Disability Research* in 2007, while MarilynWaring and Christa Fouché edited and contributed to *Managing mayhem: Work–life balance in New Zealand* (2007).

Foundation qualifying social work degrees involve field education placements, and this aspect of social work education was addressed first by Mary Nash, Robyn Munford and Kathryn Hay, who published *Social work in context: Fields of practice in Aotearoa New Zealand* (2001). The text provided students with analysis of various practice contexts as they considered field education placement options. Later in this period, Kathryn Hay, Kieran O'Donoghue and Jenny Blagdon (2006) surveyed supervisors and student members of ANZASW regarding the aims of social work field education in the registration environment, and the issue of standardising fieldwork assessment in Aotearoa New Zealand (Hay & O'Donoghue, 2009).

Mark Henrickson published extensively on issues affecting the lesbian, gay and bisexual communities in Aotearoa New Zealand. *Lavender islands: The New Zealand study* (Henrickson, Neville, Jordan, & Donaghey, 2007) was the first national strengths-based study of lesbian, gay and bisexual (LGB) people in New Zealand. Mark also published about lavender parents; the perceptions of LGB people of primary healthcare services; lavender immigration; managing multiple identities in Māori LGB; lavender netlife; religion and spirituality in LGB New Zealanders; bullying and educational attainment; and the constitution of 'lavender families'.

The development of a strong Pasifika focus was also evident through Tracie Mafile'o's significant contribution of chapters for *Social work in context: Fields of practice in Aotearoa New Zealand* (2001), *Social work theories in action* (2005a), and *Indigenous social work around the world: Towards culturally relevant education and practice* (2008). Tracie also published on Pasifika social work theory, exploring Tongan social work

Fekau'aki (Connecting) and Fakatokilalo (Humility), the social worker–client relationship in Pasifika social work, understanding youth resilience in Papua New Guinea through life story (with U. Api), and Māori and Pasifika indigenous connections (with Wheturangi Walsh-Tapiata).

The Massey University connection with the University of the South Pacific in Fiji was reflected upon by Rachael Selby in articles on teaching and learning in Fiji (along with Wheturangi Walsh-Tapiata), and new perspectives on learning in the Fiji context. A further matter of interest related to the development of a Pasifika strategy for social work at Massey University (Meo Sewabu, Walsh-Tapiata, Mafile'o, Havea, & Tuileto'a, 2008).

Concern with local government and public administration was evident in a considerable body of work by Christine Cheyne, including decision-making, citizen participation, the role of the mayor in local governance, use of the single transferable vote (STV) in local authority elections, and community wellbeing. Richard Shaw contributed to Millar's (2001, 2006) *New Zealand government and politics*, writing on consultants and advisers, and the public service.

Staff continued to contribute significantly to commentary regarding social policy in Aotearoa New Zealand. The role of ministerial advisers was the subject of three articles published by Chris Eichbaum and Richard Shaw between 2003 and 2007. Additionally, Richard Shaw wrote on public choice and bureaucratic reform, and electoral law reform. In 2005, Christine Cheyne, Michael Belgrave and Mike O'Brien authored a third edition of *Social policy in Aotearoa New Zealand: A critical introduction*.

Barbara Staniforth and Christa Fouché added to the ongoing debate regarding registration with an article concerning 'fit and proper' (Staniforth & Fouché, 2006). In a guest editorial for the *Social Work Review*, Kieran O'Donoghue (2007) offered a critical insight into an alternative proposal for the registration of social workers.

Important contributions to the social work practice literature were also made during this period. In 2001, Robyn Munford and Garth Bennie, Mary Nash, Leland Ruwhiu, Michael O'Brien and Jill Worrall contributed chapters to *New Zealand social work: Contexts and practice,* edited by Marie Connolly (Connolly, 2001). Robyn Munford and Garth Bennie, Mary Nash and Michael O'Brien revised and contributed updated chapters to a later version of this book, which was now titled *Social work: Contexts and practice,* edited by Marie Connolly and Louise Harms (Connolly & Harms, 2009).

In 2005, *Social work theories in action,* edited by Mary Nash, Robyn Munford and Kieran O'Donoghue, was published by Jessica Kingsley Publishers. This text was favourably reviewed in the *British Journal of Social Work* by Anne Quinney (2006, pp. 165–166) from Bournemouth University, who describes the book in her review as:

> ... An important contribution to understanding the complex issues involved in working with ethnic minority groups and indigenous or First Nation people. Whilst it draws on New Zealand and Australian case material, the themes and debates addressed in the book are relevant to all social workers ... it demonstrates in a clearly written and powerful way how social work theories and methods can be applied in practice settings in the promotion of anti-oppressive social work practice.

In this book an integrated practice approach is used, with four complementary theoretical approaches — namely, ecological systems, community development, strengths-based, and attachment theories — across a range of different practice contexts. A unique feature of the book is the insights offered regarding cultural issues that are involved in the application of the social work theories. In addition to the editors' contributions, several other staff and alumni contributed chapters, which focused on the application of theory with regard to trauma, practice with people living with HIV, child protection, mental health, community development with Tonga people, Māori development, refugees and migrants, and bicultural supervision (Adamson, 2005a; Fouché, 2005; Jack, 2005; Keen & O'Donoghue, 2005; Mafile'o, 2005a; Munford & Sanders, 2005; Munford & Walsh-Tapiata, 2005; Nash, 2005; Selby, 2005a; Thomas & Davis, 2005).

Supervision in social work was another key area of research, with the programme team-teaching the Post Graduate Diploma in Social Service Supervision, and providing external training contracts to the Ministry of Social Development and Department of Corrections. In 2001, Liz Beddoe, together with Jill Worrall, edited the proceedings of the supervision conference held in 2000: *From rhetoric to reality: Keynote address and selected papers*. Other supervision topics explored included cultural supervision (Su'a-Hawkins & Mafile'o, 2004), supervision planning (Walsh-Tapiata & Webster, 2004), and supervision across disciplines (Simmons, Moroney, Mace, & Shepherd, 2007).

Kieran O'Donoghue built on his previous work, and during the period published extensively on a wide range of issues in supervision, including a series of three articles reporting the results from the first national survey of social work supervision practice in Aotearoa New Zealand (O'Donoghue, 2002, 2003, 2004, 2006, 2007, 2008; O'Donoghue, Munford, & Trlin, 2005, 2006; Hair & O'Donoghue, 2009; Tisdall & O'Donoghue, 2003).

Social work in schools (SWiS) clearly emerged as a distinct field of practice in Aotearoa New Zealand. In 2001, Michael Belgrave asked whether SWiS was delivering to children (Belgrave & Dobbs, 2001); and in 2002, Mary Ann Baskerville and Rachael Selby contributed a chapter on 'Social work in schools' in Truell and Nowland's edited book *Reflections on current practice in social work* (Jaqiery, Baskerville & Selby, 2002). In *Te Kōmako* (2004), Hayley Bell, along with A. Thorpe, addressed the issue of external supervision in school social work. A model of practice for working in a New Zealand secondary school was explored by Helen Simmons (with Charmaine Wheeler) in 2009 (Wheeler & Simmons, 2009).

Public welfare and social security was engaged by Mike O'Brien, who in 2001 commented upon the marketisation of social security in New Zealand (O'Brien, 2001). In 2005, Mike presented a review of compulsory work policies and their effects on children under the aegis of the Child Poverty Action Group. Along with Lars Harrysson, Mike edited and contributed to *Social welfare, social exclusion: A life course frame* (2007). He also co-edited the text *New Zealand, new welfare* with Neil Lunt and Robert Stephens in 2008.

S taff supervised 32 Master's theses in social policy to completion during this period. There was an emphasis on biculturalism, health, criminal justice, migration, Pasifika, public administration, social policy, and welfare.

Three doctorates were awarded in social policy. Cervin (2001) explored the predicament and potential of community groups acting as advocates for families in a context where funding providers set all the rules for 'negotiation', and highlighted the potential of community group action research projects for power reversals and enhancing democracy.

Settlement issues and the policy implications for skilled Chinese migrants were the focus of Anne Henderson's thesis. Her findings called for the need for a balanced, well-integrated institutional structure of immigration that included not only a policy to regulate the entry of immigrants, but also policies designed to meet their post-arrival needs and intergroup relations in a multicultural society (Henderson, 2002).

Neil Lunt's doctoral thesis explored the emergence of social science research in New Zealand (Lunt, 2004).

Forty-seven Master's (MSW and MPhil) level theses were completed during this period. The range of topics engaged reflects the breadth of social work practice: bicultural, Māori, child welfare, counselling, community development, disability, health, sexuality, employment/ unemployment, management/administration, mental health, older persons, Pasifika, social policy, supervision and youth.

Seven theses focused on Māori social work across a range of fields. Matire Kupenga-Wanoa (2004) explored Māori voices in a study of the perspectives of former offenders and probation officers in the criminal justice system. Moana Eruera (2005) researched kaupapa Māori. Wendy Semmons (2006) studied the experiences of pregnancy and childbirth for Māori women diagnosed with a mental illness, and Hayley Bell (2006) examined colonisation, decolonisation and social work in Aotearoa. In 2009, Hannah Walsh-Mooney focused on the value of rapport in rangatahi Māori mental health (Hannah became a lecturer in the school in 2011), while Gail Bosmann-Watene examined the factors motivating young Māori women to achieve success, and Paulé Ruwhiu explored Māori women as protectors of te ao Māori knowledge.

Another seven theses focused on the field of child welfare, with two being of particular note. Jo Field investigated the role of the practice manager in strengthening professional practice in New Zealand's Child, Youth and Family service. Jo also co-taught the MSW offering on child welfare that was introduced in 2004. Shannon Pakura (Chief Social Worker from 2000 to 2005) noted the difficulties associated with uncertainty in child protection social work. Also of note is Mathew Keen's 'Queer practice': A consideration of some psychiatric/mental health social work practitioners' constructions of gay male sexualities. Mathew's expertise is evident in his publications — he contributed the chapter 'Integrated practice in mental health social work' (along with Kieran O'Donoghue) in Social work theories in action in 2005. He is also, among others, an honorary teaching associate with Massey University.

In addition to the doctorates completed by staff discussed above, another nine were awarded in Social Work during this period. The first of these was Deborah Smith's (2001) thesis, which examined the interrelationship between social support, risk level, and safety interventions following acute assessment of suicidal adolescents. Smith found that: (a) the greater the level of negative support severity, the higher the risk level; (b) the greater the risk level, the greater the number of safety interventions implemented; (c) the presence of positive support, in addition to negative support, appeared to result in lower risk-level assessments, and (d) certain risk levels were indicative of particular safety interventions. These results contributed to revisions for the social support model, and had implications for the treatment of youth suicide, service delivery to at-risk youth, and future research.

Alison Kerr's (2002) thesis explored whether 'senior citizens' have access to the material and cultural resources that enable them to choose between different courses of action in their daily lives; whether existing inter-generational relations enable them to appropriate substantive rights and responsibilities; and the relational practices and processes, the networks and affiliations, through which citizenship is 'performed' by older people. Her recommendations focused on self-determination and social inclusion for older people through anti-ageist policies and practices at national and local levels, and on further research into the plans and aspirations of senior citizens.

The support of caregivers who looked after children in statutory care with mental health problems was the focus of Philippa Wells's (2004) thesis. This study found that caregivers identified poor levels of support from Child, Youth and Family social workers and from mental health services.

Sue Hanna's (2005) thesis explored the long-term impact of child sexual abuse on committed lesbian couples, and found that the sexual abuse impacted on the women's lives and their partners', although the effects on the partner varied over time and in intensity, depending on the length of the relationship and the degree of resolution experienced by the survivor.

She also found that, overall, the couples' relationships were positive, and that they articulated clear coping strategies. Another important finding related to seeking counselling assistance, with a large proportion of the participants having used counselling as a way of working through their experiences of child sexual abuse, and having found this to be valuable.

The contribution of leadership to effective service delivery within the Probation Service was the topic of Michael Dale's (2006) thesis. He identified how the leader's experience and competence have a bearing on confidence in the leader, and a connection between positive leadership and Probation Officer work performance and service delivery.

Jeanne Holmes's (2006) thesis critiqued the concept of 'successful ageing', and found that there was disparity between the factors that older people say produce the best possible old age, and those promoted by the concept of successful ageing. She concluded that in order to promote optimum wellbeing among older people, it was necessary to include the views and values of elders themselves.

The topic of Ee Kheng Ang's thesis (2007) was the experiences of mothers returning to paid work. She found that returners found it difficult to move back into full-time work and/or careers due to employers' views about mothers' availability and suitability for career work. In addition, government support for these mothers was also insufficient.

In 2008, Carole Hamilton completed a thesis that explored the barriers to supporting intellectually disabled people in the area of sexuality and intimacy. She found that issues of social representation, such as the 'ideal couple', and the effects of gender, age and sexual desire further upheld workers' no-support-necessary response.

The final thesis is Kate Stewart's (2008), which focused on critical incident responses in secondary schools in Aotearoa New Zealand. Her thesis sought to give young people a voice in terms of what happens to them in critical incident processes and events.

The ongoing contribution of Massey alumni to the broader social work and Aotearoa New Zealand community was reflected in the following awards:

- Jackie Sayers was awarded life membership of ANZASW in 2003.
- Sara Georgeson was invested as a Member of the New Zealand Order of Merit for services to people with disabilities in 2006.
- Raymond Clarke was awarded a Queen's Service Medal for services to the public service in 2007.
- Raewyn Clark was invested as a Member of the New Zealand Order of Merit for services to the community 2007.
- Trish Hanlen was invested as a Member of the New Zealand Order of Merit in 2008.
- Jill Worrall was invested as a Member of the New Zealand Order of Merit for services to social work in 2009.
- Merv Hancock was honoured with a Civic Award from the Palmerston North City Council in 2008.
- Dr Rajen Prasad was elected a Labour Member of Parliament on the list in 2008. Prior to this, he had retired from being New Zealand's first Chief Families Commissioner.

The following list of alumni publications is impressive in the range of issues engaged. Many of the authors are now well-established in their particular fields. For example, in the field of private practice Ken McMaster and Jane Haste have made outstanding contributions. Ken, who is a director of McMaster and Associates, is best known for his work in the family violence and sex offender field, as well as in contemporary programme design and development. Jane Haste established the Blue Couch consultancy in Palmerston North, and is well-respected in the treatment and promotion of women's and children's mental health, and the professional development of social and health service professionals. Several other alumni have established academic careers. For example:

- Yvonne Crichton-Hill is a senior lecturer, and Head of Department, Human Services and Social Work, University of Canterbury.
- Peter Matthewson is a lecturer in the Human Services programmes at Unitec Institute of Technology, Auckland.
- David McNabb is a lecturer, and formerly academic leader, in Social Practice at Unitec Institute of Technology, Auckland.
- Peter Mataira is an associate professor and the Director of Indigenous Affairs at the Myron B. Thompson School of Social Work, University of Hawaii.
- Emma Webber-Dreadon is a social work educator at the University of Waikato in Tauranga.
- Lesley Pitt is a social sciences tutor teaching on the National Certificate in Mental Health and the Bachelor of Applied Social Science (Social Work) at WINTEC (Western Institute of Technology).
- Sonya Hunt is the convenor of the Bachelor of Social Work at the University of Waikato in Tauranga.

A search of publications by alumni over this period revealed 33 publications, several of which were derived from postgraduate studies the authors had undertaken.

2001

- Afeaki, E. (2001). A practical Pacific way of social work: Embrace collectivity. *Social Work Review/Tu Mau, 13*(3), 35–37.
- Crichton-Hill, Y. (2001), Experiential learning and 'Lali'. *Social Work Review/Tu Mau, 13*(3), 30–34.
- DeSouza, S. (2001). Council for international fellowship: An international social work exchange programme. *Social Work Review, 13*(2), 23–26.
- McMaster, K. (2001). Men and social work. In M. Connolly (Ed.), *New Zealand social work: Contexts and practice* (pp. 110–121). Melbourne,

Australia: Oxford University Press.

- McMaster, K. (2001). Working with violence: Family violence as a professional issue. In M. Connolly (Ed.), *New Zealand social work: Contexts and practice* (pp. 317–330). Melbourne, Australia: Oxford University Press.
- Mila, K. (2001). Flying foxes don't fit into pigeon hole. Working as 'Pacific Island' social workers: Questions of identity. *Social Work Review/Tu Mau, 13*(3), 23–24.
- Smith, P. (2001). Statutory social work: A study of social workers expectations and realisations. *Social Work Review, 13*(4), 22–24.
- Stewart, K. (2001). The evolution of critical stress incident management within secondary schools in Aotearoa New Zealand. *Social Work Review, 13*(2), 37–42.

2002

- Matthewson, P. (2002). Risk assessment and management in mental health. *Social Work Review, 14*(4), 36–43.
- McNabb, D. (2002). A strategy for effective social work within a state mental health service in Aoteraoa/ New Zealand. *Social Work Review, 14*(3), 13–18.
- Webber-Dreadon, E., & Mollard-Wharepapa, M. (2002). What has marine science got to do with social work? *Social Work Review/Te Kōmako, 14*(2), 10–13.

2003

- Mataira, P. (2003). He Kainga Tuturu: 'Talking story' and rediscovering community. *Social Work Review/Te Kōmako, 15*(3), 12–15.

2004

- Smith, P. (2004). Defensive social work: Square peg — round hole. *Social Work Review, 16*(3), 22–25.

- Stewart, K. (2004). Critical incident responses in secondary schools in Aotearoa New Zealand: Are we doing justice to our adolescents? *Social Work Review, 16*(1), 13–18.

2005

- Pitt, L. (2005). Social work registration knowledge and power. *Social Work Review, 17*(3), 41–42.
- Stewart, K. (2005). Adult experts and adolescence voices in the field of critical incident responses. *Social Work Review, 17*(1), 31–37.

2006

- Dale, M., & Trlin, A. (2006). Leadership in the New Zealand Probation Service: The perceptions and experiences of probation officers and service managers. *Aotearoa New Zealand Social Work, 19*(3), 23–37.
- Dale, M., & Trlin, A. (2006). Probation practice as social work-viewpoints of practitioners in New Zealand. *Aotearoa New Zealand Social Work, 19*(2), 4–11.
- Douglas, M. (2007). Reflection and evaluation from an agency and student perspective: Based on a consumer evaluation. *Social Work Review, 19*(1), 51–54.
- Garland, M., & Ellis, G. (2006). Synergistic supervision. *Social Work Review, 18*(3), 31–42.
- Lynch, A. (2006). The place of structural-self reflexivity in our ongoing journey as social workers. *Social Work Review, 18*(4), 78–89.
- Mila-Schaaf, K. (2006). Vā-centred social work: Possibilities for a Pacific approach to social work practice. *Social Work Review/Tu Mau 2, 18*(1), 8–13.
- Semmons, W. (2006). What does mental illness mean for Māori? In particular Māori women diagnosed with a mental illness during the period pregnancy and child birth. *Social Work Review/Te Kōmako 9, 18*(2), 36–42.

- Wepa, D., & Te Huia, J. (2006). Cultural safety and the birth culture of Māori. *Social Work Review/Te Kōmako 9, 18*(2), 26–31.

2007

- Matthewson, P. (2007). Professional leadership in mental health. *Aotearoa New Zealand Social Work, 19*(3), 38–47.
- Rains, E. (2007). Interdisciplinary supervisor development in community health service. *Aotearoa New Zealand Social Work, 19*(3), 58–65.
- Thomas, G. (2007). The power of the therapeutic relationship: Bringing to evidence-based practice. *Aotearoa New Zealand Social Work, 19*(4), 55–66.

2008

- Hanna, S. (2008). Child protection practices in a call centre: An emerging area of social work. *Aotearoa New Zealand Social Work Review, 20*(3), 34–43.
- Hutchings, J. (2008). Does social work registration have implications for social work supervision? *Aotearoa New Zealand Social Work Review, 20*(1), 2–9.
- Mataira, P. (2008). Sitting in the fire, an indigenous approach to masculinity and male violence: Māori men working with Māori men. *Aotearoa New Zealand Social Work Review, 20*(4) (*Te Kōmako*), 35–39.
- Pearce, K. (2008) Te matauranga o ko wai au. *Aotearoa New Zealand Social Work Review/Te Kōmako, 20*(4), 46–51.
- Ruwhiu, P., Ruwhiu, L. A., & Ruwhiu, L. L. H. (2008). To tatou kupenga: Mana tangata supervision, a journey of emancipation through heart mahi for healers. *Aotearoa New Zealand Social Work Review/Te Kōmako, 20*(4), 13–34.

2009

- Parsons, J. (2009). Perinatal health of young women. *Aotearoa New Zealand Social Work Review, 21*(3), 14–25.

- Stewart, K. (2009). The development of a critical incident student team. *Aotearoa New Zealand Social Work Review, 21*(3), 46–54.

The above review reflects the ongoing contribution of the social work programme, both nationally and internationally. Particular note should be taken of the indigenous scholarship, and the emergence of a stronger Pasifika focus and voice in both the programme and the publications. An impressive number of Master's and doctoral theses were completed under the guidance of staff; this level of scholarship was achieved against the backdrop of change and the demands of teaching. Staff research publications were significant, in number, scope and depth. The publication of *Social work theories in action* was an important contribution to the Aotearoa New Zealand and international literature. Finally, the achievements and influence of social work alumni reflects not only on the alumni but also on the academic foundation received at Massey University.

The period 2001 to 2009 emerges as one of continuing challenge and development for social work in Aotearoa New Zealand. The politics of compromise became increasingly evident, and debate regarding the responsibility of the State in the provision of welfare remained contested. In particular, the issue of the welfare of children stands out as a litmus test of both political and social responsibility. Notwithstanding constant review and reorganisation, the performance of Aotearoa New Zealand in relation to the welfare of vulnerable children remained abysmal in comparison with other OECD countries.

The emergence of the SWRB and the influence of ANZASW reflected the contested nature of the political space concerning social work. While registration was introduced on a voluntary basis, the debate regarding the benefits and limitations of mandatory registration continued. The development of the Tangata Whenua Social Workers Association was important, and to some extent symbolic of the assertion of rangatiratanga by Māori for Māori.

The impact of the social work programme continued, as evidenced by the depth and breadth of scholarship from academic staff, students and alumni. However, increasingly the challenge of organisational imperatives required adroit responses from the leadership of the programme.

Chapter Five
Maintaining stability in turbulent times, 2010–2016

This chapter explores the period from 2010 to 2016, a period in which natural disasters such as the Christchurch and Kaikōura earthquakes, growing inequality, and a housing crisis have come to the fore. The events that shaped the social and political character of Aotearoa New Zealand set the scene for an exploration of the development of the social work profession. In this section, changes pertaining to government, legislation and policy, bicultural development and social issues are explored.

The political climate

During this period, the National Party provided stable government under Prime Minister John Key's leadership. When Key resigned in December 2016, he was succeeded by his deputy and finance minister, Bill English. The National Party clearly won the 2011 and 2014 general elections, and worked with ACT, United Future and the Māori Party to form a minority government.

The sense of stability was also reflected in the referenda held over this period. The first was the 2011 voting system referendum, concerning whether to keep the existing MMP voting system or to change to another voting system, with the existing MMP system being retained. Two further referenda were held in 2015 and 2016 on the New Zealand flag. The outcome of these referenda was that the current New Zealand flag was retained.

The legislative and policy changes between 2010 and 2016 included the review of the Family Court, mental health, the definition of marriage, the Vulnerable Children Act 2014, and the community investment strategy.

A Family Court review discussion document released by the Ministry of Justice in 2011 found that current court processes were complex, uncertain and too slow; the system lacked a focus on children and vulnerable people; and there was insufficient support for resolving parenting matters out of court. Changes took effect in 2014, and it was expected that the workload of the Family Court would reduce. A key feature was the introduction of a dispute resolution service, enabling people in non-urgent or non-violent cases to access mediation instead of going before a judge. A significant consequence of these reforms was that from 1 April 2014 the government stopped funding counselling for couples through the Family Court. This policy decision ultimately contributed to the demise of Relationships Aotearoa (Formerly Marriage Guidance and Relationships Services) in 2015.

In the mental health field, the Mental Health Commission consulted on developing *Blueprint II for Mental Health*. The first *Blueprint*, published in 1998, had successfully championed the recovery approach, and the drive to provide access to services for the estimated 3 per cent of people most seriously affected by mental health and addiction issues. In conjunction with the development of the *Blueprint*, the Ministry of Health led the development of a five-year service development plan which articulated government policy on developments in health-funded services. In combination, the documents emphasise the need to continue to make changes in order to meet future needs. Key themes identified included earlier and more effective responses; improved equity of outcomes for different populations; increased access to services; and the effective use of resources and improved partnerships across the whole of government.

A focus on rights was evident in the Marriage (Definition of Marriage) Amendment Act 2013, which became law in August 2013. The Act enabled couples to marry regardless of their gender or sexual orientation. The new statutory definition of marriage in the Marriage Act defined 'marriage' as 'the union of 2 people, regardless of their sex, sexual orientation, or gender identity'.

The *Green Paper for Vulnerable Children* was launched in July 2011 by Minister for Social Development Paula Bennett. Nearly 10,000 public submissions were made, and in October 2012 the *White Paper for Vulnerable Children* was released. The implementation of the recommendations contained in the White Paper are articulated in the Children's Action Plan.

The White Paper embodied not only strong influences of the global neoliberal agenda in welfare, but also a shift in the welfare state's role towards children and their families. This was neatly encapsulated by the 'discourse of responsibilisation', which placed emphasis on making individuals responsible for functions and risks that were previously the responsibility of the State. This position rested on the notion of the rational actor, who is self-directing and autonomous — but it failed to take account of context. The increasing emphasis on responsibilisation raises questions about the implications for service users who are vulnerable and unable to make changes themselves. Liebenberg, Ungar and Ikeda (2015) observed that in many areas of social service (such as mental health, child welfare and corrections), the practice context (including policy, practices and funding) reflected the influence of the responsibilisation discourse (see also Garry, 2009; Peeters, 2013; Phoenix & Kelly, 2013).

The White Paper shaped the subsequent Vulnerable Children Act 2014, and CYF policy and practice changes. The Vulnerable Children Act 2014 was the legislative response to the intense public debate regarding the rights and protection of children. The NZ Police and the Ministries of Health, Education, Justice and Social Development had new, legislated responsibilities, and the heads of these government departments were accountable for protecting and improving the lives of vulnerable children.

Child protection policies were also being adopted as standard by Te Puni Kōkiri, the Ministry of Business, Employment and Innovation (Housing), the district health boards, and school boards of trustees. Other key changes included the following:

- Every person in the central government children's workforce will be safety checked (screened and vetted).
- Persons with serious convictions will be prohibited from working closely with children, unless granted an exemption.
- Parents who seriously abuse or kill children will have to prove that they are safe to parent if they go on to have another child.
- Courts can curtail and define the guardianship rights of birth parents in extreme cases.
- Children removed from their parents due to severe abuse and neglect can be placed with home-for-life carers, who can provide a safe, stable home.

The Children's Action Plan provided the framework for the implementation of these changes, which aimed to protect the most vulnerable children in New Zealand. The establishment of Children's Teams was intended to provide the mechanism for implementing the action plan. Children's Teams brought together practitioners and professionals from the iwi/Māori, health, education and the social services sectors to develop a single plan to help and support each vulnerable child.

In April 2015, in response to continuing concern regarding the performance of Child, Youth and Family, the Minister for Social Development established the Modernising Child, Youth and Family Expert Panel to oversee the development of a new child-centric operating model for CYF. The terms of reference for the review focused on whether CYF's current operating model was delivering improved outcomes for children and young people, and what changes were required to improve these outcomes. The composition of the Expert Panel was considered controversial by the exclusion of clear social worker representation. Following extensive consultation, the *Expert Panel Final Report* was released in April 2016.

The key recommendation contained in the report was the establishment of a new department to replace CYF (Ministry for Vulnerable Children, Oranga Tamariki) that would provide a single point of accountability for vulnerable children. A fundamental premise for the new organisation would be a shift in focus from managing immediate risk and containing short-term costs to one concerned with long-term outcomes for children and families. Underlying the recommendations was a shift in philosophy: the new entity would no longer be a social welfare department, but a social investment one.

A related social policy initiative, the Community Investment strategy was launched in June 2015; this resulted in the previous Family and Community Services (part of MSD) becoming Community Investment. In line with the broader social investment approach, the strategy had the goal of more targeted spending to assist vulnerable persons and communities. The strategy set out the priorities for investment within a results-measurement framework based on evidence regarding what worked and how services should be developed and delivered. Partnership with providers and communities was regarded as essential to the successful implementation of the strategy.

The welfare system was reviewed in 2010 by the Welfare Working Group (WWG), which was established by Cabinet to undertake an expansive and fundamental review of New Zealand's welfare system. Chaired by Paula Rebstock, the WWG's primary task was to identify how to reduce long-term welfare dependency. The final recommendations of the WWG included the reciprocal obligation of working-age persons to successfully provide for their own wellbeing through paid work, while those unable to secure employment should be supported and encouraged by policy settings and a responsive service delivery agency to find paid work. Concern was expressed at the need to improve social outcomes for Māori and children, with the social and inter-generational consequences of growing up in benefit-dependent households being noted as 'deeply concerning'. Particular attention was focused on reducing the forward liability and the associated reduction in long-term welfare dependency. The use of contracted not-for-profit, private sector and community responses was advocated.

Continuing concern about family violence was evident in the establishment of the Glenn Inquiry by businessman and philanthropist Sir Owen Glenn, in 2012. The Inquiry, which sought to address child abuse and family violence in Aotearoa New Zealand, attracted controversy, however, with the government responding that coordinated planning was already in place. In 2014, the Inquiry released *The People's Blueprint*, which included a proposal for the establishment of a new Family Violence Court. Bill Wilson QC, the Inquiry chairman, stated that the report filled 'a vacuum successive governments have struggled to fill'.

The construction of biculturalism continued, as evidenced through the Whānau Ora initiative, the appointment of Sir Jerry Mateparae as governor-general, and the replacement of the controversial Foreshore and Seabed Act.

The Ministry of Social Development, the Ministry of Health and Te Puni Kōkiri launched the Whānau Ora initiative in 2010, in response to the report of the Taskforce on Whānau-Centred Initiatives (2010). The taskforce report (p. 6) stated clearly that Te Tiriti o Waitangi remains a key instrument to guide national development.

Whānau Ora is a whānau-centred approach to empowering whānau to achieve better health, education, housing, skills development, and economic outcomes. Te Puni Kōkiri was charged with the role of brokers in matching the needs and aspirations of whānau and families with initiatives and services to achieve Whānau Ora outcomes. In Budget 2015, almost $50 million was secured to fund approximately 230 navigators (practitioners who work with whānau) up until 2019, so that they could continue to support thousands of whānau.

In 2011, the controversial Foreshore and Seabed Act 2004 was replaced with the Marine and Coastal Area (Takutai Moana) Act 2011. Crown ownership of the foreshore and seabed was replaced with a 'no ownership' regime. Under this legislation, iwi could apply to the court or negotiate with the Crown for recognition of customary rights; however, these interests could not prevent existing rights and uses, such as fishing, aquaculture and public access.

In August 2011, Lieutenant General Sir Jerry Mateparae was sworn in as New Zealand's twentieth governor-general, replacing Sir Anand Satyanand. Sir Jerry was the second Māori to hold the office, after Sir Paul Reeves; he had been Chief of the New Zealand Defence Force between 2006 and 2011. Sir Jerry is descended from Ngāti Tūwharetoa and Ngāti Kahungunu, and also has links to Tūhoe and tribes in the upper Whanganui River.

On 4 September 2010, a 7.1 magnitude earthquake caused widespread damage in Canterbury, particularly in Christchurch; 377 people suffered injuries, while over 1000 were injured in its aftermath. This was followed, on 22 February 2011, by a 6.3 magnitude earthquake that struck Christchurch, causing major damage to the city, killing 185 people and injuring 3129. Prime Minister John Key declared a national state of emergency, the first in 60 years.

Apart from physical injuries, affected residents also experienced secondary, recovery-related issues that have included dealing with aftershocks, damaged homes, insurance claims, poor roading, and the loss of community facilities. Mental health issues have been on the increase since the first major Christchurch earthquake and there was an impact on migration. In 2013, the *Aotearoa New Zealand Social Work Review* published a special issue that included the following observations made by Kate van Heugten regarding the impact of the earthquakes on social workers:

> The challenges they identified included the taxing nature of
> work involving emotional labour in a context of shared trauma;
> environmental stress; complex demands and fewer resources;
> ethical dilemmas and moral distress. (van Heugten, 2013, p. 35)

A work-based disaster occurred in November 2010 at the Pike River coal mine, northeast of Greymouth, when a series of gas explosions killed 29 workers underground. A subsequent inquiry acknowledged the level and value of the support given to the families by a range of agencies from the time of the first explosion. The Pike River disaster brought the adequacy of health and safety legislation and practices under intense scrutiny, and contributed to the Health and Safety at Work Act 2015, which took a duty-of-care focus, with greater responsibility being placed on senior leaders.

The 7.8 magnitude Kaikōura quake on 14 November 2016 resulted in two deaths and Kaikōura being cut off by road from the rest of New Zealand for several weeks. Like Christchurch, the region continued to experience ongoing stress with regards to the possibility of further quakes, continuing aftershocks, the remediation work needed, insurance claims (and difficulties associated with these) and significant disruptions to the tourism, and agricultural and marine industries, some irreversible.

These significant and traumatic events both tested and defined the collective consciousness and resilience of New Zealanders. Of course, the other side of this is that there has consequently been a boom in infrastructure industries such as building.

The development of social work

In this section, some key developments in the broader social work environment are considered, with particular reference to the Aotearoa New Zealand Association of Social Workers (ANZASW), the Social Workers Registration Board (SWRB), and Child, Youth and Family (CYF).

In November 2014, ANZASW held a fiftieth-anniversary event in Christchurch. Its founding president, Merv Hancock, welcomed participants to the Reunion Day in a recorded video with Dr Mary Nash, and his words and contribution were acknowledged by a standing ovation. The workshops covered a range of subjects: Innovations in Health Social Work; Whānau-Family-Aiga Practice; Community Development; Indigenous Practice; Working with Culturally and Linguistically Diverse Populations; Social Work in the Digital Age; Disaster and Emergency Management.

A special issue of *Aotearoa New Zealand Social Work Review* 26(2&3) contained an editorial by Kieran O'Donoghue, who observed:

> This issue provides a diverse picture of social workers' views,
> reflections, thoughts and research about the profession in
> Aotearoa and its journey over the past 50 years. It highlights
> that there is much that the profession has achieved and that
> there is much work ahead of us as we strive to make a difference
> and enhance the well-being of individuals, families/whanau,
> communities and the wider societies. (O'Donoghue, 2014, p. 2)

Following the acceptance of the Tangata Whenua Social Workers Association (TWSWA) into membership of the International Federation of Social Workers (IFSW), it was necessary for Aotearoa New Zealand to establish a coordinating body, as there can be only one IFSW member per country. In October 2014, ANZASW and TWSWA established a memorandum of understanding that set out the relationship between ANZASW and TWSWA in order to reach collective decisions on IFSW matters.

In 2014, a revised international definition of 'social work' was approved at the Melbourne Global Social Work Congress by the IFSW, the International Association of Schools of Social Work (IASSW) and the International Council of Social Welfare (ICSW). The three organisations also promoted The Global Agenda. This agenda recognised the role of social workers in achieving change, social justice, and the universal implementation of human rights, building on the wealth of social initiatives and social movements.

In 2011, the SWRB issued a *Mandatory SWRB registration discussion document* that resulted in the *Mandatory social worker registration: Report from the discussion paper* in 2012. Notwithstanding the considerable support for mandatory registration, the *Vulnerable Children's White Paper* of 2012 did not recommend the introduction of mandatory registration. The White Paper made reference to Child, Youth and Family and district health boards working towards ensuring that social work staff be either registered or eligible to register. Further, the Children's Action Plan contained actions to promote and support social worker registration; for example, through employment and funding contracts.

In 2012, the SWRB initial Paper Based Competency was introduced, and the SWRB also reviewed the programme recognition standards and benchmarked the four-year Bachelor's degree and two year Master's degree as the required standard for all education providers from 2017.

The SWRB conference 'Protecting the public E tiaki ana i te hapori — enhancing the profession E manaaki ana i nga mahi' was held at Te Papa in 2013. The conference was a celebration of 10 years of the Social Workers Registration Act 2003, and was promoted as 'an opportunity to create a vision for social work and the social service sector from academic, practitioner and regulatory perspectives'. The published conference proceedings were edited by Jan Duke, Mark Henrickson and Liz Beddoe. Among the papers was 'Cultural encounter: A framework of ethical practice for transnational social workers in Aotearoa', co-authored by Helen Simmons (Massey University), Wheturangi Walsh-Tapiata (Te Wānanga o Aotearoa), Litea Meo-Sewabu (Massey University) and Antoinette Umugwaneza (New Zealand Red Cross Refugee Services).

A critical review of 10 years of the Social Workers Registration Act 2003 was the subject of a 2013 issue of *Aotearoa New Zealand Social Work Review* 25(3). In his editorial, Kieran O'Donoghue noted that the launch of the establishment of the SWRB in 2003 'was an occasion of much celebration for the profession and hope in regard to registration enhancing the credibility of social work as a profession and providing a system that set the bar through competence and accountability'. Kieran observed that in 2014 the question of mandatory registration was no longer in question, but the key question remained as to when this requirement would be enacted.

In April 2014, the SWRB and the Australian Association of Social Workers (AASW) entered into a mutual recognition agreement to mutually recognise social workers who are credentialled or registered in Australia and New Zealand.

Later the same year, the SWRB held a social services sector hui in Wellington, with the aim of reviewing the preparation and support provided to student and graduate social workers. The hui resulted from concerns being raised by employers about the need for social work graduates to be able to meet the needs of the client groups that employers represented, and the recognition by educators that the current funding model for social work education and the lack of work-based entry to practice programmes meant that new graduates' transition to employment was not ideal.

Two years later, another hui was held. This time the agenda was a further revision of the programme recognition standards.

The issue of the mandatory registration of social workers was again raised when Carmel Sepuloni, Labour Member of Parliament for Kelston, introduced the Social Workers Registration (Mandatory Registration) Amendment Bill 2015. This Bill was defeated at its first reading on 14 October 2015 by one vote.

In June 2016, the Social Service Select Committee initiated an inquiry into the Social Workers Registration Act. The terms of reference of the inquiry were to consider:

- Whether registration of social workers should be mandatory and the potential challenges to registration at present.
- The adequacy of current competence assessments and other pre-requisites for registration.
- How fitness to practise social work was assessed by the Board.
- The level of oversight of social workers by the Social Workers Registration Board.
- The process and powers of the Complaints Assessment Committee.
- The adequacy of grounds of discipline and sanctions available to the Social Workers Complaints and Disciplinary Tribunal.
- The appropriateness of suspension and cancellation of registration and practising certificates as sanctions for non-compliance.

Twenty-nine submissions were received by the select committee, with Associate Professor Kieran O'Donoghue making both a written and an oral submission on behalf of the School of Social Work. Most of the submissions were in favour of mandatory registration.

On 14 March 2016, the SWRB issued an updated Code of Conduct (2016). This Code of Conduct was clearly a twenty-first century document, and provided clear guidance with regard to social workers' use of digital technology and social media, as well as clear guidance in regard to social workers' role in relation to enduring powers of attorney and protection and promotion of personal and property rights.

Over this period Child, Youth and Family (CYF) was the subject of both scrutiny and change, derived from the Children's Action Plan and the Green and White papers on vulnerable children and the Expert Advisory Panel reports. The arrival from the Great Britain of Paul Nixon as Chief Social Worker in 2010 to some degree marked out the beginning of the changes in this period. Prior to his appointment, Paul had an extensive background in care and protection, and had previously been Head of Social Work Services in North Yorkshire, England. Paul contributed to the development of Children's Teams and the Children's Action Plan. His office also produced *Workload and casework review: Qualitative review of social worker caseload, casework and workload management report* (OCSW, 2014). This review identified key areas for change and improvement in systems and practice. The findings included:

- That effective leadership, support systems and processes alongside manageable workloads make a significant difference to a social worker's ability to deliver high-quality practice.
- That key perfomance indicators (KPIs) send messages about what activities are most important. Current performance indicators were seen to focus strongly on quantitative measures, in comparison with qualitative measures.
- That frontline social workers did not have enough time or resources to manage their caseloads properly.

The scrutiny of the performance of CYF continued with the release of the Office of the Children's Commissioner's report, *State of care*, in 2015. The report set out clear expectations for CYF, including best practice; that children be treated with care and respect; and that children should be better off as a result of State intervention. However, the findings of the report were that CYF practice was not consistent; CYF practice was not child-centred; and that it was inconclusive whether children had benefitted from State intervention. Interestingly, a central critique surrounded the focus of CYF in keeping children safe, in comparison with a focus on improving long-term outcomes for children.

The report also articulated a range of expectations regarding the purpose of CYF, and the outcomes that the agency should achieve. These included being more child-centred; investing more in supporting care placements; addressing workforce capacity and capability issues; improving cultural capability; improving data collection and analysis; and establishing clearer expectations of other State agencies that have responsibility for the outcomes of children.

The government's concern with effectiveness and efficiency was further evidenced in the request in June 2014 that the Productivity Commission investigate ways to improve how government agencies commission and purchase social services. The final report was released in mid-September 2015. It made recommendations about how to make social services more responsive, client-focused, accountable and innovative.

A significant recommendation was for increased devolution of decision-making powers and responsibilities to autonomous or semi-autonomous organisations with separate governance, in comparison with the current centralised models controlled by ministers and chief executives. Further, it was argued that devolution was likely to increase the development of local ideas and innovation, and result in a more effective alignment between client circumstances and the available services. Underpinning the report was the goal of client empowerment, and greater accountability for improving client outcomes.

Social work in Aotearoa New Zealand during the period 2010 to 2016 continued to undergo change that had clearly been influenced by the New Right political agenda. ANZASW continued to maintain its relevance within a challenging political environment. These challenges were noted as the association celebrated its fiftieth anniversary; in particular, the need to be responsive to population change, technological advance, and to stake out a strong identity for the social work profession. The SWRB consolidated its growing influence on the social work profession via programme accreditation and the promulgation of policy (such as the Code of Conduct), and the protection of the status of registered social workers. The issue of mandatory registration remained firmly in the spotlight. The role of the State welfare agency CYF remained under intense scrutiny, being subject to both internal and external review, which has culminated in the establishment of a new entity, the Ministry for Vulnerable Children Oranga Tamariki in August 2016 (Tolley, 2016).

The social work programme at Massey continued to develop against a backdrop of innovation and change within the wider university. In 2010, the university marked its fiftieth anniversary as New Zealand's pre-eminent provider of distance education. To mark the occasion, *From a distance — 50th jubilee of distance learning* was written by Emeritus Professor Tom Prebble. Of interest was the observation that over the 50 years teaching methods had progressed from stapled cyclostyled study notes to an online, digital learning environment. In 2014, Massey University celebrated 50 years of being an autonomous university.

As part of the university, the social work programme and its staff had important connections with other schools and programmes. One notable example was the connection with the School of Māori Studies / Te Pūtahi-a-Toi, and Professor Mason Durie.

Professor Mason Durie was made a Knight Companion of the New Zealand Order of Merit for services to public health and to Māori health in the 2010 New Year's Honours. Sir Mason (Rangitāne, Ngāti Kauwhata, Ngāti Raukawa) joined Massey in 1988, established the School of Māori Studies / Te Pūtahi-a-Toi, and was Head of School for 14 years before being appointed Massey's first Assistant Vice-Chancellor Māori in late

2002, a role that was later expanded to include Pasifika. He was Deputy Vice-Chancellor from 2009, and retired from Massey in 2012.

Mason Durie was instrumental in the roll-out and success of a programme called Te Rau Puawai. Te Rau Puawai was established in 1999 as a mentoring programme that provides financial, study and pastoral support to Māori students, in order to increase the capacity of the Māori mental health workforce. Social work students and staff have always been involved in Te Rau Puawai, with staff as mentors and board members (for example, Wheturangi Walsh-Tapiata, and Dr Suzanne Phibbs from the School of Public Health).

In 2013, Te Rau Puawai, now led by Robyn Richardson, transferred from Te Pūtahi-a-Toi / Māori Studies to the School of Social Work in the College of Health. This was symbolic, as it highlighted the importance of Te Rau Puawai as a health initiative. Between 1999 and 2015, 109 Social Work and five Social Policy graduates have been supported by Te Rau Puawai.

The period 2010 to 2016 was one of significant change and development for Social Work and Social Policy. The Herman-Barretta Trust was established in 1989 to support students studying for their first professional degree in social work at Massey, in recognition of the escalating costs of tertiary education and of the need to assist students pursuing their education in the spirit of access and social justice. From 1989 to 2010, 36 grants were awarded, a total of $8,269.10.

On 5 November 2010, the trustees resolved to dissolve the Herman-Barretta Trust; while several fundraising events had been held over the years, and a number of staff and graduates had donated teaching fees and made special donations, income remained low and administrative costs were high. The remaining funds were contributed to the MUSA Student Assistance Programme to be reserved for BSW and MSW (Applied) applicants who meet the criteria of the Assistance Programme.

In 2010, the position of Director of Social Work and Social Policy was advertised, and Dr Kieran O'Donoghue was appointed in August

Bachelor of Social Work graduate Masina Paewai. **SCHOOL OF SOCIAL WORK**

Social work students at a Te Rau Puawai hui. *From left*: Denise Faithfull, Doll Bennett, Caroline Tana-Tepania and Hinekahu Gotty. **SCHOOL OF SOCIAL WORK**

2010 to lead the programme. A university restructuring in 2012 saw the disestablishment of the College of Education, with the college becoming an institute within the College of Humanities and Social Sciences, and the development of the College of Health. The latter was established on 1 January 2013, with Professor Paul McDonald, a public health specialist from Waterloo University, Ontario, Canada, appointed as Pro Vice-Chancellor. Social Work and Social Policy, as part of a School of Health and Social Services, was transferred from the College of Humanities and Social Sciences to the College of Health.

In October 2013, Professor Steve LaGrow was appointed Deputy Pro Vice-Chancellor of the College of Health, and Dr Kieran O'Donoghue was appointed Acting Head of School. Kieran was confirmed as Head of School from 1 January 2014, and Lareen Cooper became the Director of Social Work and Social Policy. Further organisational change was imminent, with the health staff transferring into the School of Public Health. From 1 January 2015, the School of Social Work was established, with Associate Professor Kieran O'Donoghue as Head of School and Lareen Cooper as Associate Head of School.

Recently, there have been changes in the university's senior management with the resignation of Paul McDonald in July 2016, and Vice-Chancellor Steve Maharey's resignation at the end of December 2016. The beginning of 2017 saw the appointments of Professor Jan Thomas as Vice-Chancellor and Professor Jane Mills as the new Pro Vice-Chancellor of the college.

On 22 January 2015, the fortieth anniversary of the establishment of social work as an academic discipline within the university was celebrated, together with the launch of the School of Social Work. Present and speaking at this occasion was the Vice-Chancellor, the Honourable Steve Maharey, Emeritus Professor Graeme Fraser and Professor Robyn Munford. In welcoming staff, former staff, alumni and professional practice colleagues, Associate Professor Kieran O'Donoghue commented that:

Over the past 40 years, the social work programme has produced more than 2000 graduates from its recognised professional social work qualifications. In our library there are 116 Masters theses and 32 PhD theses pertaining to social work. Our graduates make a significant impact on people's lives and contribute to a humane and just society. A number of our graduates are leaders in health social work, or advisers in the Chief Social Worker's Office and/or Managers of Non-government organisations . . . Our School has world-class staff who deliver programmes from the Albany and Manawatū campuses as well as by distance. As a School we have an international reach through our publications, research, and service. We are deeply connected with the community through placements from Northland to Invercargill and even overseas — and through service in the form of supervision, presentations and workshops and through Te Rau Puawai. Finally, we are engaged in researching diverse populations and the impact of social problems, social work practices, and the social work profession. (O'Donoghue, welcoming speech).

This was the last formal event at the university that Merv Hancock attended, and he and Professor Robyn Munford cut the celebratory fortieth anniversary cake.

Merv Hancock's contribution to Palmerston North and its community workers was honoured in 2012 with the naming of Hancock Community House, home to some 15 voluntary agencies. The Palmerston North City Council contributed $850,000 to the $2.2 million project, with the balance coming from a range of grants. A dawn blessing led by Rangitāne representative Wiremu Te Awe Awe welcomed people to come in and breathe life into the facility. Vice-Chancellor Steve Maharey gave a speech describing Merv as the father of modern social work.

In November 2012, Merv was awarded an Honorary Doctorate

DLitt (Honoris causa). Emeritus Professor Graeme Fraser read the citation that recognised Merv's pioneering work, his influence on the professionalisation of social work, and his outstanding national contribution in the field of social work education. Merv commented 'I'm extremely honoured and deeply appreciative of the award', adding it was not just an award for him, but that it also recognised the long social work history at Massey, and all of those in the field.

The structure and content of social work programmes continued to evolve between 2010 and 2016. In 2010, a review of courses in the BSW resulted in the renaming of courses and the inclusion of two courses, 179.155 Helping Skills and 179.230 Wellbeing of Pacific Peoples, as compulsory papers. The MSW and MSW (Applied) were separated into two degrees (MSW and Master of Applied Social Work [MASW], effective from 2011).

Academic reform resulted in some papers being deleted from the MSW schedule; these included Social Work with Older Persons, Working with Migrants and Refugees, and Trauma in Social Work.

The move from the College of Humanities and Social Sciences to the College of Health also resulted in the discontinuation of the Post Graduate Diploma in Arts (Social Work), and the development of a Post Graduate Diploma in Social Work, as well as the development of a professional doctorate in social work. In 2015, the Doctor of Social Work was approved by the Committee on University Academic Programmes, with the degree to commence in 2017. The Doctor of Social Work (DSW) is the first professional social work doctorate offered in New Zealand, and consists of a combination of course work and a 65,000-word research thesis.

In 2016, amendments were made to strengthen the Māori knowledge curriculum in the BSW. This involved the inclusion of compulsory Māori Studies papers in year one and year two. The first-year paper, 150.103 Nau

Merv Hancock and Professor Robyn Munford celebrate the fortieth anniversary of social work at Massey, January 2015. **SCHOOL OF SOCIAL WORK**

mai e noho: Engaging with Māori, equips students with a range of skills to engage with Māori communities, including common expressions in te reo, an understanding of key traditional concepts, customary practices tikanga, the importance of the Treaty of Waitangi, and the nature and structure of Māori social and political organisations. The second-year paper, 150.205 Mātauranga Māori, builds on the first, with a focus on heritage and contemporary Māori knowledge, as well as exploring the origins and relevance of traditional belief systems and the contemporary cultural-political contexts of mātauranga paradigms in areas such as research, education, justice, science, business, social development and the environment.

Another important development has been in the area of online learning. In 2015, Dr Nicky Stanley-Clarke, Dr Awhina English and Dr Polly Yeung were awarded an academic fellowship of $9775.50 for a project entitled 'Cutting the Distance in Distance Education: Enhancing Digital Toolbox for Social Work Students in the Bachelor of Social Work (BSW) Programme'. This project has developed a digital tool-kit across the year one and year two policy and practice papers that enhanced distance students' course completion and satisfaction.

Other changes during this period included the end of delivery of the social work programme at the Wellington campus. Hanny Naus was the last staff member, and she continued her association with the programme as an external supervisor and as a staff visitor for students on placement. The Certificate and Diploma of Whānau Development were transferred to the School of Māori Studies, and the Certificate of Pacific Development to the School of Psychology.

In 2013, there was a joint university qualification review and the SWRB programme re-recognition review (comprising a desk audit and site visit). The SWRB programme re-recognition panel comprised: Dr Jan Duke (Registrar of Regulation and Education, SWRB), Professor Richard Hugman (University of New South Wales), Dr Jane Maidment (University

Paulé Ruwhiu (staff member and PhD candidate) and Hannah Mooney (lecturer) reflect on the fourth-year student mural. The mural is completed each year and hangs on the seventh floor of the Social Science Tower. The theme is the bicultural journey of the students through the programme. **MASSEY UNIVERSITY ARCHIVES**

Associate Professor Ksenija Napan teaches a social work class in Albany.
MASSEY UNIVERSITY ARCHIVES

of Canterbury and ANZASW President), Associate Professor Te Kani Kingi (School of Public Health), Martine Hartley (CYF) and Zandra Vaccarino (recent graduate). The joint panel was chaired by Professor Mandy Morgan, (School of Psychology). The outcome of the SWRB process was that both the BSW and MASW were further recognised until 31 December 2018 on both the Albany and Palmerston North campuses. The Social Work Qualifications Review panel report gave 15 commendations which were directly related to the quality of teaching, staff, and the overall programme. In 2016, the SWRB completed the mid-point re-recognition visit, which was also very positive about the staff and the direction of the programme.

Several key staff died during this period: Andrew Trlin, Merv Hancock and Eve Hessey. Former Associate Professor Andrew Drago Trlin died peacefully at home surrounded by his family on 17 December 2014. Andrew had worked at Massey University in a range of academic positions from 1967 until his retirement in 2005. He was recipient of the Plaketa Award Matica Iseljenika Hrvatske, Zagreb, Yugoslavia, 1981; Medical Research Council of New Zealand grantee, 1978; member of the social planning sub-committee of Palmerston North City Council, 1983–1986; member of the International Union Science Study Population, New Zealand Demographic Society, and the New Zealand Geography Society. Andrew served as a member of the New Zealand Human Rights Review Tribunal (2004-2014), and was a life member of the New Zealand Population Association.

Distinguished Professor Paul Spoonley observed: 'His Master's thesis from Victoria University of Wellington — *From Dalmatia to New Zealand: A survey of Yugoslav settlement and assimilation, 1967* — highlighted two elements that were to be constant themes in his subsequent academic life: the challenges of immigration and settlement and an interest in his own community' (Spoonley, 2015). In 1979, Dunmore Press published *Now respected, once despised: Yugoslavs in New Zealand*. This book brought together Andrew's extensive material on the Yugoslav/Dalmatian community. Prior to his death, Andrew completed *Foundations: Early Croatian immigration to New Zealand*, which was published in 2016.

Merv Hancock died on 7 May 2016, and was farewelled at the Wesley Broadway Church in Palmerston North; he was in his ninetieth year. Associate Professor Kieran O'Donoghue stated that Merv Hancock's contribution could be underestimated:

> Merv Hancock was the founding father of the modern social work profession within New Zealand. Locally, he made a significant contribution to the Palmerston North community as a city councillor, public servant and private social services consultant. He was the inaugural director of the Social Work Unit at Massey University that established the first four-year Bachelor of Social Work degree in New Zealand . . . The social work scholarship that emerged from Massey University has built upon the foundation and standards set by Merv Hancock. He remains an inspiration to numerous social workers, and was a life member of the Aotearoa New Zealand Association of Social Workers as well as the founding president of that body.

Kieran added that:

> Merv was the epitome of a professional social worker. He was civic-minded and an active community citizen. When the university awarded him with his Honorary Doctorate in 2012, it honoured both him and his tremendous legacy within the field of social work, and his tremendous service to the community and people of Palmerston North. He has been a tremendous role

model, mentor and supervisor to many in social work, and is greatly loved and greatly missed.

Professor Robyn Munford delivered the eulogy at Merv's funeral, and remembered Merv as a man who took the time to make personal connections with people, and who could bring together diverse groups to make something happen:

> He had the ability to see how people, often with different perspectives, could come together for the greater good. Merv was a man with a big heart and a big intellect. He loved ideas and he had a deep love of learning. For Merv, knowledge was powerful and to be shared.

> Many of us have benefitted greatly from Merv's commitment to making ideas come alive, and from his incisive and analytical thinking and his deep understanding and insights into life's challenging issues. Merv was an historian, a sociologist, an educator and a practitioner, and he showed us over many years and in many ways how to make things happen, and to change the things that needed to be changed.

On 18 June 2016, Eve Hessey passed away. Eve was a former senior lecturer, who joined the social work team in 1978 and left in 1980 to work for the Auckland Health Board. From 1982, Eve led the Auckland College of Education Social Work programme. The following condolences were expressed by Professor Robyn Munford and W. Randolph Herman:

> You inspired many social work students and especially women students. You taught us to be analytical but to never forget our humanity. You taught me to chase my dreams, to be courageous

and to support others to also achieve their dreams. I loved your sense of humour and sense of fun. I remember your smile and that sparkle in your eyes as you shared a story with us. You have made a difference for so many, you have had a life well lived. Your legacy in New Zealand is with those social work students and colleagues you supported and inspired. Farewell Eve, our friend and colleague. Arohanui, Robyn Munford

It is with great sadness that I write a tribute to Eve. She and I came to New Zealand about the same time to teach in the new social work program at Massey University. I came fresh from practice in the USA and was a 'bit green' in the world of teaching and research. But the synergy that Merv created with faculty from all over the globe created an amazing program that has gone on to be a leader in social work education in New Zealand. I learned so much from Eve; her commitment to social justice and exacting practice standards were an inspiration to all of us as we learned to work together. Her directness and strong opinions could be daunting at times, but I learned so much about the necessity to speak up and stand up for what is important. She was an amazing asset to global social work education. My deepest regards to her loving family and friends. Randy Herman

There were several significant staffing changes between 2010 and 2016, with longstanding colleagues Wheturangi Walsh-Tapiata, Justine Webster, Jan Rimmer and Barbara Staniforth moving on. Wheturangi and Barbara have both stayed in social work education, and each holds a leadership position in their respective programmes at Te Wānanga o Aotearoa and the University of Auckland. Justine and Jan both returned to practise in leadership positions.

There were also three retirements over this period: Associate Professor

Academic staff appointments and changes, 2010–2016

- 2010: Dr Polly Yeung and Awhina English appointed as lecturers at Palmerston North.
  - Lareen Cooper appointed as a senior lecturer at Palmerston North.
  - Lynsey Ellis and Claudine Hutchings employed as tutors at Albany.
  - Wheturangi Walsh-Tapiata, Simon Nash and Justina Webster resigned.
  - Associate Professor Mike O'Brien retired.
- 2011: Dr Michael Dale and Nicky Stanley-Clarke appointed to Palmerston North campus.
  - Dr Shirley Julich appointed to Albany campus.
  - Jan Rimmer resigned.
  - Lynsey Ellis appointed as a professional clinician at Albany.
  - Hannah Mooney appointed as lecturer at Palmerston North.
- 2012: Dr Barbara Staniforth resigned to work at the University of Auckland, to lead its Master of Professional Social Work.
  - Dr Eileen Oak, senior lecturer, and Moses Faleolo, lecturer, started at Albany.
  - Dr Fiona Te Momo moved to the School of Māori Studies.
- 2013: Paulé Ruwhiu joined the school as an assistant lecturer, and Jane Parsons employed as a lecturer for Hannah Mooney on maternity leave in Palmerston North.

- 2014: Associate Professor Ksenija Napan joined the School at the Albany campus.
- 2015: Tracie Mafile'o returned to Massey University as a senior lecturer at the Palmerston North campus.
  - Andrea (Ange) Watson commenced work as a part-time tutor at Palmerston North.
- 2016: Paora Moyle joined the school as an assistant lecturer at Palmerston North.
  - Fiona Wilson and Sarah Vaelua employed as job-sharing practice-teaching associates at Palmerston North.
  - Dr Eileen Oak resigned to take up a position at University College in Dublin, Eire.

Michael O'Brien (2010), Dr Mary Nash (2012) and Rachael Selby (2015).

The development of the social work programme over the period: 2010 to 2016 reflected the rapidly changing social, political and tertiary education environments, as Massey University sought to become the 'Engine of the new New Zealand'. The emergence of the separate School of Social Work within the College of Health reflected both the status of the social work programme and the influence that it has had nationally and internationally. The programme remained responsive to the academy, and to the broader social work profession. There was cause for celebration with the fortieth anniversary of the programme, and also time to reflect on the contribution of previous staff members whose influence continues to provide direction.

The contribution of the School of Social Work to the broader social work environment continued during the period 2010 to 2016. In keeping with earlier periods, this was again evident in staff publications, theses completed, and recognition gained by both staff and alumni.

Over this period, staff made significant contributions to the field both locally and internationally. Professors Robyn Munford and Jackie Sanders were active with regard to children and youth. Together, they attended a meeting of the international resilience research project in Beijing from 11 to 17 October 2013. Researchers from Canada, China, Colombia and South Africa also attended the meeting. During this meeting, they had opportunities to meet with staff and postgraduate social work students who were working on resilience research in China.

In 2014, Professor Robyn Munford and Associate Professor Jackie Sanders (Jackie was promoted to Professor in 2015) hosted a meeting of the Pathways to Resilience international research team (colleagues from Canada, Colombia and South Africa) in Auckland. This meeting also included a well-attended seminar with NGO providers, to support the translation of the research findings into practice. Locally, Robyn and Jackie were invited by the Lead of the Workforce Work-stream for the Children's Action Plan to act as advisers for the development of a competency framework for the children's workforce. Robyn also presented a keynote address at the conference of the Association of Children's Welfare Agencies, in Sydney, Australia. The address focused on social and community work practice and family change.

Prior to his retirement, Associate Professor Mike O'Brien chaired the alternative welfare working group, which was set up by Catholic social justice agency Caritas, Anglican Church representatives and the Beneficiary Advocacy Federation, with the aim of ensuring that beneficiaries and community groups were part of the debate on government welfare reforms. Mike also delivered the Merv Hancock Address at the ANZASW Congress in Christchurch in 2010.

Dr Nicky Stanley-Clarke, pictured here with her twin daughters, Poppy and Rose, on their fifth birthday, graduates with a PhD, 2013. **MASSEY UNIVERSITY ARCHIVES**

Associate Professor Jackie Sanders, Professor Robyn Munford and Dr Martin Sullivan at Massey Graduation, 2013. **SCHOOL OF SOCIAL WORK**

Associate Professor Mark Henrickson and Dr Polly Yeung assumed leadership roles within the APASWE in 2011, with Mark being vice-president and Polly acting as the treasurer. Associate Professor Mark Henrickson has since made the following extensive contribution to the international social work community:

- Member of International Planning Committee, Global Social Work Congress 2014, Melbourne.
- Member of Planning and Scientific Committees, Social Workers Registration Board/Kāhui Whakamana Tauwhiro 10th Anniversary Conference, November 2013, Wellington.
- As the vice-president of the Asia Pacific Association for Social Work Education (APASWE) and as the Asia Pacific representative to the International Association of Schools of Social Work (IASSW), he was a member of a panel providing consultation to the National Institute of Social Development in Colombo, Sri Lanka.
- Mark also served as a peer consultant for the National Institute of Social Development of Sri Lanka Social Work Curriculum review.
- Asia-Pacific representative to the Board of the International Association of Schools of Social Work (IASSW).
- A director of the board of the Asia Pacific Association of Social Work Education (APASWE).
- Executive member of the Council on Social Work Education in New Zealand (CSWEANZ) — treasurer 2012–2015.
- Elected as the treasurer for the International Association of Schools of Social Work (IASSW) for a four-year term in 2014.
- Facilitated the Asia Pacific Association of Social Work Educators (APASWE) workshop on the amplification of the new definition of social work, 14 July 2014, Melbourne, Australia.

Kieran O'Donoghue's contributions to the social work profession over this period included being a member of the External Experts Group for the Child,

Professor Jackie Sanders and Professor Robyn Munford have contributed significantly to social work, particularly in the area of child and youth resilience.
JANE USSHER

Youth and Family (CYF) Supervision Project. This project sought to improve the quality of supervision within CYF. Kieran represented both the Council of Social Work Education in Aotearoa New Zealand and the New Zealand universities at Social Workers Registration Board sector meetings. He also facilitated the reunion day at the ANZASW C50 event in 2014. Kieran and Dr Mary Nash edited *Aotearoa New Zealand Social Work*, the ANZASW journal, for seven years, until September 2015. Their tenure was the longest of any editors of this journal. In 2015 and 2016, Kieran was involved in contributing to the development of social work supervision in Singapore through being invited to be a keynote speaker at a Supervision Seminar in 2015, and providing consultancy advice and workshops for the National University of Singapore, the Social Work Accreditation and Advisory Board and the Ministry of Social and Family Development.

Dr Kathryn Hay made a leading contribution to field education through the establishment and chairing of the Field Education sub-committee of the Council on Social Work Education in Aotearoa New Zealand. Kathryn also led and supported the development of an international placement for a small group of fourth-year students in Cambodia in 2015, while Dr Polly Yeung provided mentoring and coaching in social work and community development for New Humanity Cambodia during 2014 and 2015. Another example of the international impact of the staff was the delegation of presenters — Mark Henrickson, Polly Yeung, Kieran O'Donoghue, Helen Simmons and Nicky Stanley-Clarke — who attended the Global Social Work Congress in Melbourne, Australia, in 2014.

At a national level, Helen Simmons was a member of the organising committee for the ANZASW C50 Conference, held in November 2014 in Christchurch, and Lareen Cooper was appointed as a member of the SWRB's Complaints Assessment and Disciplinary Tribunal.

The work in the Pacific also continued, with Dr Tracie Mafile'o and Dr Kathryn Hay being part of a Massey University delegation that signed a renewed memorandum of understanding with the University of the

The group that travelled to Cambodia. *Back row, from left*: Alex Dentener (Massey), Hannah Morris (Massey), Chris Lichti (Justice Reach). *Front row*: Kath Hay, Gina Barnes (Massey), Georgea Hinii (University of Waikato), Su Hodkinson (RSW), Rochelle Doyle (University of Waikato), 13 August 2015.
KATHRYN HAY COLLECTION

South Pacific. Tracie also led developments towards establishing a Pacific regional resource centre through the International Association of Schools of Social Work (IASSW).

There were notable staff achievements in this period. Mark Henrickson and Helen Simmons received a Vice-Chancellor's Sustained Teaching Excellence Award, in 2011 and 2014 respectively. Mark Henrickson was also awarded the most prestigious international lecture for social work educators, the Eileen Younghusband Award (Memorial Lecture) at the International Social Work Congress, Seoul, South Korea, in June 2016. The lecture was established to commemorate Eileen Younghusband, an IASSW President from 1961 to 1968, who died in a car accident while on a lecture tour in the United States. Mark's lecture, entitled 'Promoting the dignity and worth of all people: The privilege of social work', was very well received and was submitted to the *International Social Work* journal for publication.

The College of Health, Albany, Lecturer of the Year Award was awarded to Associate Professor Ksenija Napan in 2015. Also in 2015, Associate Professor Kieran O'Donoghue was awarded a Certificate of Excellence for the Research category and the Quality and Innovation Trophy in the Inaugural Aotearoa New Zealand Association of Social Workers (ANZASW) Quality and Innovation Awards.

Significant contributions to the development of social work knowledge and practice through research have also been made during this period. Staff made several unseen contributions to research. These include editorial and peer review work nationally and internationally, with several staff on editorial boards and reviewing for leading journals (e.g. *British Journal of Social Work, Journal of Social Work, Qualitative Social Work, Journal of Social Work Practice*, and *International Social Work*). Other unheralded contributions was the support that staff gave to emerging student and practitioner researchers, and the examination of Master's and doctoral theses for other institutions both nationally and internationally.

Professors Robyn Munford and Jackie Sanders led the way through their ongoing longitudinal studies focused on youth resilience and youth transitions, funded by the Ministry of Business, Innovation and Employment (MBIE). Information and key findings from their research are now included in the Child, Youth and Family Practice Centre. The PARTH practice model developed by Professors Robyn Munford and Jackie Sanders from research findings was promoted and used across the statutory and NGO sectors. They also published extensively with other project members, including Professor Michael Ungar and Associate Professor Linda Liebenberg from Canada, and Professor Linda Theron from South Africa.

Associate Professor Mark Henrickson undertook important research with regard to HIV throughout this period. His work included an evaluation of the training of HIV counsellors offered throughout the Pacific Islands countries and territories, and a New Zealand Health Research Council grant of $584,036 to research HIV risks and concerns among African communities in New Zealand. In 2014, Mark was awarded a grant (US$17,564) from Empower Pacific and UNICEF to evaluate HIV counselling in antenatal clinics in Fiji, and to rewrite and present refresher training workshops to trainers in Fiji, Kiribati, Vanuatu and the Solomon Islands. He was also funded (NZ$4,795) by Te Marae Ora Cook Island Ministry of Health to produce the national integrated strategic plan for sexual and reproductive health.

Dr Shirley Julich and Dr Eileen Oak undertook funded research in the area of sexual violence, and were awarded two contracts by Rape Prevention Education. The first was to prepare a comprehensive report on the evidence base for the provision and delivery of sexual violence prevention programmes and initiatives in high-school settings, and the second was to evaluate the Rangatahi Sexual Health Project.

Dr Kathryn Hay's research over this period focused on field education and the readiness of graduates to practise. Kathryn's funded research included a project concerned with advancing the sustainability and quality of social work field education, and membership of the team led by Open Polytechnic's Neil Ballantyne that secured Ako Aotearoa funding ($300,000) for a collaborative sector-wide project into social workers' readiness to practise in the field. In addition, following the successful international placement in Cambodia in 2015, Kathryn and Simon Lowe, from the University of Waikato, were successful in securing an Ako Aotearoa best practice publication grant for a booklet on international fieldwork placements.

Dr Polly Yeung led two important evaluation projects in this period. The first was an evaluation of the impact of the Non-Government Organisation (NGO) Study Awards on social work students and their organisations. The research team — Dr Polly Yeung, Hannah Mooney, Dr Awhina English and Associate Professor Kieran O'Donoghue — made an agreement with Community Investment to conduct independent research, funded by the Massey University Research Fund. The study investigated the impact of the awards on helping recipients complete their study, and how becoming qualified enabled their social work practices to contribute positive outcomes for family, whānau, children and community. The study found the NGO Study Awards to be highly successful in improving the confidence, competence and practice of the participants, as well as vital to the successful completion of their study programme. Despite this success, the Ministry of Social Development (MSD) decided to stop funding the awards from 2017. The second evaluation project was a partnership with Metlifecare Ltd to evaluate 'The Eden Alternative', which is a model of person-directed care.

Seven staff members completed doctorates in the period between 2010 and 2016. Kieran O'Donoghue completed the first doctoral study on social work supervision in Aotearoa New Zealand. His thesis explored

Associate Professor Mark Henrickson, recipient of a Vice-Chancellor's Sustained Teaching Excellence Award in 2011, here teaching at Massey's Albany campus. **MASSEY UNIVERSITY ARCHIVES**

Jane Haste (née Parsons), Associate Professor Kieran O'Donoghue and Helen Simmons at the Massey Defining Excellence Awards in March 2015. **MASSEY UNIVERSITY ARCHIVES**

how social work supervision was constructed within Aotearoa New Zealand, and found that it was primarily from a professional standpoint, and was influenced by bicultural, indigenous and multicultural discourses. He also identified several improvements within the professional and organisational systems that supported supervision as well as within its practice, and recommended that the future research and development agenda for social work supervision both internationally and within Aotearoa New Zealand needed to focus on theory-building, responding to the dynamics of culture and difference within supervision, and the professionalisation of supervision (O'Donoghue, 2010).

Barbara Staniforth's thesis was focused on the tension between the individual counselling component of social work and the profession's commitment to social change. Barbara found that most social workers in this country did some counselling, but it was a unique counselling shaped by Aotearoa New Zealand's historical context and the profession's commitment to biculturalism. Her study has significance for the developing professional identity of social work, as well as its teaching and practice, both in this country and internationally (Staniforth, 2010).

Kathryn Hay's thesis examined the likelihood of a Pasifika human rights mechanism being advanced by the leaders of the Pacific Islands Forum. She found that there was moderate evidence of the preconditions necessary for the development of this policy idea, and that the receptivity and political will of the Pacific leaders would ultimately determine agenda success for sub-regional human rights arrangements (Hay, 2011).

Awhina English joined Massey University at the beginning of 2010. She completed her doctoral thesis through the University of Otago in 2012. Awhina's thesis explored the current experiences of Māori social workers within government, non-government, Māori and iwi (tribal) social service organisations. The findings included the identification of the motivations for Māori to become social workers, and their diverse identities. In addition, Māori social workers have developed a range of practices that have positive results for Māori whānau and are underpinned by tikanga Māori. The results also included ways organisations are currently supporting Māori social work practices, and the thesis provided recommendations for how organisations could be better equipped to support Māori social workers to use their practices for the benefit of Māori whānau (English, 2012).

Developing an understanding of service development in statutory mental health organisations was the topic of Nicky Stanley-Clarke's thesis. Her findings demonstrated an approach for understanding service development within statutory mental health organisations which could be used as a guide for policy-makers, managers and clinicians facilitating service development within this environment. In addition, the organisational case study methodology used in the study generated new theory related to service development and archetype transformation within statutory mental health providers in Aotearoa/New Zealand (Stanley-Clarke, 2013).

The two remaining theses were focused on issues affecting Pasifika peoples. The first of these was Moses Faleolo's (2014) study into why young Samoan males are attracted to youth gangs. Using a life-history approach, Moses found that various socio-cultural strains weakened controls and led the young men into gangs, where they were 're-socialised' by their new gang peers. It also revealed gang members' reasons for both joining and leaving gangs, and the extent to which Samoan cultural values and practices shaped gang values and practices.

The second study was Litea Meo-Sewabu's exploration of the cultural constructs of health and wellbeing amongst Fijian women in a Fijian village and in Whanganui, Aotearoa. From the study, Litea developed a social policy framework that incorporated the 'culturally embedded agency' of Fijian women, which in turn contributed to the beginning of a new approach to health and wellbeing not only for Fijian women but also for Pasifika and indigenous women globally.

In addition to the staff doctoral completions, eight doctorates were awarded over this period; four in Social Policy and four in Social Work.

Irene De Haan's social policy thesis investigated how new parents in diverse circumstances experienced the transition to parenthood and the types of support they found useful at this time. She found that the parents in her study were unprepared for the realities of life with a baby, and that current policy and service provision did not always meet actual needs. She recommended improving the flexibility of services, and customising services to meet the needs and preferences of specific groups of new parents (De Haan, 2011).

The perspectives on poverty of people living in New Zealand communities was the subject of Sheryl Bourke's thesis. She found that the language used to discuss poverty in New Zealand located 'real poverty' in overseas 'third world' countries, while stigmatising, racialising and spiritualising a New Zealand 'type' of poverty. In addition, she explored the governing processes that surrounded those living on social welfare benefits, and how these processes endorsed a sense of marginalised citizenship status for the beneficiary population (Bourke, 2013).

Ram Aryal's thesis focused on the experiences of people living with HIV (PLHIV) in Nepal; in particular, the processes by which they reconstructed their identities. He proposed an identity model based on the economic and social empowerment of the PLHIV, for their identity transformation and the situations they experienced in the contemporary Nepalese socio-political context (Aryal, 2014). He also found that the participants' access to resources often determined the degree of family and social stigma and discrimination.

Mothers' views of smacking in child discipline were explored in Patricia Thompson's thesis. Two clear social perspectives were found: 'a smack is more than a smack' and 'a smack is nothing more than a smack'. The findings contributed to a more socially embedded understanding of parent–child relationships, and added a new perspective to the existing literature on the physical discipline of children (Thompson, 2015).

Eight Master's theses majoring in Social Policy were completed over this period. These theses engaged diverse topics, including iwi social services; criminal justice; disability; Pasifika; poverty; and women's issues.

The first of the four Social Work doctorates was Lesley Read's study of the nature of grandparenting. Read identified three distinct models of grandparenting; namely, the full-time care grandparent with parental responsibilities; the grandparent providing regular supplementary care to assist parent/s to fulfil the parenting needs of their children; and the grandparent with a role characterised as voluntary and varied, outside parent-type responsibilities. She found that grandparents across all models had a strong emotional commitment to adult children's families, and learnt a model of grandparenting from their experience of their grandparents and observing their parents. Read (2010) also highlighted the need for social policies to be sensitive to the needs of grandparents, particularly those raising their grandchildren.

Catherine Campbell's thesis considered how young people in Canada constructed their career pathways after they graduated from secondary school. She found that participants used five strategies as they found a career-related place: navigating, exploring, drifting, settling and committing. In addition, career design principles were identified that provide guidelines for how young people could engage in the process of finding a career-related place in a way that was proactive, while at the same time accepting that career pathways may be uncertain (Campbell, 2011).

Effective health social work practice in an acute hospital was the topic of Linda Haultain's thesis. Haultain (2011) found that in the acute hospital, a health social worker was more likely to be effective if she had been able to make a successful adaptation to this predominately medically driven practice context. At the heart of this adaptation was the quality of the relationships between the practitioner, the multi-disciplinary team, the patient and their whānau.

Ian Hyslop's exploration of the nature of the knowledge generated and applied in social work practice was the fourth thesis. He found that the relational engagement particular to social work produces a contextual knowing that was aligned with critical social humanism. This knowledge was resistant to the rational-technical knowledge form which is privileged in the ascendant neoliberal political climate.

Over this period, 22 Social Work Master's theses (MSW and MPhil) were completed on topics, including adoption; child welfare; criminal justice; health; older persons; Pasifika; spirituality; supervision; welfare; and youth. Two theses focused on Māori social work practice. Paora Moyle's thesis explored Māori social workers' experiences with regard to family group conferencing and child protection practice (Moyle, 2013). Maria Haenga-Collins's thesis was concerned with the closed adoption of Māori children into Pākehā families, and the impact this has had on their belonging and whakapapa.

The social work alumni have continued to make significant impact over this period, with several alumni recognised in the awarding of the following New Zealand honours:

- Betty Sio was awarded a Queen's Service Order for services to the Pacific Island community in 2011.
- Wendy Hawke was made a Member of the New Zealand Order of Merit for services to inter-country adoption in 2014.
- Laurel Taufauata was awarded a Queen's Service Order for services to health and the Pacific community in 2014.
- Rahera Ohia was awarded a Queen's Service Order in 2014.
- Haami Piripi was made a Member of the New Zealand Order of Merit for services to Māori in 2014.
- Emeline Afeaki-Mafile'o became a Member of the New Zealand Order of Merit for Services to the Pacific community in 2016.
- Shelley Campbell became a Member of the New Zealand Order of Merit for services to health and people with disability in 2016.

In addition to the above, several other alumni received awards or significant appointments. For example, Emeline Afeaki-Mafile'o won the inaugural Women of Influence Award for Community Service and Social Enterprise in 2013, while Jane Haste (née Parsons) received Massey University's Distinguished Young Alumni Award in 2015. Two former staff members, Mary Ann Baskerville-Davies and Hanny Naus, were made life members of ANZASW. In addition to this, alumni served on the SWRB; these include Toni Hocquard, Sara Georgeson, Leisa Moorhouse and Dianne Wepa. Another of our alumni, Barbara Gilray, was employed as the professional social work adviser to the SWRB.

Massey alumni have continued to make significant contributions to the social work and broader social services sector. This is exemplified by the contribution of Graeme Munford, director of ACROSS Te Kotahitanga o te Wairua, an Anglican, Catholic and community support service providing social work, counselling and foster care services to families in Palmerston North. Graeme is widely respected in the social service sector and has maintained close links with the Massey School of Social Work as a guest lecturer. ACROSS has provided field education placement experiences for Massey students over many years.

A literature search found that since 2010, 37 articles have been published by social work alumni and students. Several of these publications were derived from research undertaken as part of a Master's study, while others reflected the individual's particular expertise in practice, social work leadership, or interest in the social work issues of the day.

2010

- Cooper, B., & Parsons, J. (2010). Dialectical behaviour therapy: A social work intervention. *Aotearoa New Zealand Social Work, 21*(4) & *22*(1), 83–91.
- Crichton-Hill, Y. (2010). Changing landscapes: Responding to domestic violence in New Zealand. *Aotearoa New Zealand Social Work/Tu Mau, 22*(4), 12–19.

- Fry, K. (2010). Social work clinical leadership in allied health. *Aotearoa New Zealand Social Work, 21*(4) & 22(1), 109–113.
- Koro, T., Walden, N., Smith, T., Dewar, A., Muller, K., Ndeke, A., . . . Simmons, H. (2010). Nga Haerenga o Le Laumei: Pathways to cultural protection through language preservation. *Aotearoa New Zealand Social Work Review/Tu Mau, 22*(4), 44–56.
- McNabb, D. (2010). Professional leadership for social work in mental health services in Aotearoa New Zealand. *Aotearoa New Zealand Social Work 21*(4) & 22(1), 103–107.
- Pitt, L. (2010). Woolsheds, wet weather gear, and the west coast: Social work practice in Taranaki. *Aotearoa New Zealand Social Work, 22*(3), 39–47.
- Ramacake, S. (2010). Fijian social work practice. *Aotearoa New Zealand Social Work/Tu Mau, 22*(4), 38–43.
- Smith, P. (2010). Whatever happened to Tuatapere? A study of a small rural community. *Aotearoa New Zealand Social Work, 22*(3), 27–38
- Todman, A., & Mulitalo-Lauta, P. (2010). The social work alert system: An account of a new inititative in the emergency department at Middlemore hospital. *Aotearoa New Zealand Social Work, 21*(4) & 22(1), 44–45.
- Virtue, C., & Fouche, C. (2010). Multiple holding: A model for supervision in the context of trauma and abuse. *Aotearoa New Zealand Social Work, 21*(4) & 22(1), 64–72.

2011
- Apaitia-Vague, T. (2011). Social work and food: A discussion. *Aotearoa New Zealand Social Work, 23*(3), 63–70.
- Apaiata-Vague, T., Pitt, L., & Younger, D. (2011). Fit and proper: A dilemma for social work educators. *Aotearoa New Zealand Social Work, 23*(4), 55–64.
- Hanlen, P. (2011). Social service manager and student information provision *Aotearoa New Zealand Social Work, 23*(4), 65–75.

- Phillips, S., & Pitt, L. (2011). Maternal mental health making a difference. *Aotearoa New Zealand Social Work, 23*(3), 31–37.

2012

- Eruera, M. (2012). He kōrari, he kete, he kōrero. *Aotearoa New Zealand Social Work, 24*(3 &4), 12–19.
- Lipsham, M. (2012). Āta as an innovative method and practice tool in supervision. *Aotearoa New Zealand Social Work, 24*(3&4), 31–40.

2013

- Dobi, S., & Ross, A. (2013). Thinking beyond the contract: A journey to collaborative community social work. *Aotearoa New Zealand Social Work Review, 25*(1), 43–53.
- Gilray, B. (2013). Social worker registration: A decade of development, debate and delivery. *Aotearoa New Zealand Social Work Review, 25*(3), 25–34.
- Henderson, E., & Fry, K. (2013). Implementing registration within a health organisation setting. *Aotearoa New Zealand Social Work Review, 25*(3), 11–18.
- Kanyi, T. (2013). Lack of outcome research on care and protection family group conference. *Aotearoa New Zealand Social Work Review, 25*(1), 35–42.
- Pitt, L. (2013). What's happening in Taranaki? Social workers and the environment. *Aotearoa New Zealand Social Work Review, 25*(4), 52–61.
- Smith, P. (2013). Registration: Ten years on within a non-government organisation. *Aotearoa New Zealand Social Work Review, 25*(3), 19–24.
- Smith, P. (2013). Whose culture is it anyway? Social working in a rural community. *Aotearoa New Zealand Social Work Review, 25*(1), 14–23.
- Winkelmann, G. (2013). Social work in health — the way ahead. *Aotearoa New Zealand Social Work Review, 25*(4), 85–88.

2014

- Fraser, S., & Simpson, S. (2014). 'Always take the weather with you' — Aotearoa New Zealand social work in a dynamic global society. *Aotearoa New Zealand Social Work Review*, 26(2 & 3), 29–38.

- McNabb, D. (2014). 30 years' membership and a 50th birthday — where to next for ANZASW? *Aotearoa New Zealand Social Work Review*, 26(2 & 3), 61–71.

- Moyle, P. (2014). A model for Māori research for Māori practitioners. *Aotearoa New Zealand Social Work/Te Kōmako*, 26(1), 29–38.

- Moyle, P. (2014). Māori social workers' experiences of care and protection: A selection of findings. *Aotearoa New Zealand Social Work/Te Kōmako*, 26(1), 55–64.

- Nash, M. (2014). Their stories — our history: John Fry, President of the Association 1972–4. *Aotearoa New Zealand Social Work Review*, 26(2 & 3), 39–47.

- Phillips, C. (2014). Spirituality and social work: Introducing a spiritual dimension into social work education and practice. *Aotearoa New Zealand Social Work Review*, 26(4), 65–77.

- Ross, A. (2014). The social work voice: How could unions strengthen practice? *Aotearoa New Zealand Social Work Review*, 26(4), 4–13.

- Sayers, J. (2014). Reminiscences of anti-racism training in the 1980s. *Aotearoa New Zealand Social Work Review*, 26(2 & 3), 81–85.

- Smith, P. (2014). The why, what, where of social work: A personal reflection on the social work role over a thirty-year period. *Aotearoa New Zealand Social Work Review*, 26(2 & 3), 75–80.

- Thomson, C. (2014). Reflections on the social work profession on the 50th anniversary of ANZASW: Those who fail to learn from history are doomed to repeat it. *Aotearoa New Zealand Social Work Review*, 26(2 & 3), 3–5.

- Thorburn, N., & De Hann, I. (2014). Children and survival sex: A social work agenda. *Aotearoa New Zealand Social Work Review*, 26(4), 14–21.

2015

- Panelli, R., Mongston, T., & Young, F. (2015). 'Moving beyond violence': Exploring new ways to support women and develop networked approaches following intimate partner violence. *Aotearoa New Zealand Social Work, 27*(3), 14–28.
- Rushton, J. (2015). Volunteer peer supervision: In an ever-changing social service environment. *Aotearoa New Zealand Social Work, 27*(3), 68–77.

The above review reflects the ongoing contribution of the social work programme both nationally and internationally. Professional and academic leadership was demonstrated, in particular by Professors Robyn Munford's and Jackie Sanders' distinguished research on youth wellbeing; Associate Professor Mark Henrickson's national and international contribution to social work education, sexuality and HIV research; Dr Kathryn Hay's leadership in the area of field education; and Associate Professor Kieran O'Donoghue's expertise in social work supervision.

Since Kieran's appointment as director of Social Work in 2010, and subsequent promotion to head of school in 2014, the school continued to build on the long-established foundation of the social work programme in order to ensure that the programme remained at the forefront of social work education and research in Aotearoa New Zealand. The record of commissioned research, publications and doctoral completions described above was impressive. The programme remained relevant to the current social work environment and continued to enjoy strong enrolments in both undergraduate and postgraduate degrees and diplomas. Finally, Massey social work alumni continued to contribute to and shape social work practice.

The impact and influence of Massey University in defining social work in Aotearoa New Zealand was particularly evident at the 2016 conference and seminar 'Social work in changing times: Towards better outcomes', held 17–19 November 2016 at Massey University, Palmerston North, attended by 209 registrants.

Day one of the event was a seminar concerned with the wellbeing of children and young people, while the other two days focused on the conference theme of 'social work in changing times: towards better outcomes'.

On the final day of the conference, a Bachelor of Social Work fortieth anniversary reunion dinner was held at Wharerata, the beautiful homestead on the Massey grounds, attended by 45 alumni and current staff. Professor Robyn Munford, foundation class member, traversed highlights of the 40 years of the programme, paying special tribute to Merv Hancock and Ephra Garrett. Memories and humorous anecdotes were shared, with a uniting theme being the significance of the BSW as a foundation for social work practice in Aotearoa New Zealand.

The keynote speakers for the conference were Professor Robbie Gilligan, Professor of Social Work and Social Policy at Trinity College Dublin; Dr Awhina Hollis-English; Paulé Ruwhiu; the Hon Steve Maharey; Professor Robyn Munford; and Jane Haste. Professor Gilligan's first keynote stressed the importance of a reviewed commitment to a truly child-centred approach in children's services and policy development. It sought to 'unpack' what being 'child-centred' means — both at the level of daily practice with individual children, but also more broadly at an organisational or policy level. He argued that being child-centred was an essential step in rising to the challenge of promoting the wellbeing of children and young people. Dr Hollis-English's keynote told a story of one whānau hauā within her whānau, and her personal experiences within disability services. She shared from the perspective of being tangata whenua, an academic, a researcher and a mother, and provided suggestions for better outcomes in changing times, beginning with the decolonisation and demystification of disability discourse and te ao Māori.

On the second day, Professor Gilligan spoke about the remarkable turbulence in the social, political and economic environments in which social work operated globally. He noted that social work found itself at the beating heart of many of the big social questions of our time: poverty, abuse and violence in institutional systems and in personal relationships, the protection of displaced and vulnerable citizens, gender inequality, the relationship between the family and the State, the extent and nature of future public investment in welfare state provision, and much more. He raised questions such as: How can social workers deal with such tensions and uncertainties as these play out in the lives of the people they serve and in the policy arena in which they operate? How can their morale be sustained? How can their work be effective? What should inform their practice? How should they achieve a balanced response to the competing demands of all kinds that they confront? How can their contribution be validated and celebrated? His aim in this presentation was to not so much hand out simple answers, but rather to propose guiding principles that may help the good ship social work steer a true course though exceptionally stormy waters.

Paulé Ruwhiu's keynote address discussed the importance of looking at the past in order to move forward as a pertinent part of te ao Māori. Paulé presented her PhD thesis, which explored the process of decolonisation and the experiences of Māori social work students, practitioners and educators. It is important for Paulé to continue to advocate for decolonisation education for social work, in terms of what this looks like inside the social work profession. This involves ensuring that social workers have gone through a process of 'Kō wai au?' ('Who am I?') This is applicable when working with whānau, hapū and iwi. Paulé presented a journey through her doctorate research, which included privileging the voices of the participants.

The Hon Steve Maharey's keynote address was a sociological analysis of the new times in which we live, from both a local and a global standpoint. Steve then discussed the implications that these times and the current issues have for social work, in terms of how to make sense of them through the use of a sociological imagination.

Professor Robyn Munford explored the context of social and community work practice in Aotearoa New Zealand. Drawing on examples from practice, Robyn presented a critical examination of the challenges faced by social and community workers, and the tensions they faced in their daily practice. She highlighted how social and community workers attend to the immediate needs of individuals, families and communities, while building an understanding of social change and the relationship between personal issues and the broader social and political context. Robyn argued for practice that makes a difference; this required social and community workers being courageous in confronting inequality and marginalisation and speaking up for social justice.

The final keynote was by Jane Haste, private practitioner, therapist and supervisor, and Massey University's Distinguished Young Alumni of 2015. Jane's presentation reviewed the concept of a dialectical paradigm and how it sits with social work, together with how it can be incorporated to negotiate and find a useful 'space between' opposing polarities in our work to generate positive outcomes for clients and colleagues. A key area that was presented was the consideration of 'what works', using emerging practices of mindfulness and service delivery within a 'business' model to improve outcomes in health and wellbeing.

During the conference, the Doctor of Social Work programme was officially launched, followed by a book launch for the new text *Social work in Aotearoa New Zealand — exploring fields of practice* by Dr Kathryn Hay, Dr Michael Dale and Lareen Cooper. This book included links to 37 video clips of social workers explaining their fields of practice. QR codes and URL links appear at key points throughout the book, giving immediate links to the videos and other websites and resources. The book also included graphics of social work theories and models, selected transcripts from the interviews, and photographs of the social workers in

The Hon Steve Maharey delivers his address to social workers at the 'Social work in changing times' conference, November 2016. **SCHOOL OF SOCIAL WORK**

Associate Professor Kieran O'Donoghue, Professor Robbie Gilligan, Professor Robyn Munford and Dr Awhina Hollis-English taking part in a panel discussion at the 'Social work in changing times' conference, November 2016. **SCHOOL OF SOCIAL WORK**

their organisations. The book was designed to help social work students make informed decisions about where to undertake the minimum 120 days of field placement required during their study.

This chapter has shown that the political dominance of the New Right National-led Coalition Government with its neo-conservative agenda placed emphasis on welfare reform, responsibilisation, and a reduction on the role of the State in civil society during this period. The construction of professional social work practice was influenced not only by ANZASW, but also increasingly by the SWRB. The question of professional identity remained central to the position of social work, and, notwithstanding debate on the issue, mandatory registration offered the greatest prospect of professional legitimacy for social work in what is an increasingly contested space.

The School of Social Work responded successfully to challenges within the academy, was subject to external scrutiny, and consolidated its reputation as a leading social work programme. The social work team continued to contribute on both the national and international stage. It had a reputation for producing social work graduates who are able to articulate the relationship between theory and practice, are aware of the requirements of bicultural practice, were committed to social justice, were aware of the influence of social policy, and who were competent practitioners. The staff, students and alumni made a contribution to teaching, research and publications, and received recognition for their excellence by way of awards and honours. The conference 'Social work in changing times: Towards better outcomes' epitomised the success of the social work programme, and provided cutting-edge analysis and commentary. The Massey School of Social Work stood ready to embrace the challenges of the future.

Dr Michael Dale, Dr Kathryn Hay and Lareen Cooper at the launch of their book *Social Work in Aotearoa New Zealand — exploring fields of practice*, 2016.
SCHOOL OF SOCIAL WORK

Staff members Dr Tracie Mafile'o and Dr Moses Faleolo (Albany) at the book launch. **SCHOOL OF SOCIAL WORK**

Chapter Six
The future picture

O ver the past 40 years, Massey University's social work programme has successfully negotiated the changing needs of the social service sector, and the broader social and political environment. The development of the programme has been presented in terms of the political and social context, developments in social work, and the development and contribution of the programme. A summary of salient points drawn from each of the preceding chapters provides the backdrop for a consideration of the future picture for both the Massey social work programme, and social work in Aotearoa New Zealand.

During this period, the emergence of neoliberalism (characterised by economic deregulation and the diminution of the welfare state) and the political dominance of the National Party was evident. There were also developments in Māori political consciousness and organisation, evidenced through Māori self-determination, a focus on race relations and biculturalism, and the significance of te reo. Further, a developing social consciousness was reflected in concern with issues affecting race relations, women and the needs of children and disabled persons.

The social work programme at Massey University was established within this broader social context. Concern with social justice is a hallmark of the social work mandate, and this was reflected in the core characteristics of the programme, which included engagement with the need for political analysis, recognition of the role of social policy, a commitment to bicultural practice, and the development of a strong connection with the social work practice community.

The political and social landscape during this period witnessed the role of the Labour Party in promoting economic policy characterised by market-led restructuring and deregulation; a change in the structure and role of the State, with an emphasis on cost, efficiency and effectiveness; and a reduction of the role of the State regarding public welfare. A drive to improve effectiveness, responsiveness and efficiency in the delivery of State-funded services was evident in legislative and policy changes in health, education, criminal justice and social welfare. Of great significance was a will to address concerns regarding racism within government organisations. *Pūao-te-Āta-tū — The daybreak report*, and the subsequent changes embraced within the Children, Young Persons, and Their Families Act 1989, were seen to provide the opportunity for a service that would be more responsive to Māori.

For social work, the drive to improve the effectiveness, responsiveness and efficiency of State services, including those concerned with social welfare, heralded an era where evidence-based policy and interventions would have a significant impact on social work practice. During this period, there was concern with the professionalisation of social work, with continued debate regarding curriculum, training, qualifications and accountability. At Massey University, much of the focus of the early period concerned the development and accreditation of the social work programme within the university and academia, and in particular the vision of social work as a graduate discipline. The stewardship exercised by the foundation staff set a benchmark against which subsequent programme development and achievement have been considered.

The defining characteristic of the social and political context during the period 1993 to 2000 reflected a continuing scaling-back of the State and the emergence of the 'third way', with a focus on civic responsibility, earned rights and individual autonomy. Within this framework, the foundations were laid for a social development approach to welfare that balanced market-driven policy with a commitment to support those in need. The new MMP voting system ushered in a new era of political compromise that was to afford voice to previously marginalised populations.

Of note was the ongoing concern exhibited regarding the performance of the statutory State agency responsible for the care and protection of children and young persons. There was a need for additional resources from the government, and a need to change the culture and operations of the department. The performance of this statutory agency can be seen as an indicator of the challenges faced by the broader social work sector, including the application of managerialism, and issues surrounding curriculum, training, qualifications and accountability.

At Massey University, the publication of *Social work in action* was a milestone for staff and alumni contributors. Moreover, the depth of Māori scholarship over this period was both impressive and a reflection of a commitment to the development of bicultural practice within the programme. The depth and breadth of scholarship from academic staff, students and alumni were having an impact, as was the contribution of graduates who were occupying a range of social work roles.

The years between 2001 and 2009 were characterised by the social reforms of the Fifth Labour Government, the rise of the Māori Party, the regulation of social work and tertiary education, and repositioning in the form of organisational change and in response to the Global Financial Crisis. Notwithstanding constant review and reorganisation of the State child welfare agency, the performance of Aotearoa New Zealand in relation to the welfare of vulnerable children remained abysmal in comparison with other OECD countries.

The emergence of the SWRB and the influence of ANZASW reflected the contested nature of the political space concerning social work. While registration was introduced on a voluntary basis, the debate regarding the benefits and limitation of mandatory registration continued. The development of the Tangata Whenua Social Workers Association was important, and to some extent symbolic of the assertion of rangatiratanga by Māori for Māori.

The Massey University social work programme remained responsive to both the university and the external social work environment. In the face of increasing competition, organisational change with a focus on achieving greater synergies between academic focus, research and business efficiency, and the demands of PBRF, the programme developed new offerings, and the profile of Massey staff within the social work arena developed further.

Between 2010 and 2016 the retention of MMP, and government by the National-led coalition, enabled the continuation of a New Right political agenda and provided stable government in unstable times. This was evident in legislative and policy changes that were underpinned by a social investment perspective, in contrast with previous approaches to welfare, and the notion of responsibilisation permeated welfare reform. The role of the State welfare agency CYF has remained under intense scrutiny, being subject to both internal and external review that has culminated in the establishment of a new entity.

The development of the university's social work programme over this period reflects the rapidly changing social, political and university environments. The emergence of the separate School of Social Work within the College of Health reflects both the status of the social work programme and the influence of the head of school and senior academics. The programme has remained responsive to the academy, and to the broader social work profession. There has been cause for celebration with the fortieth anniversary of the programme, and also time to reflect on the contribution of previous staff whose influence continues to provide direction to the programme.

The notion of the 'sociological imagination' was first proposed by American sociologist C. Wright Mills, who defined it as the individual's ability to connect personal experience to society at large:

> Perhaps the most fruitful distinction with which the sociological imagination works is between 'the personal troubles of milieu' and 'the public issues of social structure'. (Mills, 1970, p. 14)

Mills considered that the role of the social scientist was to explore how personal problems inform societal problems. This perspective maintains currency in framing the key challenges facing social work. Social work should seek to understand social change and the relationship between personal issues and the broader social and political context. Professor Robyn Munford argued in her conference presentation that the personal is political, and asked: 'How do we support individuals while at the same time challenge the structural conditions that create miserable lives?' (Munford, 2016). This requires social workers to consider the contextual factors that contribute to the psychosocial challenges faced by clients; practice should be considered in the context of rising inequality and poverty. Social work should develop a deeper understanding of structural issues, and work towards developing solutions. Kieran O'Donoghue articulated in his conference delivery the connection between the sociological imagination and social work:

> It is to have both a sociological imagination in which one understands the connection between personal and public troubles and events, as well as a social work imagination which is an optimism, faith and unswerving belief in the potential of people and a tireless effort to work in each moment as an ambassador for a humane, socially just society. (O'Donoghue, 2016)

Against this backdrop, discussion now turns to the question of the future challenges facing social work and the Massey social work programme. There are three sections: the macro trends that provide the context for international social work; the political environment that has been shaped by neoliberalism, including the construction of welfare; and the potential social work response to the identified challenges.

At the 'Social work in changing times' conference, outgoing Massey University Vice-Chancellor Steve Maharey identified a number of themes that influence the broader international context characterised as 'new times'. First, increasing globalisation that is characterised by diversity, fragmentation and differentiation. There is also increased interaction across nations, races or ethnicities, religions and cultures. Second, allied to this globalisation is the impact of migration, including changing public perceptions towards migrant and new settler groups. Third, the economic challenge to continue to meet the social and welfare needs of growing populations. Fourth, is the impact of technological development that shapes both economies and responses to social needs. And, finally, there is concern with the environment and how to meet the demand for goods and services in a sustainable manner.

The pre-eminence of neoliberal political thought and policy has shaped the Aotearoa New Zealand social and political landscape since the mid-1990s. Reflective of this has been the focus on individualism and responsibilisation. The construction of welfare will continue to present challenges in terms of both access to support and the meeting of associated costs. Previous State approaches to welfare have been superseded by a social investment approach that has yet to meet the needs of those who fall through the ever-widening safety net — the isolated and marginalised who have been 'left behind'. The question of financial and income insecurity needs to be addressed in light of the ageing population.

For Professor Robyn Munford, the focus on outcomes and targeting in response to risk and harm reflects the drive for the resolution of what are perceived to be immediate or acute issues. However, this does not sufficiently engage deeper contextual issues. Aotearoa New Zealand currently experiences high rates of unemployment (particularly among young people and minority groups), and the nation's record regarding child poverty, abuse and neglect is shameful. Further, imprisonment rates are increasing, and affordable and accessible housing and health care are out of reach for an increasing number of New Zealanders. Professor Munford raised the challenge regarding our mutual obligation to others, and asked: 'Who are the winners and who are the casualties of free market capitalism?' (Munford, 2016).

For social work, challenges are apparent in the following dominant discourses: welfare and health discourses (the biomedical, legal and economic); the influence of the social and behavioural science discourses (psychology, psychiatry, psychotherapy) and sociological ideas; and alternative and emerging discourses, such as citizen rights, spirituality, environmental sustainability and indigenous development (Healy, 2014).

What will be the response of social work in Aotearoa New Zealand to these challenges? The social work profession's experience of this climate shift is apparent in how its professional purpose is being shaped and defined by the dominant discourses. A unique feature of the Aotearoa New Zealand social work practice context is responsibility for a Te Tiriti o Waitangi-based society. In particular, members of the Aotearoa New Zealand Association of Social Workers (ANZASW) are required to understand tangata whenua perspectives; avoid imposing monocultural values and concepts on tangata whenua; and be actively anti-racist in their practice (Hay, Dale, & Cooper, 2016). It is contingent upon social workers in Aotearoa New Zealand to reflect on the position of the Treaty of Waitangi in social and community work practice, and the relationship between tangata whenua and their Treaty partners. Practitioners should critically reflect on their position and use of self, and understand their own position and practice approaches (Munford, 2016).

In order to support social work clients to achieve self-determination and to effect social change, both the sociological and social work imagination offer direction. It will be important for social work to continue to engage both multiple perspectives and competing discourses. The adoption of strength-based and mana-enhancing practice offers an alternative to the negative, often corrosive discourse of responsibilisation.

Social work practice is firmly based on relationships, and it is contingent upon practitioners to focus on developing transformative relationships, and to listen to and appreciate the experiences of clients. Social workers should adopt a critical lens and consider whether practices and policies actually result in transformative change.

Two prominent schools of thought regarding social work theories are intended to guide and explain practice which retain currency: the empirical practice movement, and the reflective tradition (Healy, 2014). In the empirical practice tradition, the primary purpose of social work knowledge is to provide guidance for accurate assessment, diagnosis and problem-solving activities. Schön (1995) identifies 'technical-rationality' as a dominant epistemology for professional practice that is reliant on the scientific paradigm. This approach is evident in the focus that exists on risk, assessment, measurement of outcomes and effectiveness. The reflective tradition develops an epistemology of practice that can account for the intuitive processes that practitioners may bring to a practice context, often characterised by 'complexity, instability, uniqueness and value conflict' (Schön, 1995, pp. 48–49). The focal point of this type of practice is the nature of the relationship between practitioner and client, a relationship that Schön (1995, p. 295) characterises as a 'reflective conversation'. It is the ability to develop a practice approach that is a synthesis of empirical theory, client knowledge and inductive reasoning that distinguishes the reflective approach.

Bearing this distinction in mind, in his address at the conference Kieran O'Donoghue (2016) asked: To what extent are social service organisations becoming 'data driven' as opposed to 'client-centred'? He argues that the empirically based 'what works' question is questionable, and a legacy of a twentieth-century universal uniform narrative which is now challenged by a complex, diverse, pluralist, contextual, interconnected world in which the specifics of when, where, how, for whom and in what circumstances matter. Kieran contrasts the 'what works' perspective with the reflective, relational, mana-enhancing, strengths and communitarian heart of social work, which emphasises the artistry of the practice in the uncertainty of the here and now, the kanohi ki te kanohi of relationships, the hopes, dreams and possibilities for the future, and the interconnectedness of people with each other and their family, whānau and communities.

Professor Robbie Gilligan also drew attention to the relational foundation of social work practice with the reminder that the 'small is not trivial', pointing out the significance and transformative potential of small actions (both positive and negative) on the lived experiences of the client (Gilligan, 2016). A focus on the life and experience of the client offers the prospect of change at the individual level, and this focus should not be overlooked.

A t Massey, it will be important to have leadership of the programme that understands practice and the requirements of the sector. As it has successfully achieved in the past, the programme will be required to constantly review itself in terms of the critical interface around key social issues both in Aotearoa New Zealand and internationally. This should be carried out against the backdrop of a commitment to the principles and values that were the foundation of the programme:

- To develop and maintain a connection between theory, research and practice, and a connection between social work and social policy.
- To maintain strong connections with the social work sector, and to encourage staff to engage in research, thus contributing to an

indigenous construction of practice.

- To develop a bicultural programme and include a focus on Māori development.
- To recognise the importance of having Māori and Pasifika students in the programme, and of respecting their voice within the profession of social work.

At times it has been challenging to meet the needs of the university and the college, and it has been difficult to constantly keep a focus on the needs of social work. Linked to this is the issue of adequate resourcing within the tertiary sector, which is likely to remain an ongoing challenge. In particular, the costs of study may impact on the student profile and result in some potential students choosing other options.

There remains an ongoing challenge to harness emerging new ideas in the sector in teaching and research; for example, person-centred practice and models of recovery and advocacy in the disability and mental health fields. Structural issues such as poverty, and children and youth growing up in impoverished material circumstances, including poor access to adequate housing and health care, and the needs of marginalised populations, will need to stay firmly on the agenda of social work practice, education and research.

The new Doctor of Social Work programme will meet an increasing demand in Aotearoa New Zealand and around the globe for advancing practice-based research among practising social workers. It is particularly relevant for social workers in the fields of health (including mental health), child and family practice, social work in schools, social service organisations, policy and practice advisers in government, and social work education and training providers. It will also be important to retain a balance between teaching and research, and to enable staff to have opportunities to complete research and maintain a focus on research-informed teaching.

The ongoing negative impact of colonisation on indigenous people must be continually engaged. It is imperative that the programme maintain and grow its focus on bicultural practice, while responding to the diverse needs of a changing client population. Critical research, writing and teaching needs to be dedicated to issues of Māori social work and indigenous social work in order to attract Māori students to social work, and retain them. Māori students and staff should be encouraged to bring their values to the programme.

There is also the need to continually consider how to make a critical contribution to Māori social work and to issues in local communities. In order to achieve these goals, there should be a focus on Māori theories informing practice, Māori models of practice, and the impact of Māori frameworks inside statutory and non-government organisations. Social work educators need to understand Whānau Ora and how it reflects rangatiratanga, and how to develop, retain and maintain a deep understanding of Māori whānau and communities.

Feedback from previous Māori staff indicates that one of the significant strengths of the Massey University social work programme is that it creates social workers who have a strong critical analysis, and that Massey has made a valuable contribution to social work leadership. However, looking to the future, they had some ideas of how Massey University can improve.

Wheturangi Walsh-Tapiata felt that it is important that the Massey social work programme and staff continue to 'battle' for the kaupapa, which includes a commitment to recruit Māori staff, to develop these staff to advance in their careers, and encourage and support staff relationships and responsibilities to the community, whānau, hapū and iwi. She challenged Massey University to strongly consider significant ways to practise biculturalism, with examples like co-teaching, fully integrated Māori content (not just paper-specific) and dual heads of school.

Leland Ruwhiu highlighted the importance of strengthening the Māori voice, and ways to grow strong indigenous social work professionals —

from both a male and female perspective/worldview (acknowledging the strong wāhine contribution to date). He wants to see more emphasis and research on Māori theories and Māori models of practice, and see these integrated right through the programme and in practice.

Rachael Selby was concerned about the reduction of the caucusing model. She noted that specific tutorials for Māori students contributed to them developing 'a greater understanding of their own backgrounds and who they were and what they could contribute'. Rachael also encouraged Massey to continue to recruit Māori postgraduate students, particularly utilising the supernumery position.

All three identified the importance of continuing to contribute to community. Concern was also expressed that the mandatory registration of social workers could potentially become colonising and restrict social workers' ability to act as agents of social change. The programme will need to continue to meet the requirements of registration, including the changing policy on the accreditation of social work programmes. A challenge for all social work programmes and social workers will be the achievement and demonstration of competence to work with and engage with Māori.

Much has been achieved by the social work programme in terms of defining social work in Aotearoa New Zealand but there is still much to do. Quoting from the 1994 conversation between Professor Robyn Munford, Dr Mary Nash and Merv Hancock seems apposite. When asked: 'What does the future hold for social work?' Merv encapsulated the challenge and promise of social work for the future:

The future holds as much uncertainty as the past. It is very important to live with uncertainty and accept it. The uncertainty of the world economy is always present, and anybody who suggests that it is not uncertain is a rogue and a vagabond. However, although uncertainty is the order of the day, the future is in a sense what one makes of it. Social work can make a contribution to defining the kind of society we live in. Therefore it needs to maintain a level of optimism about itself. (Merv Hancock, in Munford & Nash, 1994, p. 13)

References

Adamson, C. (2005a). Complexity and context: An ecological understanding of trauma practice. In M. Nash, R. Munford, & K. O'Donoghue (Eds.), *Social work theories in action* (pp. 64–79). London, United Kingdom: Jessica Kingsley Publishers.

Adamson, C. (2005b). *Complexity and context: Staff support systems in mental health after critical incidents and traumatic events.* (PhD thesis, Wellington, New Zealand: Massey University.) http://mro.massey.ac.nz/handle/10179/1573.

Anderson, R. H. (1997). Interpreting therapeutic process: A constructivist perspective. *Journal of Constructivist Psychology, 10,* 297–319.

Aotearoa New Zealand Association of Social Workers. (2014) ANZASW Digital History Project. http://www.socialworkhistory.nz/

Aryal, R. P. (2014). *The reconstruction of identity in people living with HIV in Nepal.* (PhD thesis, Auckland, New Zealand: Massey University.) http://mro.massey.ac.nz/handle/10179/6956

Barnes J., & Harris, P. (2011). Still kicking? The Royal Commission on Social Policy, 20 years on. *Social Policy Journal of New Zealand 37,* 1–13. https://www.msd.govt.nz/about-msd-and-our-work/publications-resources/journals-and-magazines/social-policy-journal/spj37/37-still-kicking-the-royal-commission-on-social-policy-20-years-on.html

Barrett, P. (1997). *Male breadwinner households and work: Alterations in the transition to a liberal welfare regime.* (PhD thesis, Palmerston North, New Zealand: Massey University.) http://mro.massey.ac.nz/handle/10179/2553

Barretta-Herman, A. (1983). Social work at the interface: The social worker in a bureaucracy. *New Zealand Social Work, 8*(September), 16–17.

Barretta-Herman, A. (1990a). The effective social service staff meeting. In R. Sligo (Ed.), *Business communication: New Zealand perspectives* (pp. 136–146). Palmerston North, New Zealand: Software Technology New Zealand Ltd.

Barretta-Herman, A. (1990b). *The restructuring of the Department of Social Welfare and implications for social work practice, 1986–1988.* (PhD thesis, Palmerston North, New Zealand: Massey University.) http://mro.massey.ac.nz/handle/10179/3918

Barretta-Herman, A., & Cruse, W. (1989). New Zealand women social work managers: A survey. *Social Work Review, 1*(3–4), 4–8.

Baskerville, M. A., & Durrant, P. (1996). Private practice: A social work option in New Zealand. *Social Work Review, 8*(1), 14–19.

Beddoe, L., & Worrall, J. (1997). The future of fieldwork in a market economy. *Asia Pacific Journal of Social Work and Development, 7*(1), 12–32.

Beddoe, L., & Worrall, J. (2001). *From rhetoric to reality: Keynote address and selected papers.* Auckland, New Zealand: Auckland College of Education.

Belgrave, M. (2000). *Evaluation of the Social Workers in Schools pilot programme: Final report.* Wellington, New Zealand: Department of Child, Youth and Family.

Belgrave, M. (2005). The Tribunal and the past: Taking a roundabout path to a new history. In M. Belgrave, M. Kawharu, & D. Williams (Eds.), *Waitangi revisited: Perspectives on the Treaty of Waitangi* (pp. 35–55). Melbourne, Australia: Oxford University Press.

Belgrave, M., & Dobbs, T. (2001). Social workers in schools: Delivering to children? *Social Work Now, 18,* 33–37.

Belgrave, M., Kawharu, M., & Williams, D. (Eds.). *Waitangi revisited: Perspectives on the Treaty of Waitangi.* Melbourne, Australia: Oxford University Press.

Bell, H. (2006). *Exiting the matrix: Colonisation, decolonisation and social work in Aotearoa — the voices of Ngāti Raukawa ki te Tonga kaimahi whanau.* (MPhil thesis, Palmerston North, New Zealand: Massey University. http://mro.massey.ac.nz/handle/10179/662

Bell, H., & Thorpe, A. (2004). External supervision: What is it for a social worker in schools? *Te Kōmako VII, Social Work Review XVI(2),* 12–14.

Bennie, G. (1995) *Social work supervision: An annotated bibliography.* Palmerston North, New Zealand: Department of Social Policy and Social Work, Massey University.

Bennie, G. (1996). *Supported employment and disabled people in New Zealand: From assimilation to transformation.* (PhD thesis, Palmerston North, New Zealand: Massey University.) http://mro.massey.ac.nz/handle/10179/2710

Benton, R., Benton, N., Croft, C., & Waaka, A. (1991). *Kahukura, the possible dream,* Wellington: New Zealand Council for Education and Training in the Social Services.

Berridge, D., Cowan, L., Cumberland, T., Davys, A., McDowell, H., Morgan, J., & Wallis, P. (1985). *Institutional racism in the Department of Social Welfare,* Department of Social Welfare, Auckland, New Zealand.

Blagdon, J. Taylor, M., & Keall, B. (1994). Update on social work registration. *Social Work Review, 6*(4), 24.

Bosmann-Watene, G. (2009). *He putiputi, he taonga, he rangatira: The factors motivating young Maori women to achieve success.* (MSW thesis, Palmerston North, New Zealand: Massey University.)

Boston, J., Martin, J., Pallot, J., & Walsh, P. (1996). *Public management: The New Zealand model.* Auckland, New Zealand: Oxford University Press.

Bourke, S. R. (2013). *Perspectives on poverty.* (PhD thesis, Auckland, New Zealand: Massey University.) http://mro.massey.ac.nz/handle/10179/4695

Boyles, P. (1998). *Enabling participation through partnership: Emancipatory research — the potential for change for disabled people.* (PhD thesis, Palmerston North, New Zealand: Massey University.) http://mro.massey.ac.nz/handle/10179/2432

Bradley, J. (1994). Iwi and the Maatua Whangai programme. In R. Munford & M. Nash, (Eds.), *Social Work in Action* (pp. 178–198), Palmerston North, New Zealand: Dunmore Press.

Bradley, J. (1995a). 'Before you tango with our whanau, you better know what makes us tick.' An indigenous approach to social work. *Social Work Review/Te Kōmako, 7*(1), 27–29.

Bradley, J. (1995b). The resolve to devolve: Māori and social services. *Practice Journal of the New Zealand Children and Young Persons Service, 1*(July), 29–35.

Bradley, J., Jacob, E., & Bradley, R. (1999). Reflections on culturally safe supervision, or why Bill Gates makes more money than we do. *Social Work Review/Te Kōmako, 11*(4), 3–6.

Briar, C. (1996). *Working for women? Gendered work and welfare policies in twentieth-century Britain.* London, England: Taylor and Francis.

Briar, C., Munford, R., & Nash, M (Eds.). (1992). *Superwoman: Where are you? Social policy and women's experience.* Palmerston North, New Zealand: Dunmore Press.

Brook, J. (1997). Sexual abuse with people with disabilities. *Social Work Review, 9*(3), 16–17.

Brown, M. (2000), *Care and protection is about adult behaviour: The Ministerial Review of the Department of Child, Youth and Family Services.* Wellington, New Zealand: Department of Child, Youth and Family. https://www.msd.govt.nz/documents/about-msd-and-our-work/publications-resources/archive/2000-care-and-protection-is-about-adult-behaviour.pdf

Campbell, C. G. (2011). *A study of the career pathways of Canadian young adults during the decade after secondary school graduation.* (PhD thesis, Palmerston North, New Zealand: Massey University.) http://mro.massey.ac.nz/handle/10179/3070

Cervin, C. (2001). *Action research, power and responsibility: The predicament and potential of New Zealand community groups.* (PhD thesis, Auckland, New Zealand:

Massey University.) http://mro.massey.ac.nz/handle/10179/2114

Cheyne, C. (1993a). History of CWL. In A. Else (Ed.), *Women together: A history of women's organisations in New Zealand. Nga ropu wahine o te Motu*. Wellington, New Zealand: Daphne Brassell and Associates.

Cheyne, C. (1993b). History of Sophia. In A. Else (Ed.), *Women together: A history of women's organisations in New Zealand. Nga ropu wahine o te Motu*. Wellington, New Zealand: Daphne Brassell and Associates.

Cheyne, C. (2000). Fin de siècle neo-liberalism: Governmentality and post-social politics. *Sites: A journal for South Pacific Cultural Studies, 38*, 2–5.

Cheyne, C., O'Brien, M., & Belgrave, M. (1997). *Social policy in Aotearoa New Zealand: A critical introduction*. Auckland, New Zealand: Oxford University Press.

Cheyne, C., Belgrave, M., & O'Brien, M. (2005). *Social policy in Aotearoa New Zealand: A critical introduction* (3rd ed). Auckland, New Zealand: Oxford University Press.

Child, Youth and Family Practice Centre (2016). *Knowledge and practice*. http://www.practicecentre.cyf.govt.nz/knowledge-base-practice-frameworks/#ChildYouthandFamilyPracticeFrameworks5 (Accessed 14 October 2016.)

Cockburn, G. (1994). Supervision in social work: A brief statement of the essentials. *Social Work Review, 6*(5&6), 37.

Coney, S., & Bunkle, P. (June 1987). An unfortunate experiment. *Metro*, pp 47–65.

Connolly, M. (Ed.) (2001). *New Zealand social work: Contexts and practice*. Melbourne: Oxford University Press.

Connolly, M. (2007). Practice frameworks: Conceptual maps to guide interventions in child welfare. *British Journal of Social Work, 37*(5), 825–837. doi:10.1093/bjsw/bcl049

Connolly, M., & Harms, L. (Eds.) (2001). *New Zealand social work: Contexts and practice* (2nd ed.) Melbourne: Oxford University Press.

Cooper, L. (1993). Mandatory reporting. *Social Work Review 6*(2), 29–31.

Craig, W. (1983). *A community work perspective*. Palmerston North, New Zealand: Massey University.

Craig, W. (1991). *From rocking the cradle to rocking the system: Women, community work and social change in Aotearoa*. (PhD thesis, Palmerston North, New Zealand: Massey University.) http://mro.massey.ac.nz/handle/10179/3111

Cram, F. (2012). *Safety of subsequent children: Māori children and whānau. A review of selected literature*. Wellington, New Zealand: Families Commission. http://www.superu.govt.nz/sites/default/files/SoSC-Maori-and-Whanau.pdf

Dale, M. P. (2006). *Probation practice, leadership and effective service delivery: A qualitative study of the perspectives of probation officers and service managers in the New Zealand Probation Service.* (PhD thesis, Palmerston North, New Zealand: Massey University.) http://mro.massey.ac.nz/handle/10179/1476

Davys, A. (2002). *Perceptions through a prism: Three accounts of good social work supervision.* (MSW thesis, Palmerston North, New Zealand: Massey University.) http://mro.massey.ac.nz/handle/10179/5754

De Haan, I. A. (2011). *A good start: Supporting families with a first baby.* (PhD thesis, Auckland, New Zealand: Massey University.) http://mro.massey.ac.nz/handle/10179/3226

Department of Social Welfare. (1994). *Te Punga: Our bicultural strategy for the nineties.* Wellington, New Zealand: Department of Social Welfare.

Department of Social Welfare. (1998). *Towards a code of social and family responsibility; he kaupapa kawenga a whanau hapori: Public discussion document.* Wellington, New Zealand: Department of Social Welfare.

Duke, J., Henrickson, M., & Beddoe, L. (Eds.) (2014). *Protecting the public — Enhancing the profession E tiaki ana i te Hapori — E manaaki ana i nga mahi: Edited proceedings from the Social Workers Registration Board Conference 2013.* Wellington, New Zealand: Social Workers Registration Board. http://www.swrb.govt.nz/doc-man/ppep-conference-1/219-swrb-ppep-conference-proceedings

Dyson, R. (2003). CYF baseline review findings released. Wellington, New Zealand. https://www.beehive.govt.nz/release/cyf-baseline-review-findings-released

Ellis, G. (1997). Have you supervised a student lately? (And if not, why not?) *Advances in Social Work and Welfare Education, 2*(1), 83–96.

Ellis, G. (1998). *Through the looking glass: Fieldwork supervisors' perceptions of their role and needs for support, education and training.* (MSW thesis, Palmerston North, New Zealand: Massey University.) http://mro.massey.ac.nz/handle/10179/5824

Ellis, G., Nixon, A., & Sayers, J. (1996). Education and training needs of workers in the voluntary sector. In *Sharing our stories: Palmerston North Community Services Council 1971–1996* (pp. 48–49). Palmerston North, New Zealand: Palmerston North Community Services Council.

English, A. N. R. (2012). Pūao-te-Āta-tū: Informing Māori social work since 1986. *Aotearoa New Zealand Social Work Review/Te Kōmako, 24*(3&4), 41–48.

Eruera, M. M. (2005). *He kōrero kōrari: Supervision for Māori: Weaving the past, into the present for the future.* (MPhil thesis, Auckland, New Zealand: Massey University.) http://mro.massey.ac.nz/handle/10179/6471

Faleolo, M. M. (2014). *'Hard-hard-solid!' Life histories of Samoans in Bloods youth gangs in New Zealand.* (PhD thesis, Auckland, New Zealand: Massey University.)

http://mro.massey.ac.nz/handle/10179/6532

Field, J. (2004). *Strengthening professional practice: The role of practice manager in New Zealand Child, Youth and Family.* (MSW thesis, Palmerston North, New Zealand: Massey University.) http://mro.massey.ac.nz/handle/10179/6268

Fouché, C. (2005). An ecological understanding of HIV practice in South Africa. In M. Nash, R. Munford, & K. O'Donoghue (Eds.), *Social work theories in action* (pp. 50–63). London, England: Jessica Kingsley Publishers.

Garry G. C. (2009). Responsibilization strategy of health and safety: Neo-liberalism and the reconfiguration of individual responsibility for risk. *British Journal of Criminology, 49*(3), 326–342. doi:10.1093/bjc/azp004

Gibbs, A. (1988). *Unshackling the hospitals: Report of the Hospital and Related Services Taskforce.* The Taskforce, Ministry of Health, New Zealand.

Gilligan, R. (2016). What are some of the critical issues for social work in these changing times? Keynote address to Social work in changing times: Towards better outcomes conference, 18 November 2016. (Unpublished paper) Palmerston North: Massey University.

Haenga Collins, M. (2011). *Belonging and whakapapa: The closed stranger adoption of Māori children into Pākehā families.* (MSW thesis, Palmerston North, New Zealand: Massey University.) http://mro.massey.ac.nz/handle/10179/3195

Hamilton, C. A. (2008). *'In our house we're not terribly sexual': Exploring the barriers to supporting intellectually disabled people in the area of sexuality and intimacy.* (PhD thesis Palmerston North, New Zealand: Massey University.) http://mro.massey.ac.nz/handle/10179/843

Hair, H. J., & O'Donoghue, K. (2009). Culturally relevant, socially just social work supervision: Becoming visible through a social constructionist lens. *Journal of Ethnic and Cultural Diversity in Social Work. 18*(1–2), 70–88.

Hanna, S. (2005). *Breaking another silence: The long-term impacts of child sexual abuse on committed lesbian couples:* (PhD thesis, Auckland, New Zealand: Massey University.) http://mro.massey.ac.nz/handle/10179/1552

Harrysson, L., & O'Brien, M. A. (2007). Introduction. In L. Harrysson & M. O'Brien (Eds.), *Social welfare, social exclusion: A life course frame* (pp. 1–5). Lund, Sweden: Varpinge Ord & Text.

Harrysson, L., & O'Brien, M. A. (2007). Conclusion. In L. Harrysson & M. O'Brien (Eds.), *Social welfare, social exclusion: A life course frame* (pp. 195–203). Lund, Sweden: Varpinge Ord & Text.

Haultain, L. R. (2011). *From the cleaners to the doctors: Exploring the dimensions of effective health social work practice in an acute hospital.* (PhD thesis, Auckland, New Zealand: Massey University.) http://mro.massey.ac.nz/handle/10179/3255

Hay, K. (2000). *Contracting for care: Constraints and opportunities.* (MPhil thesis, Palmerston North, New Zealand: Massey University.) http://mro.massey.ac.nz/handle/10179/9948

Hay, K. (2011). Can collaboration and competition co-exist? Building a cross-institutional community of practice. *Asia-Pacific Journal of Cooperative Education, 12*(1), 31–38.

Hay, K., Dale, M., & Cooper, L. (2016). *Social work in Aotearoa New Zealand — exploring fields of practice.* Palmerston North, New Zealand: Massey University Press.

Hay, K., & O'Donoghue, K. (2009). Assessing social work field education: Towards standardising fieldwork assessment in New Zealand. *Social Work Education, 28*(1), 42–53.

Hay, K. S., O'Donoghue, K. B., & Blagdon, J. (2006). Exploring the aims of social work field education in the registration environment. *Social Work Review, 18*(4), 20–28.

Healy, K. (2014) *Social work theories in context: Creating frameworks for practice* (2nd ed.). Basingstoke, Hampshire; New York, NY: Palgrave Macmillan.

Henderson, A. M. (2002). *The settlement of skilled Chinese immigrants in New Zealand: Issues and policy implications for socioeconomic integration.* (PhD thesis, Palmerston North, New Zealand: Massey University.) http://mro.massey.ac.nz/handle/10179/1988

Henrickson, M., Neville, S., Jordan, C., & Donaghey, S. (2007). Lavender islands: The New Zealand study. *Journal of Homosexuality, 53*(4), 223–248.

Hera, J. (1995). *Reclaiming the last rites (rights): Women and after-death policy, practices and beliefs in Aotearoa/New Zealand.* (PhD thesis, Palmerston North, New Zealand: Massey University.) http://mro.massey.ac.nz/handle/10179/3129

Herman, W. R. (1983). *Formal and informal support systems in a rural town and county report of the research on mental health in Dannevirke borough and county.* (MPhil thesis Palmerston North, New Zealand: Massey University.)

Holmes, J. (2006). *Successful ageing: A critical analysis.* (PhD thesis, Palmerston North, New Zealand: Massey University.) http://mro.massey.ac.nz/handle/10179/3884

Human Rights Commission. (1982). Report of the Human Rights Commission on Representations by the Auckland Committee on Racism and Discrimination, Children and Young Persons Homes Administered by the Department of Social Welfare.

Jack, R. (2005). Strengths-based practice in Stutory Care and Protection Work. In M. Nash, R. Munford & K. O'Donoghue (Eds.), *Social work theories in action* (pp. 174–188). London, England: Jessica Kingsley Publishers.

Jackson, M. (1988). *The Maori and the criminal justice system — he whaipaanga hou: A new perspective: Part 2.* Wellington, New Zealand: Department of Justice.

Jakobs, J. V. (2005). *Messy bedrooms: Issues for parents of teenagers.* (MPhil thesis, Palmerston North, New Zealand: Massey University.)

Jaqiery, N., Baskerville, M., & Selby, R. (2002). Social work in schools (SWIS). In R. Truell & L. Nowland (Eds.), *Reflections on current practice in social work* (pp. 81–98). Palmerston North, New Zealand: Dunmore Press.

Keen, B. M. T. (2001). *'Queer practice': A consideration of some psychiatric/mental health social work practitioners' constructions of gay male sexualities.* (MSW thesis, Palmerston North, New Zealand: Massey University.) http://mro.massey.ac.nz/handle/10179/7069

Keen, M., & O'Donoghue, K. (2005). Integrated practice in mental health social work. In M. Nash, R. Munford, & K. O'Donoghue (Eds.), *Social work theories in action* (pp. 80–92). London, England: Jessica Kingsley Publishers.

Kerr, A. L. (2002). *Senior citizens? Old age and citizenship in provincial New Zealand communities.* (PhD thesis, Palmerston North, New Zealand: Massey University.) http://mro.massey.ac.nz/handle/10179/2001

King, M. (2004). *The Penguin history of New Zealand.* Auckland, New Zealand: Penguin Books.

Kiro, C. (2000). Maori research and the social services — Te Puawaitanga o te tohu. *Social Work Review/Te Kōmako, 12*(4), 26–32.

Kiro, C. A. (2001). *Kimihia mo te hauora Maori: Maori health policy and practice.* (PhD thesis, Auckland, New Zealand: Massey University.) http://mro.massey.ac.nz/handle/10179/2166

Kupenga-Wanoa, M. (2004). *Māori voices from within: A study of the perspectives of former offenders and probation officers in the criminal justice system.* (MSW thesis, Palmerston North, New Zealand: Massey University.) http://mro.massey.ac.nz/handle/10179/6086

Lee, J. (1996). The empowerment approach to social work practice. In F. Turner (Ed.), *Social work treatment* (4th ed.) (pp. 218–249). New York, NY: Free Press.

Liebenberg, L., Ungar, M., & Ikeda, J. (2015). Neo-liberalism and responsibilisation in the discourse of social service workers. *British Journal of Social Work, 45,* 1006–1021. doi:10.1093/bjsw/bct172 (Advance access publication 2013, November 10.)

Lunn, M. (1997). What am I . . . for her? Feminism and disability with/in the postmodern. (PhD thesis, Palmerston North, New Zealand: Massey University.) http://mro.massey.ac.nz/handle/10179/2576

Lunn, M., & Munford, R. (2007). 'She knows who she is! But can she find herself in the analysis?' Feminism, disability and research practice. *Scandinavian Journal of Disability Research, 9*(2), 65. doi: 10.1080/15017410601079460

Lunt, N. (2004). *Contested inheritance: The emergence of social science research in New Zealand.* (PhD thesis, Auckland, New Zealand: Massey University.) http://mro.massey.ac.nz/handle/10179/1619

Lunt, N., O'Brien, M., & Stephens, R. (2008). New Zealand, new welfare. Melbourne, Australia: Cengage Learning Australia.

Mafile'o, T. (2001). Social work and the Pasifika dimension. In M. Nash, R. Munford, & K. Hay (Eds.), *Social work in context: Fields of practice in Aotearoa New Zealand* (pp. 113–121). Palmerston North, New Zealand: School of Sociology, Social Policy and Social Work, Massey University.

Mafile'o, T. (2005a). Community development: A Tongan perspective. In M. Nash, R. Munford, & K. O'Donoghue (Eds.), *Social work theories in action* (pp. 125–139). London, England: Jessica Kingsley Publishers.

Mafile'o, T. (2005b). *Tongan metaphors of social work practice: Hangē ha pā kuo fa'ú.* (PhD thesis, Palmerston North, New Zealand: Massey University.) http://mro.massey.ac.nz/handle/10179/1697

Mafile'o, T. (2008). Tongan social work practice. In M. Gray, J. Coates, & M. Yellow Bird (Eds.), *Indigenous social work around the world: Towards culturally relevant education and practice.* (pp. 117–127). Surrey, England: Ashgate.

Mafile'o, T., & Api, U. K. (2009). Understanding youth resilience in Papua New Guinea through life story. *Qualitative Social Work, 8*(4), 469–288. doi:10.1177/1473325009246522

Mafile'o, T., & Walsh-Tapiata, W. (2007). Maori and Pasifika indigenous connections. *AlterNative: Journal of Indigenous Scholarship, 3*(2), 128–145.

Maharey, S., & O'Brien, M. (Eds.). (1986). *Alternatives: Socialist essays for the 1980s.* Palmerston North, New Zealand: Department of Sociology, Massey University.

Martinson, R. (1974). What works? Questions and answers about prison reform. *The Public Interest, 35,* 22–54.

Mataira, P. (2000). *Nga kai arahi tuitui Māori: Māori entrepreneurship. The articulation of leadership and the dual constituency arrangements associated with Māori enterprise in a capitalist economy.* (PhD thesis, Auckland, New Zealand: Massey University.) http://mro.massey.ac.nz/handle/10179/2267

Maynard, K., Coebergh, B., Anstiss, B., Bakker, L., & Huriwai, T. (1999). Ki te arotu: Toward a new assessment: The identification of cultural factors which may pre-dispose Māori to crime. *Social Policy Journal of New Zealand Te Puna Whakaaro, 13,* 43–54.

McCarthy, J., & Lambie, I. (1995). Overview of problem initial assessment (part 1) and interview assessment techniques with family and offenders (part 2). *Social Work Review, 7*(2) 5–12.

McMaster, K. (1992). *Feeling angry, playing fair: A guide to change.* Auckland, New Zealand: Reed.

McMaster, K., & Swain, P. (1989). *A private affair: Stopping men's violence to women.* Wellington, New Zealand: GP Books.

McNabb, D. (1997). Registration for New Zealand social workers. *Social Work Review, 9*(4), 43–45.

McNabb, D. (2014). 30 years' membership and a 50th birthday — where to next for ANZASW? *Aotearoa New Zealand Social Work, 26*(2 & 3), 61–71.

McPherson, M. J. (2000). *The nature and role of the extended family in New Zealand, and its relationship with the State: Based on a study of a provincial city.* (PhD thesis, Palmerston North, New Zealand: Massey University.) http://mro.massey.ac.nz/handle/10179/2171

Meo-Sewabu, L., Walsh-Tapiata, K. W., Mafile'o, T. A., Havea, S., & Tuileto'a, R. (2008). Developing a Pacific strategy for social work at Massey University, New Zealand. *The Fiji Social Workers Journal, 3,* 13–30.

Mills, C. Wright. (1970). *The Sociological imagination.* Harmondsworth, England: Penguin.

Milne, S. (1998) *Shifting ground: The position of women parenting alone in Auckland and their access to housing in a restructured environment.* (PhD thesis, Auckland, New Zealand: Massey University.) http://mro.massey.ac.nz/handle/10179/2447

Minster of Education. (1988). *Tomorrow's schools: The reform of education administration in New Zealand.* Wellington, New Zealand: Government Printer.

Ministerial Advisory Committee on a Maori Perspective for the Department of Social Welfare. (1986). *Pūao-te-Āta-tū (Daybreak).* Wellington, New Zealand: Department of Social Welfare.

Moyle, P. (2013). *From family group conferencing to Whānau Ora: Māori social workers talk about their experiences.* (MSW thesis, Palmerston North, New Zealand: Massey University.) http://mro.massey.ac.nz/handle/10179/4731

Mulengu, A. P. (1994). *From job creation to training, 1840–1990: A descriptive analysis of the development and demise of job creation policy as the mainstay of state responses to unemployment in New Zealand.* (PhD thesis, Palmerston North, New Zealand: Massey University.) http://mro.massey.ac.nz/handle/10179/2945

Munford, R. (1989). *The hidden costs of caring women who care for people with intellectual disabilities.* (PhD thesis, Palmerston North, New Zealand: Massey University.)

Munford, R. (1999). An examination of current practices in the provision of care: Exploring these practices in social work education. *Social Work Education, 17*(1), 57–75. doi:10.1080/02615479811220061

Munford. R. (2016). Keynote address. *Social Work in Changing Times: Towards Better Outcomes — Conference 17–19 November*. School of Social Work, Massey University.

Munford, R., & Bennie, G. (2001). Social work and disability. In M. Connolly (Ed.), *New Zealand social work: Contexts and practice* (pp. 157–167). Melbourne, Australia: Oxford University Press.

Munford, R., Georgeson, S., & Gordon, J. (1994). Social work with people with disabilities and their families. In R. Munford & M. Nash (Eds.), *Social work in action* (pp. 265–295). Palmerston North, New Zealand: Dunmore Press.

Munford, R., & Nash, M. (1994a). A feminist contribution to social work. In R. Munford & M. Nash (Eds), *Social work in action* (pp. 234–250). Palmerston North, New Zealand: Dunmore Press.

Munford, R., & Nash, M. (Eds.). (1994b). *Social work in action*. Palmerston North, New Zealand: Dunmore Press.

Munford, R., & Opie, A. (1996). Exploring effective strategies for enhancing social workers' contributions in multi-disciplinary teams. *Social Work Review, 8*(4), 3–7.

Munford, R., & Rumball, S. (2000). Women in university power structures. In M-L. Kearney (Ed.), *Women, Power and the Academy: From Rhetoric to Reality* (pp.92–98). New York, United States: Berghahn Books.

Munford, R., & Sanders, J. (1999). *Supporting families*. Palmerston North, New Zealand: Dunmore Press.

Munford, R., & Sanders. J. (2003). *Making a difference in families: Research that creates change*. Crows Nest, NSW, Australia: Allen and Unwin.

Munford, R., & Sanders, J. (2005). Working with families: Strengths-based approaches. In M. Nash, R. Munford & K. O'Donoghue (Eds.), *Social work theories in action* (pp. 158–173). London, England: Jessica Kinglsey Publishers.

Munford, R., & Sanders. J. (2006). *Strength-based social work with families*. Melbourne, Australia: Thomson.

Munford, R., Sanders, J., Maden, B., & Maden, E. (2007). Blending whānau/family development, parent support and early childhood education programmes. *Social Policy Journal of New Zealand, 32*, 72–87.

Munford, R. & Walsh-Tapiata, W. (1999). *Strategies for change: Community development in Aotearoa New Zealand*. Palmerston North. New Zealand: School of Social Policy and Social Work, Massey University.

Munford, R., & Walsh-Tapiata, W. (2005). Community development: Principles into practice. In M. Nash, K. O'Donoghue, & R. Munford (Eds.), *Social work theories in action*. London, England: Jessica Kingsley Publishers.

Napan, K. (1998a). *Evaluation of the 'contact–challenge method' in social work practice education*. (PhD thesis, Auckland, New Zealand: Massey University.) http://mro.massey.ac.nz/handle/10179/2440

Napan, K. (1998b). The contact–challenge method: In pursuit of effective teaching and learning in social work. *Social Work Review, 9*(1&2), 43–47.

Nash, M. (1987). *Women and social work: A study of feminist social work student placements*. (Master of Arts in Social Work thesis, Palmerston North, New Zealand: Massey University.) http://mro.massey.ac.nz/handle/10179/9960

Nash, M. (1993). The use of self in experiential learning for cross-cultural awareness: An exercise linking the personal with the professional. *Journal of Social Work Practice, 7*(1), 55–61.

Nash, M. (1998a). *People, policies and practice: Social work education in Aotearoa/ New Zealand from 1949–1995*. (PhD thesis, Palmerston North, New Zealand: Massey University.) http://mro.massey.ac.nz/handle/10179/2014

Nash, M. (1998b). That terrible title, 'social worker': A time of transition in social work history, 1949–1973. *Social Work Review, 10*(1), 12–18.

Nash, M. (2001). Social work in Aotearoa New Zealand: Its origins and traditions. In M. Connolly (Ed.), *New Zealand social work: Contexts and practice* (pp. 32–43). Melbourne, Australia: Oxford University Press.

Nash, M. (2005). Responding to settlement needs: Migrants and refugees and community development. In M. Nash, R. Munford & K. O'Donoghue (Eds.), *Social work theories in action* (pp. 140–154). London, England: Jessica Kingsley Publishers.

Nash, M., Munford, R., & Hay, K. (2001). *Social work in context: Fields of practice in Aotearoa New Zealand*. Palmerston North, New Zealand: School of Sociology, Social Policy and Social Work, Massey University.

Nash, M., Munford, R., & O'Donoghue, K. (Eds.) (2005). *Social work theories in action*. London, England: Jessica Kingsley Publishers.

Nash, S. (2007). *Integrating citizens' agendas in New Zealand local government environmental planning and decision-making: An examination of two wastewater planning processes and implications for deliberative democracy*. (PhD thesis, Palmerston North, New Zealand: Massey University.) http://mro.massey.ac.nz/ handle/10179/780

New Zealand Council for Education and Training in the Social Services (NZCETSS). (1991). *Education and training in the social services*. Wellington, New Zealand: NZCETSS.

O'Brien, M. (1991). *The problem of poverty: Ideology, the state and the 1972 Royal Commission on Social Security*: (PhD thesis. Palmerston North, New Zealand: Massey University.)

O'Brien, M. (1994). The case of the neglected triplets: Policy, class, poverty. In R. Munford, & M. Nash, *Social work in action* (pp. 391–409). Palmerston North, New Zealand, Dunmore Press.

O'Brien, M. (2001). A hydra-like creature? The marketization of social security in New Zealand. In J. Dixon & M. Hyde (Eds.), *The marketization of social security* (pp. 143–166). Westport, CT: Quorum Books/Greenwood Publishing Company.

O'Brien, M. (2005). A just profession or just a profession? Social work and social justice. *Social Work Review, 17*(1), 13–22.

O'Brien, P. O., & Sullivan, M. J. (Eds.). (2005). *Allies in emancipation: Shifting from providing service to being of support.* Melbourne, Australia: Thomson/Dunmore Press.

O'Donoghue, K. (1998). *Supervising social workers. A practical handbook.* Palmerston North, New Zealand: School of Policy Studies and Social Work, Massey University.

O'Donoghue, K. (1999). *Professional supervision practice under new public management: A study of the perspectives of probation officers and service managers in the community probation service.* (MPhil thesis, Palmerston North, New Zealand: Massey University.) http://mro.massey.ac.nz/handle/10179/751

O'Donoghue, K. (2002). Global vision, local vision, personal vision and social work supervision. *Social Work Review, 14*(4), 20–25.

O'Donoghue, K. (2003). *Restorying social work supervision.* Palmerston North, New Zealand: Dunmore Press.

O'Donoghue, K. (2004). Social workers and cross-disciplinary supervision. *Social Work Review, 16*(3), 2–7.

O'Donoghue, K. (2006). An introduction to social work supervision practice: Defining and describing the terrain towards an ideal practice. *Today's Children are Tomorrow's Parents: Journal of the Network for the Prevention of Child Maltreatment, 17–18*, 93–103.

O'Donoghue, K. (2007). Clinical supervision within the social work profession in Aotearoa New Zealand. In D. Wepa (Ed.), *Clinical supervision in Aotearoa/ New Zealand: A health perspective* (pp. 12–25). Auckland, New Zealand: Pearson Education.

O'Donoghue, K. (2008). Towards improving social work supervision in Aotearoa New Zealand. *Aotearoa New Zealand Social Work Review, 20*(1), 10–21.

O'Donoghue, K. (2010). *Towards the construction of social work supervision in*

Aotearoa New Zealand: A study of the perspectives of social work practitioners and supervisors. (PhD thesis, Palmerston North, New Zealand: Massey University.) http://mro.massey.ac.nz/handle/10179/1535

O'Donoghue, K. (2013). Editorial. The Social Workers Registration Act (2003) — 10 years on, *Aotearoa New Zealand Social Work Review, 24*(3), 1–2.

O'Donoghue, K. (2014). Editorial. 50th anniversary issue. *Aotearoa New Zealand Social Work Review, 26*(2&3), 1–2.

O'Donoghue, K. (2015). Issues and challenges facing social work supervision in the twenty-first century. *China Journal of Social Work, 8*(2), 136–149. doi:10.1080/1752 5098.20151039172

O'Donoghue, K. (2016). Keynote address. *Social Work in Changing Times: Towards Better Outcomes — Conference 17–19 November*. School of Social Work, Massey University.

O'Donoghue, K., Baskerville, M., & Trlin, A. (1999). Professional supervision in the new managerial climate of the Department of Corrections. *Social Work Review, 11*(1), 8–15.

O'Donoghue, K., & Maidment, J. (2005). The ecological systems metaphor in Australasia. In M. Nash, R. Munford, & K. O'Donoghue (Eds.), *Social work theories in action* (pp. 32–49). London, England: Jessica Kingsley Publishers.

O'Donoghue, K., Munford, R., & Trlin, A. (2005). Mapping the territory: Supervision within the association. *Social Work Review, 17*(4), 46–64.

O'Donoghue, K., Munford, R., & Trlin, A. (2006). What's best about social work supervision according to association members. *Social Work Review, 18*(3), 79–91.

Office of the Chief Social Worker. (2014). *Workload and casework review: Qualitative review of social worker caseload, casework and workload management report*. Wellington, New Zealand: Office of the Chief Social Worker.

Pakura, S. (2008). *Experts in uncertainty: Social work in child protection*. (MSW thesis, Palmerston North, New Zealand: Massey University.) http://mro.massey.ac.nz/handle/10179/6496

Payne, M. (1991). *Modern social work theory: A critical introduction*. Basingstoke, England: Macmillan.

Peeters, R. (2013). Responsibilisation on government's terms: New welfare and the governance of responsibility and solidarity. *Social Policy and Society, 12*(4), 583–595.

Phoenix, J., & Kelly, L. (2013). You have to do it for yourself: Responsibilization in youth justice and young people's situated knowledge of youth justice practice. *British Journal of Criminology, 53*(3), 419–437.

Prasad, R. (1986). *Transitions in foster care: The development of training programs for foster care workers.* (PhD thesis, Palmerston North, New Zealand: Massey University) http://mro.massey.ac.nz/handle/10179/3582

Prasad R. (1988a). *A methodology for developing training programs for foster care.* (AFCR publication MO54). King George, VA: American Foster Care Resources, Inc.

Prasad, R. (1988b). *Foster care research: Emerging practice principles.* (AFCR publication MO52). King George, VA: American Foster Care Resources Inc.

Prasad, R. (1988c). *Foster care training: Developmental and implementation.* (AFCR publication MO54). King George, VA: American Foster Care Resources Inc.

Prasad, R. (1988d). *Towards a theoretical framework in foster care: A framework for the management of, and research into, transitions in foster care.* (AFCR publication MO53). King George, VA: American Foster Care Resources, Inc.

Prasad, R. (Ed.). (1993). *Book of readings: 79651 Integrated practice in welfare and development.* Palmerston North, New Zealand: Massey University.

Prebble, T. (2010). *From a distance — 50th jubilee of distance learning.* Palmerston North, New Zealand: Massey University.

Quinney, A. (2006) Social work theories in action. *The British Journal of Social Work,* 36(1), 165–166. doi:10.1093/bjsw/bch407

Read, L. (2010). *What is this thing called grandparenting? The social, economic and political influences on the role in New Zealand.* (PhD thesis, Palmerston North, New Zealand: Massey University.) http://mro.massey.ac.nz/handle/10179/2225

Reid, W., & Epstein, L. (1972). *Task-centred casework.* New York, United States: Columbia University Press.

Report of the Taskforce to Review Education. (1988). *Administering excellence: Effective administration in education* [The Picot Report]. Wellington, New Zealand: Government Printer.

Richards-Ward, L. (1996). *From the ward to the home: Caring for a family member diagnosed with schizophrenia in New Zealand.* (PhD thesis, Palmerston North, New Zealand: Massey University.) http://mro.massey.ac.nz/handle/10179/2759

Ruwhiu, L. (1994). Maori development and social work. In R. Munford & M. Nash (Eds.), *Social work in action* (pp. 126–143). Palmerston North, New Zealand: Dunmore Press.

Ruwhiu, L. (1999). *Te puawaitanga o te ihi me te wehi: The politics of Māori social policy development.* (PhD thesis, Palmerston North, New Zealand: Massey University.) http://mro.massey.ac.nz/handle/10179/3529

Ruwhiu, P. A. (2009). *Ka haere tonu te mana o ngā wahine Māori: Māori women as protectors of te ao Māori knowledge.* (MSW thesis, Palmerston North, New

Zealand: Massey University.) http://mro.massey.ac.nz/handle/10179/1793

Sanders, J. (2004). *Subject child: The everyday experiences of a group of small town Aotearoa/New Zealand children.* (PhD thesis, Palmerston North, New Zealand: Massey University.) http://mro.massey.ac.nz/handle/10179/1624

Schön, D. (1995). *The reflective practitioner: How professionals think in action.* Aldershot, England: Arena.

Scott, D. (1990). Practice wisdom: The neglected source of practice research. *Social Work, 35,* 564–568.

Selby, R. (1994). My whānau. In R. Munford & M. Nash (Eds.), *Social work in action* (pp. 144–151). Palmerston North, New Zealand: Dunmore Press.

Selby, R. (1995). Watch out for the quick sand; ethics in practice. *Social Work Review/ Te Kōmako, 7*(1), 19–20.

Selby, R. (2005). Dreams are free: Nga moemoea a te hapu. In M. Nash, R. Munford, & K. O'Donoghue (Eds.), *Social work theories in action* (pp. 113–124). London, England: Jessica Kingsley Publishers.

Selby, R., & Field, M. (1999) Social Workers in Schools in the year 2000: A new professional presence in our schools. *Social Work Review/Te Kōmako, 11*(4), 12–15.

Selby, R., & Laurie, A. (Eds.). (2005). *Maori and oral history: A collection.* Wellington, New Zealand: National Oral History Association of New Zealand.

Selby, R., & Walsh-Tapiata, W. (2002). Reflections on teaching and learning in Fiji. In K. Sanga, C. Chu, C. Hall & L. Crowl (Eds.), *Re-Thinking Aid Relationships in Pacific Education* (pp. 251–260). Wellington, New Zealand: Victoria University of Wellington, He Parekereke.

Selby, R., Ruwhiu, L., & Walsh-Tapiata, W. (1996). *Māori and the social services: An annotated bibliography.* Palmerston North, New Zealand: Massey University.

Semmons, W. (2006). What does mental illness mean for Māori? In particular Māori women diagnosed with a mental illness during the period pregnancy and child birth. *Social Work Review/Te Kōmako, 18*(2), 36–42.

Shaw, R. (1994). Radical social work. In R. Munford & M. Nash, *Social work in action* (pp. 410–429). Palmerston North, New Zealand: Dunmore Press.

Shaw, R. (2000). Model without a cause: Public choice and bureaucratic reform in New Zealand. *New Zealand Sociology, 15*(2), 251–283.

Shaw, R. (2001a). Advisers and consultants. In R. Miller (Ed.), *New Zealand government and politics* (pp. 145–158). Auckland, New Zealand: Oxford University Press.

Shaw, R. (2001b). *Shaping the bureau or maximising the budget? Rational choice historical institutionalism and bureaucratic reform in New Zealand.* (PhD thesis,

Palmerston North, New Zealand: Massey University.)

Shaw, R. H. (2006a). Consultants and advisers. In R. Miller (Ed.), *New Zealand government and politics* (4th ed.) (pp. 257–272). Melbourne, Australia: Oxford University Press.

Shaw, R. H. (2006b). The public service. In R. Miller (Ed.), *New Zealand government and politics* (4th ed.) (pp. 273–284). Melbourne, Australia: Oxford University Press.

Sheehan, K. (2015). *Sex work advocacy in Aotearoa New Zealand: Advocates' perspectives on effecting positive change.* (MSW (Applied) research report, Palmerston North, New Zealand: Massey University.

Shirley, I. F. (1979). *Planning for community: The mythology of community development and social planning.* Palmerston North, New Zealand: Dunmore Press.

Shirley, I. F. (Ed.). (1982). *Development tracks: The theory and practice of community development.* Palmerston North, New Zealand: Dunmore Press.

Shirley, I. (1986). *Social practice within a capitalist state.* (PhD thesis, Palmerston North, New Zealand: Massey University.) http://mro.massey.ac.nz/handle/10179/3468

Shirley, I., Easton, B., Briar, C., & Chatterjee, S. (1990). *Unemployment in New Zealand.* Palmerston North, New Zealand: Dunmore Press.

Simmons, H. (2006). *Out of the closet: Experiences and expressions of spirituality in supervision.* (MPhil thesis, Palmerston North, New Zealand: Massey University.) http://mro.massey.ac.nz/handle/10179/6726

Simmons, H., Moroney, H., Mace, J., & Shepherd, K. (2007). Supervision across disciplines: Fact or fantasy? In D. Wepa (Ed.), *Clinical supervision in Aotearoa/New Zealand: A health perspective* (pp. 72–86). Auckland, New Zealand: Prentice Hall.

Simmons, H., Walsh-Tapiata, W. Meo-Sewabu, L., & Umugwaneza, A. (2014). Cultural encounter: A framework of ethical practice for transnational social workers in Aoteaora. In J. Duke, M. Henrickson L. & Beddoe (Eds.), *Protecting the public — Enhancing the profession E tiaki ana i te Hapori — E manaaki ana i nga mahi: Edited proceedings from the Social Workers Registration Board Conference 2013.* Wellington, New Zealand: Social Workers Registration Board. http://www.swrb.govt.nz/doc-man/ppep-conference-1/219-swrb-ppep-conference-proceedings

Simpson, J., Duncanson, M., Oben, G., Wicken, A., & Pierson, M. (2015). *Child Poverty Monitor 2015 technical report.* Dunedin, New Zealand: NZ Child and Youth Epidemiology Service, University of Otago.

Social Workers Registration Board. (2006). *Onboard,* 3(Summer). http://www.swrb.govt.nz/component/docman/?task=doc_download&gid=55&Itemid=

Smith, D. A. (2001). *The interrelationship between social support, risk-level and safety interventions following acute assessment of suicidal adolescents.* (PhD thesis, Palmerston North, New Zealand: Massey University.) http://mro.massey.ac.nz/handle/10179/2119

Spicer, J., Trlin, A., & Walton, J. A. (Eds.). (1994). *Social dimensions of health and disease: New Zealand perspective.* Palmerston North, New Zealand: Dunmore Press.

Spoonley, P. (2015). Andrew Drago Trlin (1942–2014). *New Zealand Sociology, 30*(1), 175–177.

Spoonley, P., Pearson, D., & Shirley, I. (Eds.), (1982). *New Zealand: Sociological perspectives.* Palmerston North, New Zealand: Dunmore Press.

Spoonley, P., Pearson, D., & Shirley, I. (1990). Introduction. In P. Spoonley, D. Pearson, and I. Shirley (Eds.), *New Zealand society: A sociological introduction* (pp. 7–9). Palmerston North, New Zealand: Dunmore Press.

Staniforth, B. (2010). *Past, present and future perspectives on the role of counselling in social work in Aotearoa New Zealand.* (PhD thesis, Auckland, New Zealand: Massey University.)

Staniforth, B. (2015). Tiromoana and Taranaki house: A tale of their times. *Aotearoa New Zealand Social Work Review, 27*(1–2), pp. 5–23.

Staniforth, B., & Fouché, C. B. (2006). An Aotearoa primer on 'fit and proper': School version. *Social Work Review, 18*(4), 11–19.

Stanley-Clarke, N. (2013). *Understanding service development in statutory mental health organisations in Aotearoa New Zealand: An organisational case study.* (PhD thesis, Palmerston North, New Zealand: Massey University.) http://mro.massey.ac.nz/handle/10179/4690

Stanley-Clarke, N. (2016). Key ideologies: The theories of social policy. In J. Maidment & L. Beddoe (Eds.), *Social policy for social work and human services in Aotearoa New Zealand: Diverse perspectives* (pp. 48–63). Christchurch, New Zealand: Canterbury University Press.

Stewart, K. J. (2008). *Adding quality to the quilt: Adolescent experiences of critical incident responses in secondary schools in Aotearoa New Zealand.* (PhD thesis, Palmerston North, New Zealand: Massey University.) http://mro.massey.ac.nz/handle/10179/796

Su'a-Hawkins, A., & Mafile'o, T. A. (2004). What is cultural supervision? *Social Work Now, 29*, 10–16.

Sutherland, D. (1996). *From unconscious to self-conscious: Cognitive rehabilitation from the perspective of symbolic interactionism.* (PhD thesis, Palmerston North, New Zealand: Massey University.) http://mro.massey.ac.nz/handle/10179/2842

Tangata Whenua Social Workers Association (2009). *Tangata Whenua Social Workers Association aims.* http://www.twswa.org.nz/

Taskforce on Whānau-Centred Initiatives (2010). *Whānau Ora: Report of the Taskforce on Whānau-Centred Initiatives.* http://www.msd.govt.nz/about-msd-and-our-work/publications-resources/planning-strategy/whanau-ora/

Thomas, C. (2005). *What's in a name? Strengths-based supervision — reality or rhetoric? An analysis of supervision in an organisation with a vision of strengths-based practice.* (MSW thesis, Palmerston North, New Zealand: Massey University.) http://mro.massey.ac.nz/handle/10179/5656

Thomas, C., & David, S. (2005). Bicultural strengths-based supervision. In M. Nash, R. Munford & K. O'Donoghue (Eds.), *Social work theories in action* (pp. 189–204). London, England: Jessica Kingsley Publishers.

Thompson, P. (2015). *To smack or not to smack, is that the question? The social perspectives on the issue of child discipline held by a cohort of mothers in Aotearoa New Zealand and what they indicate.* (PhD thesis, Palmerston North, New Zealand: Massey University.)

Tisdall, M., & O'Donoghue, K. B. (2003). A facilitated peer group supervision model for practitioners. In K. McMaster & A. Wells (Eds.), *Innovative approaches to stopping family violence* (pp. 221–232). Wellington, New Zealand: Steele Roberts.

Tolley, A. (2016). *New ministry dedicated to care and protection.* https://www.beehive.govt.nz/release/new-ministry-dedicated-care-and-protection

Trlin, A. (1979). *Now respected, once despised: Yugoslavs in New Zealand.* Palmerston North, New Zealand: Dunmore Press.

Trlin, A. (2016). *Foundations: Early Croatian immigration to New Zealand.* Auckland, New Zealand: Opuzen Press.

Trlin, A., & Spoonley, P. (Eds.). (1992). *New Zealand and international migration: A digest and bibliography.* Palmerston North, New Zealand: Massey University, Department of Sociology.

Trotter, C. (1999), *Working with involuntary clients.* London: Sage.

Van Heugten, K. (2013) Supporting human service workers following the Canterbury earthquakes. *Aotearoa New Zealand Social Work, 25*(2), 35–43.

Walsh-Mooney, H. A. (2009). *The value of rapport in Rangatahi Māori mental health: A Māori social work perspective.* (MSW thesis, Palmerston North, New Zealand: Massey University.) http://mro.massey.ac.nz/handle/10179/1363

Walsh-Tapiata, W. (1997). *Raukawa Social Services: Origins and future directions.* (MSW thesis, Palmerston North, New Zealand: Massey University.) http://mro.massey.ac.nz/handle/10179/5897

Walsh-Tapiata, W., & Webster, J. (2004). Do you have a supervision plan? *Social Work Review/Te Kōmako, 16*(2), 15–19.

Waring, M., & Fouché, C. (Eds.). (2007). *Managing mayhem: Work–life balance in New Zealand.* Wellington, New Zealand: Dunmore Press.

Webber-Dreadon, E. (1999) He taonga mo o matou tipuna (A gift handed down by our ancestors): An indigenous approach to social work supervision. *Social Work Review/Te Kōmako, 11*(4), 7–11.

Weeks, A. (1994). *A study of financial management practices in the Children and Young Persons Service in Fiscal 1994.* Wellington, New Zealand: Children, Young Persons Service, New Zealand Government.

Wells, P. (2004). *Someone to walk with me: Supporting caregivers who look after children with mental health problems in statutory care.* (PhD thesis, Palmerston North, New Zealand: Massey University.) http://mro.massey.ac.nz/handle/10179/1897

Wheeler, C., & Simmons, H. (2009). 'Loitering with intent' — a model of practice for working in a New Zealand secondary school. *Aotearoa New Zealand Social Work Review, 21*(3), 38–45.

Worrall, J. (2001a). Feminist practice in social work. In M. Connolly (Ed.), *New Zealand social work: Contexts and practice* (pp. 304–316). Melbourne, Australia: Oxford University Press.

Worrall, J. (2001b). *Grandparents raising grandchildren: A handbook for grandparents and other kin caregivers. Ma ngā kaumātua hei tautoko te tipurangi āke o ngā mokopuna.* Auckland, New Zealand: Grandparents Raising Grandchildren Trust.

Worrall, J. (2003). *Grandparents raising grandchildren: A handbook for grandparents and other kin caregivers. Ma ngā kaumātua hei tautoko te tipurangi āke o ngā mokopuna.* Auckland, New Zealand: Grandparents Raising Grandchildren Trust.

Young, G. (1994). Critical components in the supervision of child protection social workers in a statutory agency. *Social Work Review, 6*(5/6), 23–29.

Bibliography

Adams, R. S., Imray, D. J., Kirk, A. R., McDonald, F., Shirley, I. F. & Snively, S. (1981). Report of the working party on research into employment with special emphasis on youth unemployment. Wellington, New Zealand: National Research Advisory Council.

Adamson, C. (1999). Towards a social work knowledge base of traumatic events. *Social Work Review, 11*(1), 29–34.

Adamson, C. (2001). Social work and the call for evidence-based practice in mental health: Where do we stand? *Social Work Review, 13*(2), 8–12.

Adamson, C. (2006). Stress, trauma and critical incidents: The challenge for social work education. *Social Work Review, 18*(4), 50–58.

Adamson, C. (2007). Post-traumatic stress disorder: Overview. *Occupational Medicine, 57*(6), 397–398.

Afeaki, E. (2001). A practical Pacific way of social work: Embrace collectivity. *Social Work Review, 13*(3) Tu Mau, 35–37.

Afeaki-Mafileo, E. (2004). *The effects of social policy upon the Tongan kainga.* (MPhil thesis, Auckland, New Zealand: Massey University.) http://hdl.handle.net/10179/10508#sthash.6tzccZoG.dpuf

Agnew, M. B. M. (2001). *Women prisoners in the criminal justice system: Towards equal treatment and recognition of difference.* (MA (Social Policy) thesis, Palmerston North, New Zealand: Massey University.)

Allan, A. (1992). The Mason Report commentary. *Social Work Review, 4*(4), 19–22.

Anderson, R. H. (1997). Professionalism, ethics, and the career counselling professional. *New Zealand Journal of Counselling, 18,* 50–57.

Ang, E. K. (2007). *Career break or broken career? Mothers' experiences of returning to paid work.* (PhD thesis, Palmerston North, New Zealand: Massey University.) http://mro.massey.ac.nz/handle/10179/1671

Apaiata-Vague, T. (2011). Social work and food: A discussion. *Aotearoa New Zealand Social Work 23*(3), 63–70.

Apaiata-Vague, T., Pitt, L., & Younger, D. (2011). Fit and proper: A dilemma for social work educators. *Aotearoa New Zealand Social Work 23*(4), 55–64.

Appleton, C. M. (2010). *Integrity matters: An inquiry into social workers' understandings.* (MSW thesis, Palmerston North, New Zealand: Massey University.) http://mro.massey.ac.nz/handle/10179/2209

Apulu, M. T. J. (2010). *Tautua Faatamalii: (servant hood [i.e. servanthood] with absolute integrity): Engaging with Samoan young people.* (MPhil thesis, Auckland, New Zealand: Massey University.) http://mro.massey.ac.nz/handle/10179/2914

Asher, B. (1983). Class, state and health care. *Working Papers on the State, 1,* 5–20. Palmerston North, New Zealand: Sociology Department, Massey University.

Asher, B. (1984). Qualified social workers in New Zealand: Some research findings. *New Zealand Social Work, 9*(3), 5–7.

Attrill, P. M. (1999). *More than a death: Dangerous dynamics and their impact on social work practice at the Children, Young Persons and Their Families Agency.* (MSW thesis, Palmerston North, New Zealand: Massey University.) http://mro. massey.ac.nz/handle/10179/6087

Bade, K. (1993). *Policy analysis using microsimulation. (*MA (Social Policy) thesis, Palmerston North, New Zealand: Massey University.)

Barker, S. (2000). *Welfare that work tests.* (MA (Social Policy) thesis, Auckland, New Zealand: Massey University.) http://mro.massey.ac.nz/handle/10179/6451

Barratt, D. R. (2001). *Mature students: Life choice or life's necessity.* (MA (Social Policy) thesis, Palmerston North, New Zealand: Massey University.) http://mro.massey. ac.nz/handle/10179/6934

Barrett, P. (1993). The health sector reforms: A commitment to health or ideology. *Social Work Review, 5*(5), 15–19.

Barretta-Herman, A. (1982). Computers in social services. *New Zealand Social Work, 7*(1), 12–14.

Baskerville, M. A. (1983). Women in social work. *New Zealand Social Work, 8*(September), 13–16.

Baskerville, M. A. (1998). *Academic workload in the College of Humanities and Social Sciences.* (MBA research report, Palmerston North, New Zealand: Massey University).

Baxter, B. E. (1999). *Why are so few women requesting attendance at protected persons' programmes?* (MSW thesis, Palmerston North, New Zealand: Massey University.) http://mro.massey.ac.nz/handle/10179/6239

Beddoe, L., & Henrickson, M. (2005). Continuing professional social work education in Aotearoa New Zealand. *Asia Pacific Journal of Social Work and Development, 15*(2), 75–90. doi: 10.1080/21650993.2005.9755981

Beddoe, L., & Worrall, J. (1997). Fieldwork in a market economy — challenges and changes. *Advances in Social Work and Welfare Education, 2*(1), 54–63.

Beddoe, L., & Worrall, J. (1997). The future of fieldwork in a market economy. *Asia. Pacific Journal of Social Work, 7*(1), 19–32.

Beddoe, L., & Worrall, J. (Eds.). (2001). *Supervision Conference: From rhetoric to reality*. Auckland, New Zealand: Auckland College of Education.

Belgrave, M. (1996). Social workers in the classroom. *Social Work Review, 8*(2), 26–28.

Belgrave, M. (1997). *Counting the hectares: Quantifying Māori land loss in the Auckland Rangahaua Whanui district 1865–1908*. Rangahaua Whanui Wellington, New Zealand: Waitangi Tribunal.

Belgrave, M. (1997). Pre-emption, the Treaty of Waitangi and the politics of Crown purchase. *New Zealand Journal of History, 31*(1), 23–37.

Belgrave, M. P. (2001). Auckland's Mercy Hospital: A century of care. *Private Hospital Care, 1*(2), 2021.

Belgrave, M. P. (2001). Something borrowed, something new: History and the Waitangi Tribunal. In B. Dalley & J. Phillips (Eds.), *Going public: The changing nature of New Zealand history* (pp. 92–110). Auckland, New Zealand: Auckland University Press.

Belgrave, M. P. (2004). Needs and the state: Evolving social policy in New Zealand history. In B. Dalley & M. Tennant (Eds.), *Past judgement: Social policy in New Zealand history* (pp. 23–38). Dunedin, New Zealand: University of Otago Press.

Belgrave, M. P. (2004). 'Three steps forward — one step back': Individual autonomy and the Mater Hospital in Auckland. In A. Green & M. Hutching (Eds.), *Remembering: Writing oral history* (pp. 124–144). Auckland, New Zealand: Auckland University Press.

Belgrave, M., & Brown, L. (1997). *'Beyond a dollar value': The cost of informal care and the Northern Region Case Management Project*. Auckland, New Zealand: North Health.

Belgrave, M., & Dobbs, T. (2001). Social workers in schools: Delivering to children? *Social Work Now, 18*, 33–38. Retrieved from http://www.cyf.govt.nz/documents/about-us/publications/social-work-now/social-work-now-18-april01.pdf

Bell, H., & Thorpe, A. (2004). External supervision: What is it for social work in schools? *Social Work Review/Te Kōmako, 16*(2), 12–14.

Benge, D. C. (1997). *Access to tertiary education institutions in six nations, New Zealand, Australia, the United States of America, the United Kingdom, Sweden, and Japan: A comparative study of funding*. (MA (Social Policy) thesis, Palmerston North, New Zealand: Massey University.) http://mro.massey.ac.nz/handle/10179/9979

Bennie, G, & Munford, R. (1985). Individual programme planning and the mentally handicapped: Implications for practice. *New Zealand Social Work, 10*(2), 13–15.

Bevan, K. (1999). *Exploring personal and political issues of identity for white Maori women: Whakatoro te torangapu me te ake o nga kaupapa tuakiri mo nga wahine Maori ma.* (MPhil thesis, Palmerston North, New Zealand: Massey University.) http://mro.massey.ac.nz/handle/10179/2125

Blissett, W. (1999). Potential possibilities of diversification and specialisation in social work. *Social Work Review/Te Kōmako, 11*(4), 19–20.

Blyth, S. A. (1999). *Shifting to a sustainable city? Citizen participation in Wellington's Our City — Our Future strategy.* (MA (Social Policy) thesis, Palmerston North, New Zealand): Massey University. http://mro.massey.ac.nz/handle/10179/9849

Boden, J. M., Sanders, J., Munford, R., Liebenberg, L., & McLeod, G. F. H. (2016). Paths to positive development: A model of outcomes in the New Zealand Youth Transitions Study. *Child Indicators Research, 9*(4), 889–911. doi: 10.1007/s12187-015-9341-3

Bowden, A. R. (1980). *Middle management supervisors in a statutory social welfare agency: A study of the views of senior social workers.* (MSW thesis, Palmerston North, New Zealand: Massey University.) http://mro.massey.ac.nz/handle/10179/7786

Bowden, R. (1984). Changing focus. *New Zealand Social Work, 9*(2), 8–10.

Boyd, H. C. (1999). *Maverick politicians: Their beliefs and actions.* (MA (Social Policy) thesis, Auckland, New Zealand: Massey University.)

Briar, C. (1993). Employment. In R. Smithies & H. Wilson (Eds.), *Making choices: Social justice for our times — an initiative of the church leaders in 1993.* Wellington, New Zealand: Church Leaders' Social Justice Initiative.

Briar, C. (1997). Welfare myths of our time. *Broadsheet, 214*(Winter), 53–56.

Briar, C. (1997). *Working for women? Gendered work and welfare policies in twentieth-century Britain.* London, England: UCL Press.

Briar, C. (1998). Solo parents: Mother-work and/or other work? Liberal, conservative and solidaristic policies. *Labour, Employment and Work in New Zealand,* 150–156.

Briar, C. (1999). Single mothers in an international context: Mothers or workers? *Women's History Review, 8*(1), 169–188.

Briar, C. (2001). The gendering of inequalities: Women, men and work. *Women in Management Review, 16*(1), 42–46.

Briar, C. (2004). Solidarity between the sexes and the generations: Transformations in Europe. *Women in Management Review, 19*(8), 437–438.

Briar, C. (2006). Babies and bosses: Family policy directions in the OECD. *Journal of Feminist Family Therapy, 17*(3–4), 47–65.

Briar, C., & Cheyne, C. (1998). Women and social/economic policy: New feminist agendas for changing times? In R. Du Plessis & L. Alice (Eds.), *Feminist thought in*

Aotearoa/New Zealand: Differences and connections (pp. 209–215). Auckland, New Zealand: Oxford University Press.

Briar, C., & O'Brien, M. A. (2003). Comparative family policy research. In R. Munford & J. Sanders (Eds.) (2003), *Making a difference in families: Research that creates change* (pp. 193–210). Crows Nest, NSW, Australia: Allen & Unwin.

Briar, C., & Work, S. (2000). In search of gender-sensitive concepts and measures of poverty, inequality and well-being. *Social Policy Journal of New Zealand, 14*, 17–29.

Bridgland, C. (1997). *'Under someone else's roof': Tenants' knowledge and experience of tenancy rights in the Manawatu*. (MA (Social Policy) thesis, Palmerston North, New Zealand: Massey University.)

Briggs, L. E. (1992). *Women survivors of sexual abuse: Identification and disclosure.* (MSW thesis, Palmerston North, New Zealand: Massey University.) http://mro. massey.ac.nz/handle/10179/6657

Brook, J. (1988). *The demise of the New Zealand Social Work Training Council.* (MSW thesis. Palmerston North, New Zealand: Massey University.)

Brosnahan, N., Chilcott, J., Henderson, D., Holdaway, T., Miller, D., & O'Brien, M. (1983). *Surviving on the breadline: A study of low income families in Palmerston North*. Palmerston North, New Zealand: Social Work Unit, Massey University.

Brown, L. (1994). *An exploration of women's involvement in social change: Current directions in community work practice*. (MSW thesis, Palmerston North, New Zealand: Massey University.) http://mro.massey.ac.nz/handle/10179/5867

Browning, J., & Duncan, G. (2005). Family membership in post-reunion adoption narratives. *Social Policy Journal of New Zealand, 26*, 156–172.

Brunton, M., Jordan, C., & Fouche, C. (2008). Managing public health care policy: Who's being forgotten? *Health Policy, 88*(2), 348–358.

Burne, J. A. (1999). *Adventure social work: Evaluation of a New Zealand therapeutic outdoor adventure programme*. (MSW thesis, Palmerston North, New Zealand: Massey University.) http://mro.massey.ac.nz/handle/10179/6138

Burns, G. (2008). *The silent revolution: Disabled people discuss regaining power and control in their lives*. (MSW thesis, Palmerston North, New Zealand: Massey University.) http://mro.massey.ac.nz/handle/10179/7817

Caird, B. (1999). *Speaking sentences: Inside women's experiences of gender, punishment and rehabilitation*. (MA (Social Policy) thesis, Massey University.) http://mro.massey.ac.nz/handle/10179/7033

Calvert, S. J., Kazantzis, N., Merrick, P. L., Orlinsky, D. E., Ronan, K. R., & Staniforth, B. L. (2008). Professional development of New Zealand social workers who engage in psychotherapy perceptions and activities. *Aotearoa New Zealand Social Work, 19*(4), 16–31.

Cameron, S., & Wilson-Salt, A.-M. (1995). The summary of the report 'The experience of social workers working in the area of care and protection under CYF Act 1989'. *Social Work Review, 7*(2), 19–21.

Carroll, M, (1992). Birthfathers — out of sight, out of mind. *Social Work Review, 5*(1&2), 12–16.

Carroll, M. (1993). Adoption report: A business perspective. *Social Work Review, 5*(5), 24–26.

Chapman, J., & Duncan, G. (2007). Is there now a new 'New Zealand model'? *Public Management Review, 9*(1), 1–25.

Chapman, S. J. (2010). *Perceptions of the effectiveness of SWiS.* (Unpublished research report, Palmerston North, New Zealand: Massey University.)

Cheyne, C. (1990). *Made in God's image: A project researching sexism in the Catholic Church in Aotearoa-New Zealand.* Wellington, New Zealand: Catholic Commission for Justice, Peace and Development.

Cheyne, C. (1990). Strengthening democracy? New times in local government. *Sites, 20,* 117–125.

Cheyne, C. (1990). Struggles over sovereignty. *Sites, 20,* 157–162.

Cheyne, C. (1991). Postmodern culture and the development of a critical social policy. *Sites, 23,* 33–45.

Cheyne, C. (2002). Public involvement in local government in New Zealand: A historical account. In J. Drege (Ed.), *Empowering communities? Representation and participation in New Zealand's local government* (pp. 116–155). Wellington, New Zealand: Victoria University Press.

Cheyne, C. (2002). 'Shakai fukushi seisaku to kokumin seikatsu no henka' (Changes in social welfare policies and the lives of citizens). In Takahashi Fumitoshi (Ed.), *Restructuring in Japan in the 21st century — learning from New Zealand* (pp. 161–184). Kyoto, Japan: Kouyou Shobou.

Cheyne, C. (2004). Changing political leadership: The New Zealand mayor in contemporary local governance. *Political Studies, 56*(2), 51–64. doi: 10.1177/003231870405600207

Cheyne, C. (2006). Central government and its role in community planning. In M. Thompson Fawcett & C. Freeman (Eds.), *Living together: Towards inclusive communities in New Zealand* (pp. 27–41). Dunedin, New Zealand: Otago University Press.

Cheyne, C. (2006). Local government. In R. Miller (Ed.), *New Zealand government and politics* (4th ed.) (pp. 285–295). Melbourne, Australia: Oxford University Press.

Cheyne, C. (2006). New Zealand: Articulating a long-term vision for community well-being. In H. Heinelt, D. Sweeting, & P. Getimis (Eds.), *Legitimacy and urban governance: A cross-national comparative study* (pp. 173–187). Oxford, England: Routledge.

Cheyne, C., & Comrie, M. (2002). Enhanced legitimacy for local authority decision making: Challenges, setbacks and innovation. *Policy and Politics, 30*(4), 469–482.

Cheyne, C., & Comrie, M. (2002). Involving citizens in local government: Expanding the use of deliberative processes. In J. Drege (Ed.), *Empowering communities? Representation and participation in New Zealand's local government* (pp. 156–186). Wellington, New Zealand: Victoria University Press.

Cheyne, C., & Comrie, M. (2005). Empowerment or encumbrance? Exercising the STV option for local authority elections in New Zealand. *Local Government Studies, 31*(2), 185–204. doi: 10.1080/03003930500032064

Cheyne, C., & Freeman, C. (2006). A rising tide lifts all boats? A preliminary investigation into the impact of rising New Zealand coastal property prices on small communities. *Kotuitui: New Zealand Journal of Social Sciences Online, 1*(2), 105–124. doi: 10.1080/1177083X.2006.9522414

Chinnery, S. A. (1999). *Ties that bind: Attachment formation in the maltreated preadolescent child placed in long term foster care: Masking feelings, a correlate of insecure attachment.* (MSW thesis, Auckland, New Zealand: Massey University.)

Choopug, S. (2005). *Civil society in the Chi River, Northeast Thailand.* (PhD thesis, Auckland, New Zealand: Massey University.) http://mro.massey.ac.nz/handle/10179/1550

Close, P. C. (Ed.). (1989). *Family divisions and inequalities in modern society.* Basingstoke, England: Macmillan.

Conder, J., Mirfin-Veitch, B., & Sanders, J. (2008). 'I've got to think of him . . .': Relationships between parents with an intellectual disability and foster parents. *Developing Practice: The Child, Youth, and Family Work Journal, 21*(Winter), 17–25.

Conder, J., Mirfin-Veitch, B., Sanders, J., & Munford, R. (2010). Planned pregnancy, planned parenting: Enabling choice for adults with a learning disability. *British Journal of Learning Disabilities, 39*(2), 105–112. doi: 10.1111/j.1468-3156.2010.00625.x

Connor, H., Bruning, J., & Napan, K. (2016). Positive women: A community development response to supporting women and families living with HIV/AIDS in Aotearoa New Zealand. *Whanake: The Pacific Journal of Community Development, 2*(2), 14–23. http://www.unitec.ac.nz/whanake/index.php/2016/10/26/positive-women-a-community-development-response-to-supporting-women-and-families-living-with-hivaids-in-aotearoa-new-zealand/

Contraception, Sterilisation, and Abortion Act, 1977. http://www.legislation.govt.nz/act/public/1977/0112/latest/whole.html#DLM17685

Coombes, K. A. (1998). *The impact of family of origin on social workers from alcoholic families and implications for practice.* (MSW thesis, Palmerston North, New Zealand: Massey University.)

Cooper, B., & Parsons, J. (2010). Dialectical behaviour therapy: A social work intervention. *Aotearoa New Zealand Social Work, 21*(4) & *22*(1), 83–91.

Cotterell, G. A. (2001). *Welfare state retrenchment in New Zealand under National rule 1990–1996: A Marxist perspective.* (MPhil thesis, Auckland, New Zealand: Massey University.) http://mro.massey.ac.nz/handle/10179/6237

Coulter, R. A. (1999). *Unskilled youth, unemployment and training: a case study.* (MA (Social Policy) thesis, Palmerston North, New Zealand: Massey University.) http://mro.massey.ac.nz/handle/10179/7074

Craig, W. (1990). Caring and nurturing: A central theme in community work. *Te Kupu Kaimahi-a-iwi, 5,* 5–7.

Craig, W., & Gruys, M. (1983). The moral calculus of university social work education. *New Zealand Social Work, 10*(3), 4–8.

Craig, W., & Munford, R. M. (1996). Community development. In J. Bensemann, B. Findsen, & M. Scott (Eds.), *The fourth sector: Adult and community education in Aotearoa/New Zealand* (pp. 223–233). Palmerston North, New Zealand: Dunmore Press.

Crawford, R. (1985). Department of Social Welfare child and service policy and institutional racism: A perpetuation of the New Zealand colonial past. *New Zealand Social Work, 10*(2), 7–12.

Crean, P., & Baskerville, M. A. (2007). Community advocacy — a social work role? *Aotearoa New Zealand Social Work Review, 19*(4), 3–10.

Crezee, I., Julich, S. J., & Hayward, M. (2011). Issues for interpreters working in refugee settings. *Journal of Applied Linguistics and Professional Practice, 8*(3), 253–273. doi: 10.1558/japl.v8i3.253

Crichton-Hill, Y. (2001). Experiential learning and 'Lali'. *Social Work Review/Tu Mau, 13*(3), 30–34.

Crichton-Hill, Y. (2010). Changing landscapes responding to domestic violence in New Zealand. *Aotearoa New Zealand Social Work/Tu Mau, 22*(4), 12–19.

Cruse, W. (1995). Care for professional social work staff in the New Zealand Children and Young Persons Service. (MPhil thesis, Palmerston North, New Zealand: Massey University.)

Cwikel, J., Savaya, R., Munford, R., & Desai, M. (2010). Innovation in schools of social work: An international exploration. *International Social Work, 53*(2), 187–201. doi: 10.1177/0020872809355393

Dale, M. P. (1997). *Case management intervention with violent offenders: An action research approach to the development of a practice model.* (MSW thesis, Palmerston North, New Zealand: Massey University.) http://mro.massey.ac.nz/handle/10179/5837

Dale, M. (2013). Social work at Whakatipuria Teen Parent Unit. *Aotearoa New Zealand Social Work Review, 25*(1), 3–13.

Dale, M., & Trlin, A. (2006). Leadership in the New Zealand Probation Service: The perceptions and experiences of probation officers and service managers. *Aotearoa New Zealand Social Work, 19*(3), 23–37.

Dale, M., & Trlin, A. (2006). Probation practice as social work-viewpoints of practitioners in New Zealand. *Aotearoa New Zealand Social Work, 19*(2), 4–11.

Dantis, T. M. (2008). *Journeying with God: Spirituality and participation in faith related activities among Catholic youth in Whangarei.* (MPhil thesis, Palmerston North, New Zealand: Massey University.) http://mro.massey.ac.nz/handle/10179/1036

Davidson, C. (2005). *Volunteering for a job: converting social capital into paid employment.* (MPhil thesis, Auckland, New Zealand: Massey University.)

Davidson, T.-L. (2013). *To what degree do the in-work tax credit policies introduced in New Zealand (2006) and Sweden (2007) contribute to the wellbeing of sole mothers?* (MA (Social Policy) thesis, Palmerston North, New Zealand: Massey University.) http://mro.massey.ac.nz/handle/10179/4808

De Bruin, A., & Mataira, P. (2003). Indigenous entrepreneurship. In A. De Bruin and A. Dupuis (Eds.), *Entrepreneurship: New perspectives in a global age* (pp. 169–184). Aldershot, England: Ashgate.

De Jong, D. K. (2001). *The well-being of Russian and Romanian intercountry adoptees in New Zealand.* (MSW thesis, Palmerston North, New Zealand: Massey University.) http://mro.massey.ac.nz/handle/10179/6430

Dempster, B. P. (2008). *Climate calculus: Does realist theory explain the Howard government's decision not to ratify the Kyoto Protocol?* (MA (Social Policy) thesis, Palmerston North, New Zealand: Massey University.) http://mro.massey.ac.nz/handle/10179/725

De Ocampo, M. I. O. (2006). *The exploitation of children as soldiers in the Philippines: an analysis of issues and challenges in social work practice.* (MSW thesis, Auckland, New Zealand: Massey University.)

Department of the Prime Minister and Cabinet. (2016). The Official Information Act 1982. *The Cabinet Manual.* Wellington, New Zealand. https://cabinetmanual.cabinetoffice.govt.nz/8.13

Department of Social Welfare Act. (1971). Wellington, New Zealand: Government Printer.

DeSouza, S. (2000). Early social work intervention in bone marrow transplantation. *Social Work Review, 12*(1), 28–33.

DeSouza, S. (2001). Council for international fellowship: An international social work exchange programme. *Social Work Review, 13*(2), 23–26.

De Vos, A. S., Strydom, H., Fouche, C. B., & Delport, C. S. L. (2005). *Research grassroots: For the social sciences and human professions.* Pretoria, South Africa: Van Schaik Publishers.

Dewhurst, K. (2015). *Making a claim for services: Supporting vulnerable young people's engagement with services.* (MSW thesis, Palmerston North, New Zealand: Massey University.) http://mro.massey.ac.nz/handle/10179/7729

Dickson, N., Henrickson, M., & Mhlanga, F. (2012). *AfricaNZ Count: An estimate of currently resident and HIV positive Africans in New Zealand.* Report completed for the Health Research Council of New Zealand and Ministry of Health (Contract 11/965). Wellington, New Zealand: Health Research Council of New Zealand and Ministry of Health.

Dobi, S., & Ross, A. (2013). Thinking beyond the contract: A journey to collaborative community social work. *Aotearoa New Zealand Social Work Review, 25*(1), 43–53.

Douglas, M. (2007). Reflection and evaluation from an agency and student perspective: Based on a consumer evaluation. *Social Work Review, 19*(1), 51–54.

Dowdeswell, S. (1998). *No guarantees: The experiences of women in casual work.* (MA (Social Policy) thesis, Auckland, New Zealand: Massey University.) http://mro.massey.ac.nz/handle/10179/6260

Dowman, C. P. (1999). *Contestability in the resource consent process under the Resource Management Act 1991: A study of opportunities for Māori within a contestable consent process.* (MA (Social Policy) thesis, Palmerston North, New Zealand: Massey University.) http://mro.massey.ac.nz/handle/10179/8305

Drew, J. (1987). *Social work supervision a political function: A critique of cognitive interests and the impact of the capitalist welfare state.* (MSW thesis, Palmerston North, New Zealand: Massey University.) http://mro.massey.ac.nz/handle/10179/6777

Drew, R. (1998). *Brides of the state? Change and continuity in income support policy for solo mothers in New Zealand.* (MA (Social Policy) thesis, Palmerston North, New Zealand: Massey University.) http://mro.massey.ac.nz/handle/10179/5733

Duncan, G. (1993). Accident compensation: The trend towards privatisation. *Public Sector, 16*(4), 13–16.

Duncan, G. (1993). ACC reform and rehabilitation. *Social Work Review, 6*(2), 18–20.

Duncan, G. (1995). ACC reform and workplace safety and health. *Journal of*

Occupational Health and Safety — Australia and New Zealand, 11(4), 381–385.

Duncan, G. (1996). Accident compensation — 1995 and still languishing. *New Zealand Journal of Industrial Relations, 20*(III), 237–253.

Duncan, G. (1996). Employee liability and commitment. *Employment Today,* 35(September), 4–6.

Duncan, G. (1996). Is compensation bad for your back? *Australian Journal of Rehabilitation Counselling, 2*(2), 128–139.

Duncan, G. (1996). The ECA: A way with it. *Employment Today, 37*(December), 14–15.

Duncan, G. (1996). State sector service quality: A joke or a challenge? *Employment Today, 36*(October–November), 25–26.

Duncan, G. (1996). Whatever happened to no-fault compensation? *Employment Today, 35*(September), 3.

Duncan, G. (1997). The management of risk and quality in the social services. *Social Policy Journal of New Zealand, 9*(November), 66–79.

Duncan, G. (1997). Weberian rationality, post modernity and the state: Are we heading for a post-bureaucratic society? *Sites, 34,* 53–75.

Duncan, G. (2000). Mind-body dualism and the biopsychosocial model of pain: What did Descartes really say? *Journal of Medicine and Philosophy: A forum for bioethics and philosophy of medicine, 25*(4), 485–513. doi: 10.1076/0360-5310(200008)25:4;1-A;FT485

Duncan, G. (2003). Workers' compensation and the governance of pain. *Economy and Society, 32*(3), 449–477.

Duncan, G. (2004). Pouvoir et savoir: The tertiary education strategy and the will to know. *New Zealand Journal of Tertiary Education, 1,* 1–9.

Duncan, G. (2005). Child poverty and family assistance in New Zealand. *ZIAS Zeitschrift für ausländisches und internationales Arbeits-und Sozialrecht [Journal of Comparative and International Labour and Social Law], 4,* 323–352.

Duncan, G. (2005). What do we mean by 'happiness'? The relevance of subjective wellbeing to social policy. *Social Policy Journal of New Zealand, 25,* 16–31.

Duncan, G. (2007). After happiness. *Journal of Political Ideologies, 12*(1), 85–108.

Duncan, G., & Nimmo, J. (1993). Accident compensation and labour relations: The impact of recent reforms. *New Zealand Journal of Industrial Relations, 18*(3), 288–305.

Duncan, G., & Worrall, J. (2000) 'The impact of neo-liberal policies on social work in New Zealand'. (Unpublished paper, Auckland, New Zealand: Massey University.)

Duncan, G., & Worrall, J. (2000). Window on the world: Social policy and social work in New Zealand. *European Journal of Social Work, 3*(3), 283–295. doi: 10.1080/714052831

Easton, S. A. H. (2007). *A hard tweak: TeachNZ criteria and the Smith proposal.* (MPhil thesis, Palmerston North, New Zealand: Massey University.)

Eichbaum, C., & Shaw, R. H. (2003). A third force? Ministerial advisers in the executive. *Public Sector, 26*(3), 7–13.

Eichbaum, C., & Shaw, R. H. (2005). Why we should all be nicer to ministerial advisers. *Policy Quarterly, 1*(4), 18–25

Eichbaum, C., & Shaw, R. H. (2006). Enemy or ally? Senior officials' perceptions of ministerial advisers before and after MMP. *Political Science, 58*(1), 3–22. doi: 10.1177/003231870605800101

Eruera, M. (2012). He korari, he kete, he korero. *Aotearoa New Zealand Social Work/ Te Kōmako, 24*(3&4), 12–19.

Fagan, K. (2010). *Successful young adults are asked 'In your experience, what builds confidence?'* (MSW thesis, Palmerston North, New Zealand: Massey University.)

Fagan, K., Simmons, H., & Nash, M. (2012). Successful young adults are asked: 'In your experience, what builds confidence?' *Aotearoa New Zealand Social Work Review, 24*(2), 8–18.

Faleolo, M. M. (2013). 'Horsing it and fried up: Health risks for Samoans in South Auckland Bloods youth gangs.' In N. Seve-Williams, M. Taumoepeau, & E. Saafi (Eds.), *Pacific edge: Transforming knowledge into innovative practice* (pp. 49–56). Research papers from the fourth Health Research Council of New Zealand Pacific Health Research Fono Auckland, New Zealand: The Health Research Council of New Zealand.

Faleolo, M. M. (2016). 'From the street to the village': The transfer of NZ youth gang culture to Samoa. *New Zealand Sociology, 31*(2), 48–73.

Florence, J. (1996). *Culture of partnership to culture of contract: child and family support services contracting with the New Zealand Community Funding Agency.* (MSW thesis, Auckland, New Zealand: Massey University.) http://mro.massey. ac.nz/handle/10179/5466

Foley, M. A. (2007). *Bringing practice into theory: Social workers' experiences of bringing social work into attachment theory.* (MPhil thesis, Palmerston North, New Zealand: Massey University.)

Foley, M., Nash, M., & Munford, R. (2009). Bringing practice into theory: Reflective practice and attachment. *Aotearoa New Zealand Social Work Review, 21*(1&2), 39–47.

Fook, J., Munford, R., & Sanders, J. (1999). Interviewing and evaluating. In I. Shaw & J.

Lishman (Eds.), *Evaluation and social work practice* (pp. 164–81). London, England: Sage.

Fordham, A. M. (1995). *The impact of institutional-political factors of employment equity: A comparative study of the policy framework in New Zealand and Australia.* (MA (Social Policy) thesis, Palmerston North, New Zealand: Massey University.) http://mro.massey.ac.nz/handle/10179/5818

Foster, S. (2002). *An analysis of the skills and knowledge base for needs assessment and service coordination.* (MSW thesis, Palmerston North, New Zealand: Massey University.) http://mro.massey.ac.nz/handle/10179/5467

Fouché, C. B., & Delport, C. S. L. (2005). Introduction to the research process. In A. S de Vos & M. Greeff (Eds.), *Research grassroots: For the social sciences and human professions* (pp. 71–85). Pretoria, South Africa: Van Schaik Publishers.

Fouché, C. B., & de Vos, A. S. (2005). Problem formulation. In A. S. de Vos & M. Greeff (Eds.), *Research grassroots: For the social sciences and human professions* (pp. 100–110). Pretoria, South Africa: Van Schaik Publishers.

Fouche, C. B., Lunt, N., & Yates, D. (2007). *Growing research in practice: A collection of resources.* Auckland, New Zealand: Massey University.

Fouché, C. B., & Schurink, W. (2005). Qualitative research designs. In A. S. de Vos & M. Greeff (Eds.), *Research grassroots: For the social sciences and human professions* (pp. 286–313). Pretoria, South Africa: Van Schaik Publishers.

Fraser, S., & Simpson, S. (2014). 'Always take the weather with you': Aotearoa New Zealand social work in a dynamic global society. *Aotearoa New Zealand Social Work Review, 26*(2&3), 29–38.

Fry, K. J. (2001). 'The Madonna myth': The ideology of motherhood and it's [sic] *influence on women with postnatal depression.* (MSW thesis, Palmerston North, New Zealand: Massey University.) http://mro.massey.ac.nz/handle/10179/6278

Fry, K. (2010). Social work clinical leadership in allied health. *Aotearoa New Zealand Social Work, 21*(4) & 22(1), 109–113.

Garland, M., & Ellis, G. (1999) *Home improvements tools for working with families* [video], Palmerston North, New Zealand: School of Social Policy and Social Work, Massey University.

Garland, M., & Ellis, G. (2006). Synergistic supervision. *Social Work Review, 18*(3), 31–42.

Garwood, K. (1994). *Policy, planning, outputs and outcomes: A Community Corrections Division study.* (MSW thesis, Palmerston North, New Zealand: Massey University.) http://mro.massey.ac.nz/handle/10179/7274

Georgeson, S. (2000). *The Disabled Persons Assembly 1983–1999: Successes, challenges and lessons for the disability movement in New Zealand.* (MSW thesis, Palmerston North, New Zealand: Massey University.) http://mro.massey.ac.nz/handle/10179/7306

Gerrit, S., & Fouché, C. (2004). Emotional wellness and management effectiveness within the public healthcare sector. *SA Journal of Human Resource Management, 2*(1), 1–8. doi: 10.4102/sajhrm.v2i1.30

Gibbs, C. D. (2005). *Holistic health: The effectiveness of a counselling model in a primary health setting.* (MSW thesis, Palmerston North, New Zealand: Massey University.) http://mro.massey.ac.nz/handle/10179/7283

Giles, J. R., Cureen, H. M., & Adamson, C. E. (2005). The social sanctioning of partner abuse: Perpetuating the message that partner abuse is acceptable in New Zealand. *Social Policy Journal of New Zealand, 26,* 97–116

Gilray, B. (2013). Social worker registration: A decade of development, debate and delivery. *Aotearoa New Zealand Social Work Review, 25*(3), 25–34.

Glynn, L., & Dale, M. (2015). Engaging dads: Enhancing support for fathers through parenting programmes. *Aotearoa New Zealand Social Work, 27*(1&2), 59–72.

Goodwillie, C. (1995). *Bewhoherenow: philosophy of existing sense.* (PhD thesis, Auckland, New Zealand: Massey University.) http://mro.massey.ac.nz/handle/10179/4622

Goodwin, D. W. T. (1996). *'He tapu te whare tangata': Support for young Māori mothers during pregnancy, birth and motherhood.* (MSW thesis, Palmerston North, New Zealand: Massey University.) http://mro.massey.ac.nz/handle/10179/5565

Gray, M. K. (2004). *Just practice and the beginning social practitioner.* (MSW thesis, Auckland, New Zealand: Massey University.) http://mro.massey.ac.nz/handle/10179/6051

Green, S. E. N. (2001). *Multiple choice? The experiences of women with multiple sclerosis: Oppression, options, opportunities.* (MSW thesis, Palmerston North, New Zealand: Massey University.) http://mro.massey.ac.nz/handle/10179/9936

Greer, J. A. (2001). *Collaborative practice: A practice approach to joint working between agencies providing mental health services.* (MSW thesis, Palmerston North, New Zealand: Massey University.)

Haitana, G. (1995) Strengthening the collective strands . . . a must for tangata whenua healing. *Social Work Review/Te Kōmako, 7*(1), 30.

Hall, T., & Shirley, I. (1982). Development as methodology: Locality development, social planning and social action (pp. 135–163). In I. F. Shirley (Ed.), *Development tracks: The theory and practice of community development.* Palmerston North, New Zealand: Dunmore Press.

Hameed, S., Breckenridge, J., Bennett, P., Mafile'o, T., Simeon, L. & Steven, H. (2016). Local context matters: Developing good practice in workplace responses to family and sexual violence in Papua New Guinea. *SAGE Open, 6*(3):1–13. doi: 10.1177/2158244016657142

Hamilton, J. D. (2013). Historical oil shocks. In R. E. Parker & R. M. Whaples, *Routledge handbook of major events in economic history* (pp. 239–265). New York, NY: Routledge.

Hammond, V., Harrison, G., Parker, W., Patterson, B., & Hicks, D. (1996). Engagements and de facto relationships. In R. L. Fisher, B. Atkin, & D. Howman (Eds.), *Fisher on matrimonial property* (3rd ed.) (pp. 81–94). Wellington, New Zealand: Butterworths.

Hancock, M. W. (1985). *Report of the Ministerial Review Committee on the New Zealand Social Work Training Council.* Wellington, New Zealand: The Committee.

Hancock, M. W., & Asher, B. (1984). *Social services in Napier.* Napier, New Zealand: Napier City Council.

Hancock, M., & Nash, M. (2005). The first two years of NZASW 1964–1966. Reflections on re-reading the first issue of *New Zealand Social Worker. Social Work Review, 17*(1), 23–30.

Handyside, R. (1992). *A model of social work practice in the New Zealand workplace.* (MSW thesis, Palmerston North, New Zealand: Massey University.)

Hanlen, P. A. (2002). *Altruistic leaders: Voices of women in voluntary organizations.* (MSW thesis, Palmerston North, New Zealand: Massey University.) http://mro. massey.ac.nz/handle/10179/6298

Hanlen, P. (2011). Social service manager and student information provision. *Aotearoa New Zealand Social Work, 23*(4), 65–75.

Hanna, S. (2008). Child protection practices in a call centre: An emerging area of social work. *Aotearoa New Zealand Social Work Review, 20*(3), 34–43.

Hare, J. L. (2010). *Christian social workers and their sense of effectiveness in social work practice.* (MSW thesis, Auckland, New Zealand: Massey University.) http:// mro.massey.ac.nz/handle/10179/2202

Harris, A. (1996). *Maori land development schemes, 1945–1974, with two case studies from the Hokianga.* (MPhil thesis, Auckland, New Zealand: Massey University.) http://hdl.handle.net/10179/6486

Harte, A. (2004). *Employment relations in a changing world: A comparison of outcomes for New Zealand workers under neoliberalist and third way regimes.* (MA (Social Policy) thesis, Palmerston North, New Zealand: Massey University.) http:// mro.massey.ac.nz/handle/10179/5069

Havea, S. (2011). *The relationship between lotu and ako for Pacific university students in New Zealand.* (MPhil thesis, Palmerston North, New Zealand: Massey University.) http://mro.massey.ac.nz/handle/10179/3261

Havea, S. F. (1996). *The cultural preservation of Tonga: Traditional practice and current policy.* (MPhil thesis, Auckland, New Zealand: Massey University.) http://mro.massey.ac.nz/handle/10179/5890

Hawken, D. B. (1996). *Strong in their spirits: Women managers in the social services.* (MSW thesis, Auckland, New Zealand: Massey University.) http://mro.massey.ac.nz/handle/10179/5787

Hay, K. (2009). A Pacific human rights mechanism: Specific challenges and requirements. *Victoria University of Wellington Law Review, 40*(1), 195–214.

Hay, K. (2010). 'The canoe will sail when the wind is right': Moving towards sub-regional human rights arrangements in the Pacific? In *New Zealand Yearbook of International Law* (pp. 171–180). Christchurch, New Zealand: International Law Group, School of Law, Canterbury University. http://www.nzlii.org/nz/journals/NZYblntLaw/2010/7.html

Hay, K., Ballantyne, N., & Brown. K. (2014). *Hic sunt dracones*: Here be dragons! Difficulties in mapping the demand for social work placements in New Zealand. *Journal of Practice Teaching and Learning, 13*(1), 24–43. doi: 10.1921/12302130106

Hay, K., & Brown, K. (2015). Social work practice placements in Aotearoa New Zealand: Agency managers' perspectives. *Social Work Education, 34*(6), 700–715. doi:10.1080/02615479.2015.1062856

Hay, K., & Dale, M. (2014). Moving through Moodle: Using e-technology to enhance social work field education. *Asia-Pacific Journal of Cooperative Education, 15*(2), 119–128.

Hay, K., Dale, M., & Yeung, P. (2016). Influencing the future generation of social workers: Field educator perspectives on social work field education. *Advances in Social Work and Welfare Education, 18*(1), 39–54.

Hay, K., & Teppett, R. (2011). Back to the future and back again: Reflections on a student unit. *Aotearoa New Zealand Social Work Review. 23*(4), 26–33.

Hayward, J. (2012). 'Biculturalism: From bicultural to monocultural, and back', *Te Ara — the Encyclopedia of New Zealand.* http://www.TeAra.govt.nz/en/biculturalism/page-1 (Accessed 9 January 2017.)

Henderson, E., & Fry, K. (2013). Implementing registration within a health organisation setting. *Aotearoa New Zealand Social Work Review, 25*(3), 11–18.

Henderson, R., & O'Donoghue, K. B. (2013). A former president reflects on the effects of social worker registration upon the association: An interview with Rose Henderson. *Aotearoa New Zealand Social Work Review, 25*(3), 60–67.

Henrickson, M. (2005). Can anybody work with anyone? Reframing cultural competence. *Social Work Review, 17*(1), 1–2.

Henrickson, M. (2005). Lavender parents. *Social Policy Journal of New Zealand, 26,* 68–83.

Henrickson, M. (2006). Ko wai ratou? Managing multiple identities in lesbian, gay and bisexual New Zealand Māori. *New Zealand Sociology, 21*(2), 247–269.

Henrickson, M. (2006). Lavender immigration to New Zealand: Comparative descriptions of overseas-born sexual minorities. *Social Work Review, 18*(3), 69–78.

Henrickson, M. (2007). A queer kind of faith: Religion and spirituality in lesbian, gay and bisexual New Zealanders. *Aotearoa Ethnic Network Journal, 2*(2), 59–70. http://www.aen.org.nz/journal/2/2/Henricksen.html

Henrickson, M. (2007). Lavender faith: Religion, spirituality and identity in lesbian, gay and bisexual New Zealanders. *Journal of Religion and Spirituality in Social Work, 26*(3), 63–80.

Henrickson, M. (2007). Reaching out, hooking up: Lavender netlife in a New Zealand study. *Sexuality Research and Social Policy: Journal of NSRC, 4*(2), 38–49. doi: 10.1525/srsp.2007.4.2.50

Henrickson, M. (2007). 'You have to be strong to be gay': Bullying and educational attainment in LGB New Zealanders. *Journal of Gay and Lesbian Social Services, 19*(3–4), 67–85.

Henrickson, M. (2008). Deferring identity and social role in lesbian, gay and bisexual New Zealanders. *Social Work Education, 27*(2), 169–181. doi: 10.1080/02615470701709626

Henrickson, M. (2009). Sexuality, religion, and authority: Toward reframing estrangement. *Journal of Religion and Spirituality in Social Work, 28*(1–2), 48–62. doi: 10.1080/15426430802643570

Henrickson, M. (2009). Social work education and sexual minorities. In C. Noble, M. Henrickson, & I. Y. Han (Eds.), *Social work education: Voices from the Asia Pacific* (pp. 173–192). Melbourne, Australia: Vulgar Press.

Henrickson, M. (2010). Civilized unions, civilized rights: Same-sex relationships in Aotearoa New Zealand. *Journal of Gay and Lesbian Social Services, 22*(1–2), 40–55. doi: 10.1080/10538720903332214

Henrickson, M. (2015). A queer kind of faith: Religion and spirituality in lesbian, gay and bisexual New Zealanders. In S. Hunt (Ed.), *Religion and LGBTQ sexualities: Critical essays*. London, England: Ashgate.

Henrickson, M. (2015). Sexuality and social work. In J. D. Wright (Ed.) *International encyclopedia of the social and behavioral sciences* (2nd ed.) (Vol. 21, pp. 802–807).

Oxford, England: Elsevier.

Henrickson, M. (Ed.). (2017). *Getting to zero: Global social work responds to HIV*. Auckland, New Zealand: IASSW/UNAIDS, 2017.

Henrickson, M., Brown, D. B., Fouché, C., Poindexter, C. C., & Scott, K. (2013). 'Just talking about it opens your heart': Meaning-making among Black African migrants and refugees living with HIV. *Culture, Health and Sexuality, 15*(8), 910–923.

Henrickson, M., Dickson, N., Mhlanga, F., & Ludlam, A. (2013, June). *AfricaNZ Care: A report on knowledge, attitudes, behaviours and beliefs about HIV among Black Africans living in New Zealand*. Report completed for the Health Research Council of New Zealand and Ministry of Health (Contract 11/965). Auckland, New Zealand.

Henrickson, M., Dickson, N., Mhlanga, F., & Ludlam, A. (2015). Stigma, lack of knowledge and prevalence maintain HIV risk among Black Africans in New Zealand. *Australian and New Zealand Journal of Public Health, 39*(1), 32–37. doi:10.1111/1753-6405.12301

Henrickson, M., & Fisher, M. (2016). 'Treating Africans differently': Using skin colour as proxy for HIV risk. *Journal of Clinical Nursing, 25*(13–14), 1941–1949. doi: 10.1111/jocn.13212

Henrickson, M., Fisher, M., Ludlam, A., & Mhlanga, F. (2016). What do African new settlers 'know' about HIV? *New Zealand Medical Journal, 129*(1434), 36–43.

Henrickson, M., Fouché, C., Poindexter, C., Brown, D., & Scott, K. (2014). Host country responses to Black African migrants and refugees living with HIV. *Aotearoa New Zealand Social Work Review, 26*(4), 25–36.

Henrickson, M., & Neville, S. (2012). Identity satisfaction over the life course in sexual minorities. *Journal of Gay and Lesbian Social Services, 24*(1), 80–95.

Herman, W. R. (1987). Editoral. Protection of social workers from violence as an issue. *New Zealand Social Work, 12*(1&2), 1.

Hesseling-Green, N. B. (2015). *The ties that bind: An exploratory study into the relationships in open adoption*. (MSW thesis, Palmerston North, New Zealand: Massey University.) http://mro.massey.ac.nz/handle/10179/7555

Hessey, E. M. (1978). Group supervision for social workers — an experiment for growth in social work. *New Zealand Social Work, 2*(4), 12–14.

Hessey, E. M., & Fraser, G. S. (1978). Small scale research for practising social workers. In *New Zealand Association of Social Workers Conference* (pp. 28–38). Palmerston North, New Zealand: Department of University Extension, Massey University.

Hewitt, D. (2003). *Safety of female patients in sexually-integrated acute psychiatric wards in Aotearoa New Zealand*. (MA (Social Policy) thesis, Auckland, New Zealand: Massey University.)

Highet, P. (1999). *Double vision: The experience of multiple sclerosis through the eyes of women.* (MSW thesis, Palmerston North, New Zealand: Massey University.)

Hill, N. (2004). *Education, a young mother's key to success, a young mother's hope: A study of the impact of pregnancy and mothering on the educational participation and goals of young mothers.* (MPhil thesis, Auckland, New Zealand: Massey University.) http://mro.massey.ac.nz/handle/10179/7025

Hill, N., Fouché, C., & Worrall, J. (2005). Education: A young mother's hope. *Social Work Review, 17*(1), 38–48.

Hill, R. (2009). *Māori and the State: Crown–Māori relations in New Zealand/ Aotearoa, 1950–2000.* Wellington, New Zealand: Victoria University Press.

Hollis-English, A. (2016). Working with non-indigenous colleagues: Coping mechanisms for Māori social workers. *Indigenous Social Work Journal, 10*, 71–82.

Human Rights Commission Act, 1977. http://www.nzlii.org/nz/legis/hist_act/ hrca19771977n49294/

Human Rights Commission. (2016). Our story. https://www.hrc.co.nz/about/our-story/

Hunapo, B., & Ohia, R. (1986). Social work training in Aotearoa — a Maori perspective. *New Zealand Social Work, 11*(2), 11–13.

Hunt, S. (1992). *Equal employment opportunities valuing women's work?* (MSW thesis, Palmerston North, New Zealand: Massey University.) http://mro.massey. ac.nz/handle/10179/7294

Hunt, S., & King, T. (2000). Allied health: Aligned for empowerment. *Social Work Review, 12*(3), 13–19.

Hunt-Ioane, F. (2005). *Physical discipline in Samoan families.* (MSW thesis, Auckland, New Zealand: Massey University.) http://mro.massey.ac.nz/ handle/10179/6692

Hunter, M. (1997). *A job full of conflicts: The experience of women child protection social workers in New Zealand.* (MSW thesis, Auckland, New Zealand: Massey University.) http://mro.massey.ac.nz/handle/10179/6148

Hutchings, J. (2008). Does social work registration have implications for social work supervision? *Aotearoa New Zealand Social Work Review, 20*(1), 2–9.

Hutchings, J. (2012). *The prevalence, nature and views of cross-disciplinary supervision amongst social workers in Aotearoa New Zealand.* (MPhil thesis, Palmerston North, New Zealand: Massey University.) http://mro.massey.ac.nz/ handle/10179/3836

Hutchings, J., Cooper, L., & O'Donoghue, K. (2014). Cross-disciplinary supervision amongst social workers in Aotearoa New Zealand. *Aotearoa New Zealand Social Work Review, 26*(4), 53–64.

Hyslop, I. (2013). *Social work practice knowledge: An enquiry into the nature of the knowledge generated and applied in the practice of social work.* (PhD thesis, Auckland, New Zealand: Massey University.) http://mro.massey.ac.nz/handle/10179/5139

Illich, I. (1971). *Deschooling society.* New York, NY: Harper & Row.

Illich, I. (1977). *Limits to medicine: Medical nemesis — the expropriation of health.* Harmondsworth, England: Penguin.

Illich, I. (1977). The disabling professions. *Inquiry, 21,* 17–21.

Jaquiery, N., Baskerville, M., & Selby, R. A. (2002). Social work in schools (SWiS). In R. Truell & L. Nowland (Eds.), *Reflections on current practice in social work* (pp. 81–98). Palmerston North, New Zealand: Dunmore Press.

Jelicich, S., & Trlin, A. (1997). Print culture of other languages — Croatian. In P. Griffith, R. Harvey & K. Maslen (Eds.), *Book and print in New Zealand: A guide to print culture in Aotearoa* (pp. 276–281). Wellington, New Zealand: Victoria University Press.

Johnson, C. (2015). *Are we failing them? An analysis of the New Zealand criminal youth justice system. How can we further prevent youth offending and youth recidivism?* (MA (Social Policy) thesis, Auckland, New Zealand: Massey University.) http://mro.massey.ac.nz/handle/10179/7420

Johnston, R. C. (1984). *Job creation schemes and the capitalist state: Marxist analysis of job creation schemes, 1890–1912 and 1930–1935.* (MA thesis, Palmerston North, New Zealand: Massey University.)

Jülich, S. (2001). *Breaking the silence: Restorative justice and child sexual abuse.* (PhD thesis, Auckland, New Zealand: Massey University.) http://mro.massey.ac.nz/handle/10179/2110

Jülich, S. (2014). Stockholm syndrome, substantive equality and the costs of child sexual abuse. In M. Bjørnholt & A. McKay (Eds.), *Counting on Marilyn Waring: New advances in feminist economics* (pp. 105–118). Bradford, Canada: Demeter Press.

Jülich, S., & Cox, N. (2013). Good workplaces: Alternative dispute resolution and restorative justice. In J. Parker & J. Arrowsmith (Eds.), *The big issues in employment: HR management and employment relations in New Zealand* (pp. 111–133). Sydney, Australia: CCH.

Jülich, S., & Landon, F. (2014). Restorative justice and sexual violence: Overcoming the concerns of victim-survivors. In T. Gavrielides (Ed.), *A victim-led criminal justice system: Addressing the paradox* (pp. 41–56). London, England: IARS Publications.

Jülich, S. J., McGregor, K., Annan, J., Landon, F., McCarrison, D., & McPhillips, K.

(2011). Yes, there is another way! *Canterbury Law Review, 17*, 222–228.

Jülich, S. J., & Oak, E. B. (2016). Does grooming facilitate the development of Stockholm syndrome? The social work practice implications. *Aotearoa New Zealand Social Work Review, 28*(3), 10. doi:10.11157/anzswj-vol28iss3id247

Jülich, S., Oak, E., Terrell, J., & Good, G. (2014). *Primary prevention of sexual violence in Aotearoa New Zealand: A literature review.* Auckland, New Zealand: Massey University.

Kanyi, T. (2013). Lack of outcome research on care and protection family group conference. *Aotearoa New Zealand Social Work Review, 25*(1), 35–42.

Keen, B. M (1990). Social work practice with gay men with HIV/Aids. *Social Work Review, 3*(1&2), 4–13.

Kenkel, D. (2005). *Futurority: Narratives of the future.* (MA (Social Policy) thesis, Auckland, New Zealand: Massey University.) http://mro.massey.ac.nz/handle/10179/682

Kerr, A. (1993). Special education policy: A critique. *Social Work Review, 5*(5), 8–14.

Kerr, A. L. (1996). *When you lack the word: Stories from parents of children with visual and other disabilities.* (MPhil thesis, Palmerston North, New Zealand: Massey University.)

Kim, S. (2006). *Absolute solitude of the alien mind.* (MA (Social Policy) thesis, Auckland, New Zealand: Massey University.)

Koro, T., Walden, N., Smith, T., Dewar, A., Muller, K., Ndeke, A., . . . Simmons, H. (2010). Nga haerenga o le laumei: Pathways to cultural protection through language preservation. *Aotearoa New Zealand Social Work Review/Tu Mau, 22*(4), 44–56.

Korzon, J. (2011). *Fit to practice: Exploring the work experiences of registered nurses who are disabled during the course of their careers.* (MPhil thesis, Palmerston North, New Zealand: Massey University.) http://mro.massey.ac.nz/handle/10179/3837

Kruger, D. J., de Vos, A. S., Fouché, C. B., & Venter, L. (2005). Quantitative data analysis and interpretation. In A. S. de Vos & M. Greeff (Eds.), *Research grassroots: For the social sciences and human professions* (pp. 286–313). Pretoria, South Africa: Van Schaik Publishers.

Kuka, J. (2000). *The effects of raupatu on the health and wellbeing of Pirirakau: Nga aria o te raupatu e pa ana ki te hauoratanga a Pirirakau.* (MA (Social Policy) thesis, Palmerston North, New Zealand: Massey University.)

La Grow, S., Towers, A., Yeung, P., Alpass, F. & Stephens, C. (2015). The relationship between loneliness and perceived quality of life among older persons with visual impairment. *Journal of Visual Impairment and Blindness, 109*(6), 487–499.

LaGrow, S., Yeung, P., Towers, A., Alpass, F., & Stephens, C. (2011). Determinants of the overall quality of life of older persons who have difficulty seeing: The importance of the ability to get around. *Journal of Visual Impairment and Blindness, 105*(10), 720–730.

Lambert, J. (1994). *'They can't see what we see': Voices and standpoint of twelve Plunket nurses.* (MPhil thesis, Palmerston North, New Zealand: Massey University.) http://mro.massey.ac.nz/handle/10179/7054

Lambourn, A. (1999). *Reducing the use of alcohol and other drugs by high school students: High school students' perceptions of the efficacy of various prevention approaches.* (MPhil thesis, Auckland, New Zealand: Massey University.) http://mro.massey.ac.nz/handle/10179/5675

Lauta-Mulitalo, P. T. (1998). *The role of Fa'asamoa in social work in Aotearoa New Zealand.* (MSW thesis, Auckland, New Zealand: Massey University.) http://mro.massey.ac.nz/handle/10179/6212

Lee, V. (2009). *From caregiving to bereavement: Weaving the strands of identity.* (MSW thesis, Palmerston North, New Zealand: Massey University.) http://mro.massey.ac.nz/handle/10179/1314

Leigh, G. R. (2006). *The case for reintroducing universal child allowance in 21st century New Zealand.* (MA (Social Policy) thesis, Palmerston North, New Zealand: Massey University.)

Levine, S. (1979). The New Zealand election of 1978: An ambiguous verdict. *Parliamentary Affairs, 32*(4): 410–421. doi:10.1093/pa/32.4.410

Lipsham, M. (2012). Āta as an innovative method and practice tool in supervision. *Aotearoa New Zealand Social Work/Te Kōmako, 24*(3&4), 31–40.

Livingston, K. G. (1990). *Policy and politics the New Zealand Labour Party 1987 social policy debate.* (MSW thesis, Palmerston North, New Zealand: Massey University.)

Lunn, M. (2006). Becoming an academic woman: Islam, religious identity and career. *Asian Journal of Women's Studies, 12*(2), 33–63.

Lunn, M. (2007). Women academicians: Gender and career progression. *Jurnal Pendidikan Malaysia, 32*, 77–90. http://journalarticle.ukm.my/193/

Lunn, M., & Noble, A. (2008). Re-visioning science: 'Love and passion in the scientific imagination': Art and science. *International Journal of Science Education, 30*(6), 793–805.

Lunt, N. (1999). The discipline of social policy and biculturalism. *Social Policy Journal of New Zealand, 12*, 1–15.

Lunt, N. (2005). A note on political science and the metaphorical imagination.

Politics, 25(2), 73–79. doi: 10.1111/j.1467-9256.2005.00231.X

Lunt, N. (2006). Employability and New Zealand welfare restructuring. *Policy and Politics, 34*(3), 473–494.

Lunt, N. (2006). Sickness and invalid's benefits: New developments and continuing challenges. *Social Policy Journal of New Zealand, 27*, 77–99.

Lunt, N. (2006). The lingering death of social policy. *Sociology, 40*(2), 381–386.

Lunt, N., Aitkin, K., & Hirst, M. (1997). Staying single in the 90s: Single-handed practitioners in the new National Health Service. *Social Science and Medicine, 45*(3), 341–349.

Lunt, N., & Baldwin, S. (1997). Charging ahead in the community: Local authority charging policies for community care. *Health and Social Care in the Community, 5*(6), 418–420.

Lunt, N., & Davidson, C. (2000). Doing politics: Journey to the centre of the (academic) universe: 20 steps on getting published in journals. *Politics, 20*(1), 43–50.

Lunt, N., & Davidson, C. (2002). Increasing social science research capacity: Some supply-side considerations. *Social Policy Journal of New Zealand, 18*, 1–17.

Lunt, N., & Davidson, C. (2003). *Evaluating policy and practice: A New Zealand reader.* New Jersey, NJ: Pearson Prentice Hall.

Lunt, N., O'Brien, M., & Stephens, R. (2008). New welfare, New Zealand? In N. Lunt, M. O'Brien, & R. Stephens (Eds.), *New Zealand, new welfare* (pp. 3–9). Melbourne, Australia: Cengage Learning Australia.

Lunt, N., O'Brien, M., & Stephens, R. (2008). What lies ahead? In N. Lunt, M. O'Brien, & R. Stephens (Eds.), *New Zealand, new welfare* (pp. 146–153). Melbourne, Australia: Cengage Learning Australia.

Lunt, N., & Pernice, R. (1999). New Zealand disability employment policy in the 1990s. *Social Policy Journal of New Zealand, 12*, 16–34.

Lunt, N., Spoonley, P., & Mataira, P. (2002), Past and present: Reflections on citizenship within New Zealand. *Social Policy and Administration, 36*, 346–362.

Lunt, N., & Thornton, P. (1997). Researching disability employment policies. In C. Barnes & G. Mercer, *Doing disability research* (pp. 108–122). Leeds, England: Disability Press.

Lunt, N., & Thornton, P. (1998). Working opportunities for disabled people. In J. Wheelock and J. Vail (Eds.), *Work and idleness: The political economy of full employment* (pp. 131–142). Netherlands: Springer. doi: 10.1007/978-94-011-4397-4_8

Lynch, A. (2006). The place of structural-self reflexivity in our ongoing journey as social workers. *Social Work Review, 18*(4), 78–89.

Lynch, A. R. (2003). *An analysis of social work reflective practice in Aotearoa/New Zealand.* (MSW thesis, Palmerston North, New Zealand: Massey University.)

MacKay, B. J. (1995). *Kaupapa Māori and responsiveness: Management responsiveness to Māori health issues in the reformed health service of the 1990s.* (MA (Social Policy) thesis, Palmerston North, New Zealand: Massey University.) http://mro.massey.ac.nz/handle/10179/5564

MacLennan, B. J. (2000). *Deliberative democracy: Developing best practice in territorial local authorities.* (MA (Social Policy) thesis, Palmerston North, New Zealand: Massey University.) http://mro.massey.ac.nz/handle/10179/6636

Madgeskind, S. M. (2009). *Motivation for change in the discipline of children.* (MSW thesis, Auckland, New Zealand: Massey University.) http://mro.massey.ac.nz/handle/10179/1333

Mafile'o, T. (2001) Pasifikan social work theory. *Social Work Review/Tu Mau, 13*(3), 10–13.

Mafile'o, T. (2004). Exploring Tongan social work Fekau'aki (connecting) and Fakatokilalo (humility). *Qualitative Social Work, 3*(3), 239–257. doi: 10.1177/1473325004045664

Mafile'o, T. (2006). Matakainga (behaving like family): The social worker–client relationship in Pasifika social work. *Social Work Review, 18*(1), 31–36.

Mafile'o, T. (2016). Strengthening research capacity in Oceania. *Social Dialogue, 15,* 18–20.

Mafile'o, T. & Vakalahi, H. F. O. (2016). Indigenous social work across borders: Expanding social work in the South Pacific. *International Social Work* (pp. 1–16). Advance online publication. doi: 10.1177/0020872816641750

Mafile'o, T. A., & Walsh-Tapiata, W. (2007). Māori and Pasifika indigenous connections. *AlterNative: An International Journal of Indigenous Scholarship, 3*(2), 128–145.

Maharaj, A. (2004). *Ethnic peoples in Aotearoa/New Zealand: Towards effective participation in the development of social policy.* (MPhil thesis, Palmerston North, New Zealand: Massey University.) http://mro.massey.ac.nz/handle/10179/6937

Maharey, S., & O'Brien, M. (1986). Introduction: 'Common sense' and 'good sense'. In S. Maharey & M. O'Brien (Eds.), *Alternatives: Socialist essays for the 1980s* (pp. 1–6). Palmerston North, New Zealand: Department of Sociology, Massey University.

Mahina, O. (1993). The poetics of Tongan traditional history, Tala-e-fonua: An ecology-centred concept of culture and history. *Journal of Pacific History, 28*(June), 1.

Marshall, D. (1996). Would you recognise the loss and grief of adoption? *Social Work Review, 8*(2), 14–16, 20.

Mataira, P. (2000). *Te kaha o te Waiata —The power of music: Māori oral traditions* (illustrated by E. Tipu e Rea). Indigenous Religious Musics. Aldershot, England: Ashgate.

Mataira, P. (2002). Treaty partnering: Establishment of a charter for Maori community based programmes. *Social Work Review/Te Kōmako, 14*(2), 5–7.

Mataira, P. (2003). He kainga tuturu: 'Talking story' and rediscovering community. *Social Work Review/Te Kōmako, 15*(3), 12–15.

Mataira, P. (2008). Sitting in the fire, an indigenous approach to masculinity and male violence: Māori men working with Māori men. *Aotearoa New Zealand Social Work Review/Te Kōmako, 20*(4), 35–39.

Mataira, P. J. (2000). Mana and tapu: Sacred knowledge, sacred boundaries. In D. Harvey (Ed.), *Indigenous religions* (pp. 99–111). London, England: Continuum.

Mataira, P. J. (2001). *Negotiating the boundaries: The politics of cross-cultural research in the social sciences.* Auckland, New Zealand: School of Social and Cultural Studies, Massey University.

Matthewson, P. (2007). Professional leadership in mental health. *Aotearoa New Zealand Social Work, 19*(3), 38–47.

Matthewson, P. J. (1998). *Maintaining safety: The social support and monitoring of men who have completed therapy for sexual offending.* (MPhil thesis, Palmerston North, New Zealand: Massey University.)

Matthewson, P. J. (2002). Risk assessment and management in mental health. *Social Work Review, 14*(4), 36–43.

McCarthy, J., & Lambie, I. (1995). Nature of adolescent sexual offending (part 3). Treating adolescent sexual offenders. *Social Work Review, 7*(3), 18–25.

McClure, M. (2016). Auckland places — eastern suburbs: Ōrākei to the Tāmaki River. *Te Ara — the Encyclopedia of New Zealand.* http://www.TeAra.govt.nz/en/auckland-places/page-13 (Accessed 2016, November 29.)

McCraw, D. (1983). Classifying the 1981 general election. *Political Science, 35*(2), 190–197.

McCreary, J., & Shirley, I. (1982). In the rural tradition: Anthropologists come to town. In I. F. Shirley (Ed.), *Development tracks: The theory and practice of community development* (pp. 28–49). Palmerston North, New Zealand: Dunmore Press.

McGregor, K., Gautam, J., Glover, M., & Jülich, S. (2013). Health care and female survivors of childhood sexual abuse: Health professionals' perspectives. *Journal of Child Sexual Abuse, 22*(6), 761–775. doi: 10.1080/10538712.2013.811143

McKegg, K. (1997). *Anomalies of collection: A study of the validity and value of ethnic data.* (MA (Social Policy) thesis, Palmerston North, New Zealand: Massey

University.) http://mro.massey.ac.nz/handle/10179/7822

McMaster, K. (1997). *Identifying and assessing risk in men who have a history of violence towards their female partners.* (MSW thesis, Palmerston North, New Zealand: Massey University.) http://mro.massey.ac.nz/handle/10179/6644

McMaster, K. (2001). Men and social work. In M. Connolly (Ed.), *New Zealand social work: Contexts and practice* (pp. 110–121). Melbourne, Australia: Oxford University Press.

McMaster, K. (2001). Working with violence: Family violence as a professional issue. In M. Connolly (Ed.), *New Zealand social work: Contexts and practice* (pp. 317–330). Melbourne, Australia: Oxford University Press.

McNabb, D. (2002). A strategy for effective social work within a state mental health service in Aoteraoa/New Zealand. *Social Work Review, 14*(3), 13–18.

McNabb, D. (2010). Professional leadership for social work in mental health services in Aotearoa New Zealand. *Aotearoa New Zealand Social Work, 21*(4) & *22*(1), 103–107.

Melling, P. M. (1997). *Excellence in dementia care.* (MSW thesis, Palmerston North, New Zealand: Massey University.) http://mro.massey.ac.nz/handle/10179/7305

Meo-Sewabu, L. D. (2015). *'Tu ga na inima ka luvu na waqa' (The bail to get water out of the boat is in the boat yet the boat sinks): The cultural constructs of health and wellbeing amongst Marama iTaukei in a Fijian village in Lau and in a transnational Fijian community in Whanganui, Aotearoa.* (PhD thesis, Palmerston North, New Zealand: Massey University.) http://mro.massey.ac.nz/handle/10179/7577

Meo-Sewabu, L. D., & Walsh-Tapiata, W. (2012). Global declarations and village discourses: Social policy and indigenous wellbeing. *AlterNative: An International Journal of Indigenous Peoples, 8*(3), 305–317. doi: 10.1111/apv.12059

Merchant, R. L. (2010). *Who are abusing our children? An exploratory study on reflections on child abuse by media commentators.* (MSW thesis, Auckland, New Zealand: Massey University.) http://mro.massey.ac.nz/handle/10179/1612

Mertens, D., Bledsoe, K., Sullivan, M. J., & Wilson, A. (2010). Utilization of mixed methods for transformative purposes. In A. Tashakkori & C. Teddlie (Eds.), *Sage handbook of mixed methods in social and behavioral research* (pp. 193–214). Thousand Oaks, CA: Sage.

Middleton, L. A. (1998). *View to the future: Mid-life women and retirement income planning.* (MA (Social Policy) thesis, Palmerston North, New Zealand: Massey University.)

Mila, K. (2001). Flying foxes don't fit into pigeon hole. Working as 'Pacific Island' social workers: Questions of identity. *Social Work Review/Tu Mau, 13*(3), 23–24.

Mila-Schaaf, K. (2006). Va-centred social work: Possibilities for a Pacific approach to social work practice. *Social Work Review/Tu Mau, 18*(1), 8–13.

Ministry for Culture and Heritage. (2014). The 1981 Springbok rugby tour. http://www.nzhistory.net.nz/culture/1981-springbok-tour

Ministry for Culture and Heritage. (2015). Remembering carless days. https://nzhistory.govt.nz/media/photo/carless-days

Ministry for Culture and Heritage. (2016). Occupation of Bastion Point begins. https://nzhistory.govt.nz/occupation-of-bastion-point-begins

Ministry for Culture and Heritage. (2016). Wanganui Computer legislation enacted. https://nzhistory.govt.nz/big-brother-is-watching-legislation-is-passed-establishing-the-wanganui-computer-centre

Ministry of Health. (2012). Rising to the challenge: The Mental Health and Addiction Service development plan 2012–2017. Wellington, New Zealand: Ministry of Health.

Ministry of Justice. (2016). About Family Court. https://www.justice.govt.nz/family/about/

Mokomoko, C. (2000). *Kia whai te whakatekainga o nga turoro wairangi: The effectiveness of discharge planning for Maori mental health patients.* (MSW thesis, Palmerston North, New Zealand: Massey University.) http://mro.massey.ac.nz/handle/10179/5630

Mooney, H., & Dale, M. (2015). Facilitating closure. In J. Maidment & R. Egan (Eds.), *Practice skills in social work and welfare: More than just common sense* (3rd ed.) (pp. 299–313). Crows Nest, NSW, Australia: Allen and Unwin.

Mooney, H. A. (2012). Māori social work views and practices of rapport building with rangatahi Māori. *Aotearoa New Zealand Social Work Review/Te Kōmako, 24*(3&4), 49–64.

Moorhouse, L., Hay, K., & O'Donoghue, K. (2014). Listening to student experiences of supervision. *Aotearoa New Zealand Social Work Review, 26*(4), 37–52.

Moorhouse, L. M. (2013). *How do social work students perceive their fieldwork supervision experiences?* (MSW thesis, Palmerston North, New Zealand: Massey University.) http://mro.massey.ac.nz/handle/10179/4675

Morris, L. (1999). *Lone mothers and paid work.* (MA (Social Policy) thesis, Auckland, New Zealand: Massey University.) http://mro.massey.ac.nz/handle/10179/6198

Moss, M. (1999). *Rhetoric to reality: Early childhood education funding policy.* (MA (Social Policy) thesis, Palmerston North, New Zealand: Massey University.) http://mro.massey.ac.nz/handle/10179/10213

Moyle, P. (2014). A model for Māori research for Māori practitioners. *Aotearoa New*

Zealand Social Work/Te Kōmako, 26(1), 29–38.

Moyle, P. (2014). Māori social workers' experiences of care and protection: A selection of findings. *Aotearoa New Zealand Social Work/Te Kōmako, 26*(1), 55–64.

Mulitalo-Lauta, P. (2000). *Fa'a Samoa and social work within the New Zealand context.* Palmerston North, New Zealand: Dunmore Press.

Mulitalo-Lauta, P. T., Menon, K., & Tofilau, M. V. (2005). The practice of reciprocity among Pacific Island peoples in employment relations in New Zealand. *Human Resources Magazine, 10*(4), 28–29.

Mulitalo-Lauta, P. U. T., & Menon, K. (2006). Art therapy and Pacific Island peoples in New Zealand: A preliminary observation and evaluation from a Pacific Island perspective. *Social Work Review, 18*(1), 22–30.

Munford, R. (1985). Foster care for children with a handicap. *New Zealand Social Work, 10*(1), 8–9.

Munford, R. (1986). Services for people with mental handicaps: Implications for social workers. *New Zealand Social Work, 11*(2), 14–17. http://mro.massey.ac.nz/handle/10179/3494

Munford, R. (1991). The experience of women who care for people with intellectual disabilities. *Network, 1*(3), 22–37.

Munford, R. (1992). Politics of caregiving. *Social Work Review, 5*(1&2), 4–11.

Munford, R. (1992). Representative of New Zealand Council for Education and Training in the Social Services Development Group. *Presentation to the NZCYP Agency on Reviewing the Training and Competency for Social Workers.* Palmerston North, New Zealand: Social Policy Research Centre.

Munford, R. (1993). Caregiving — a shared commitment. In K. Bellard (Ed.), *Disability, family, whānau and society* (pp. 265–292). Palmerston North, New Zealand: Dunmore Press.

Munford, R. (1994). The politics of caregiving. In M. H. Rioux & M. Bach (Eds.), *Disability is not measles: New research paradigms in disability* (pp. 265–284). Ontario, Canada: Alan Roeher Institute.

Munford, R. (1994). Reclaiming our rights to citizenship. *Social Work Review, 6*(3), 4–11.

Munford, R. (1995). A position of marginalisation or inclusion? The experience of women with disabilities. *New Zealand Journal of Disabilities Studies, 1*(1) 29–59.

Munford, R. (2003). And then there was social work. *New Zealand Sociology, 18*(1), 46–54.

Munford, R., & Bennie, G., (2015). Learning disability and social work. In J. D. Wright (editor-in-chief), *International encyclopedia of the social & behavioral sciences, vol*

13 (2nd ed.) (pp. 684–689). Oxford, England: Elsevier.

Munford, R., Oka, T., & Desai, M. (2009). Qualitative social work research in the Asia-Pacific region. *Qualitative Social Work, 8*(4), 419–425. doi: 10.1177/1473325009346503

Munford, R., & Sanders, J. (2008). Drawing out strengths and building capacity in social work with troubled young women. *Child and Family Social Work, 13*(1), 2–11. doi: 10.1111/j.1365-2206.2007.00501.X

Munford, R., & Sanders, J. (2010). Embracing the diversity of practice: Indigenous knowledge and mainstream social work practice. *Journal of Social Work Practice: Psychotherapeutic Approaches in Health, Welfare and the Community, 25*(1), 63–77. doi: 10.1080/02650533.2010.532867

Munford, R., & Sanders, J. (2013). Assessment of families. In M. J. Holosko, C. N. Dulmus, & K. M. Sowers (Eds.), *Social work practice with individuals and families: Evidence-informed assessments and interventions* (pp. 237–264). Hoboken, New Jersey: John Wiley & Sons.

Munford, R., & Sanders, J. (2015). Components of effective social work practice in mental health for young people who are users of multiple services. *Social Work in Mental Health, 13*(5), 415–438. doi: 10.1080/15332985.2014.959239

Munford, R., & Sanders, J. (2015). Understanding service engagement: Young people's experience of service use. *Journal of Social Work, 16*(3), 283–302. doi: 10.1177/1468017315569676

Munford, R., & Sanders, J. (2016). Finding meaningful support: Young people's experiences of 'risky' environments. *Australian Social Work, 69*(2), 229–240.

Munford, R., & Sanders, J. (2016). Foster parents: An enduring presence for vulnerable youth. *Adoption and Fostering, 40*(3), 264–278.

Munford, R., & Sanders, J. (2016). Harnessing resistance in interventions with young people. *Journal of Social Work Practice, 1*–15. doi:10.1080/02650533.2016.1164127

Munford, R., Sanders, J., Andrew, A., & Butler, P. (2003). Action research with families/ whanau and communities. In R. Munford & J. Sanders (2003), *Making a difference in families: Research that creates change* (pp. 93–113). Crows Nest, NSW, Australia: Allen and Unwin.

Munford, R., Sanders, J., Mirfin-Weitch, B., & Conder, J. (2008). Ethics and research: Searching for ethical practice in research. *Ethics and Social Welfare, 2*(1), 50–66. doi: 10.1080/17496530801948754

Munford, R., Sanders, J., Spoonley, P., & Tisdall, M. (1996). Factors related to the achievement of positive change in families — some preliminary findings. *Social Work Review, 8*(2), 29–34.

Munford, R., Sanders, J., Spoonley, P., & Tisdall, M. (1996). *Working successfully with families.* Wellington, New Zealand: Barnardos Research Centre.

Munford, R., Sanders, J., Spoonley, P., Tisdall, M., Mulden, A., & Jock, A. (1995). Getting started on family research: Methodological concerns. *Social Work Review, 7*(3), 6–9.

Munford, R., & Sullivan, M. (1997). Social theories of disability: The insurrection of subjugated knowledge. In P. O'Brien & R. Murray (Eds.), *Human services: Towards partnership and support* (pp. 17–34). Palmerston North, New Zealand: Dunmore Press.

Munford, R., & Walsh-Tapiata, W. (2006). Community development: Working in the bicultural context of Aotearoa New Zealand. *Community Development Journal, 41*(4), 426–442. doi: 10.1093/cdj/bsl025

Munford, R. M., Sanders, J., Tisdall, M., Henare, A., & Spoonley, P. (1997). Families in context: Parental discipline strategies with children. *Childrenz Issues: Journal of the Children's Issues Centre, 1*(2), 25–28.

Munro, A. C. K. (2005). *Contrasting approaches to mandatory reporting in New Zealand and the Northern Territory of Australia: A comparative study.* (MPhil thesis, Palmerston North, New Zealand: Massey University.) http://mro.massey.ac.nz/handle/10179/9963

Napan, K., & Connor, C. (2014). Difference and diversity as a resource for learning: Teaching transcultural social practice. *International Journal of Diversity in Education, 13*(3), 79–89.

Napan, K., Ingamells, K., & Gasquoine, S. (2014). Strengths in action: A pilot study of a strengths development programme within tertiary education utilising the Clifton StrengthsQuest™ & narratives of strengths interviews. *Aotearoa New Zealand Social Work Review, 25*(4), 71–85.

Napan, K., & Oak, E. (2016). Inquiring into the spirit of social work. *Dialogue in Praxis, 5*(18), Special Issue, 30–34.

Nash, M. (1993). Dreams and reflections: Social work education. *Social Work Review, 5*(4), 32–33.

Nash, M. (1994). Social work education in Aotearoa/New Zealand. In R. Munford & M. Nash, *Social work in action* (pp. 37–57). Palmerston North, New Zealand: Dunmore Press.

Nash, M. (1997). Who drives social work education in New Zealand? *Social Work Review, 9*(4), 14–19.

Nash, M. (1999). Our history — and our professional social work identity. *Social Work Review, 11*(3), 2–5.

Nash, M. (2000). Oral history: Their stories and our history — Major Thelma Smith. *Social Work Review, 12*(3), 32–36.

Nash, M. (2001). Educating social workers in Aotearoa New Zealand. In M. Connolly (Ed.), *New Zealand social work: Contexts and practice* (pp. 265–278). Melbourne, Australia: Oxford University Press.

Nash, M. (2001). Oral history: Their stories, our history — Bertha Zurcher. *Social Work Review, 13*(1), 20–24.

Nash, M. (2002). Oral history: Their stories, our history — Anne Delamare and Bill Cox. *Social Work Review, 14*(1), 10–14.

Nash, M. (2014). Their stories, our history — John Fry, President of the Association 1972–4. *Aotearoa New Zealand Social Work Review, 26*(2&3), 39–47.

Nash, M., O'Donoghue, K., & Munford, R. (2005). *Introduction: Integrating theory and practice*. In M. Nash, K. O'Donoghue, & R. Munford (Eds.), *Social work theories in action* (pp. 15–28). London, England: Jessica Kingsley Publishers.

Nash, M., & Stewart, B. (2002). *Spirituality in social care*. London, England: Jessica Kingsley Publishers.

Nelson, A. (2000). *Perspectives on effective interventions with substance abusing adolescents in Aotearoa/New Zealand*. (MSW thesis, Palmerston North, New Zealand: Massey University.) http://mro.massey.ac.nz/handle/10179/6262

Netto, J. A., Yeung, P., Cocks, E., & McNamara, B. (2016). Facilitators and barriers to employment for people with mental illness: A qualitative study. *Journal of Vocational Rehabilitation, 44*(1), 61–72.

Neville, S., & Henrickson, M. (2006). Perceptions of lesbian, gay and bisexual people of primary healthcare services. *Journal of Advanced Nursing, 55*(4), 407–415. doi: 10.1111/j.1365-2648.2006.03944.x

Neville, S., & Henrickson, M. (2009). The constitution of 'lavender families': A LGB perspective. *Journal of Clinical Nursing, 18*(6), 849–856. doi: 10.1111/J.1365-2702.2008.02457.X

Neville, S., & Henrickson, M. (2010). 'Lavender retirement': A questionnaire survey of lesbian, gay and bisexual people's accommodation plans for old age. *International Journal of Nursing Practice, 16*(6), 586–594. doi: 10.1111/J.1440-172X.2010.01885.X

Neville, S., & Henrickson, M. (2014). HIV disease. In E. Chang & A. Johnson (Eds.), *Chronic illness and disability: Principles for nursing practice* (2nd ed.) (pp. 514–530). Chatswood, NSW, Australia: Elsevier.

Neville, S. J., & Henrickson, M. (2008). HIV/ Aids. In A. Chang & E. Johnson (Eds.), *Chronic illness and disability: Principles for nursing practice* (pp. 409–423).

Chatswood, NSW, Australia: Elsevier.

New Zealand Human Rights Commission. (1982) *Report of the Human Rights Commission on representation by the Auckland Committee on Racism and Discrimination: Children and young persons homes administered by the Department of Social Welfare.* (The Johnston Report.) Wellington, New Zealand: New Zealand Human Rights Commission.

New Zealand Social Work Training Council. (1974). *Minimum standards for an accredited course in social work.* Wellington, New Zealand: New Zealand Social Work Training Council.

Noble, C., & Henrickson, M. (2014). Towards identifying a philosophical basis for social work. In C. Noble, H. Strauss, & B. Littlechild (Eds.), *Global social work: Crossing borders, blurring boundaries* (pp. 3–14). Sydney, NSW, Australia: University of Sydney Press.

Noble, C., Henrickson, M., & Han, I. (Eds.). (2009). *Social work education: Voices from the Asia-Pacific.* Melbourne, Australia: Vulgar Press.

Noble, C., Henrickson, M., & Han, I. Y. (Eds.). (2013). *Social work education: Voices from the Asia-Pacific* (2nd ed.). Sydney, Australia: Sydney University Press.

Nsiah, J. E. (1999). *An assessment of the income allocation, living standards, housing and living circumstances of low income households in the Auckland Region in 1998.* (MA (Social Policy) thesis, Auckland, New Zealand: Massey University.) http://mro.massey.ac.nz/handle/10179/6069

Oak, E. (2015). A minority report for social work? The Predictive Risk Model (PRM) and the Tuituia Assessment Framework in addressing the needs of New Zealand's vulnerable children. *British Journal of Social Work, 46*(5), 1208–1223. doi: 10.1093/bjsw/bcv028

O'Brien, M. (1982). Disabling myths — social values. *New Zealand Social Work, 6*(4), 12–14.

O'Brien, M. (1983). Accident compensation: Whose interest? *Working Papers on the State, 1,* 69–123. Palmerston North, New Zealand: Sociology Department, Massey University.

O'Brien, M. (1984). Alternative explanations of welfare beliefs. *New Zealand Social Work, 9*(2), 10–11.

O'Brien, M. (1986). Need the poor always be with us? Wealth, incomes, social security, socialism. In S. Maharey & M. O'Brien (Eds.), *Alternatives: Socialist essays for the 1980s* (pp. 109–131). Palmerston North, New Zealand: Department of Sociology, Massey University.

O'Brien, M. (1988). Social and economic policy. *Economic Policy Network Newsletter, 5,* 1–4.

O'Brien, M. (1988). Social policy and ideology. *Working Papers on the State, 4*, 31. Palmerston North: Department of Sociology, Massey University.

O'Brien, M. (1988). Social work and social service have no class. *New Zealand Social Work Journal, 12*(4), 10–12.

O'Brien, M. (1991). Future directions for the welfare state. *Social Work Review, 4*(2&3), 37–40.

O'Brien, M. (1993). How cutting the incomes of the poorest advances economic and social policy. In P. Saunders & S. Shaver (Eds.), *National Social Policy Conference: Theory and practice in Australian social policy: Rethinking the fundamentals, July 1993.* Sydney, Australia: University of New South Wales.

O'Brien, M. (1993). *New wine in old bottles: Social security in New Zealand 1984–1990.* Sydney, Australia: University of New South Wales Social Policy Research Centre.

O'Brien, M. (1994). Ideology, poverty and unemployment. In P. Green (Ed.), *Studies in New Zealand social problems* (2nd ed.) (pp. 127–149). Palmerston North, New Zealand: Dunmore Press.

O'Brien, M. (1996). Dynamic approaches to poverty: Evidence. *Social Work Review, 8*(2), 9–13.

O'Brien, M. (1998). Social work in 2000. *Social Work Review, 10*(2), 3–8.

O'Brien, M. (2001). Doing ethical research legally: Research ethics and the law. In M. Tolich (Ed.), *Research ethics in Aotearoa New Zealand* (pp. 25–34). Auckland, New Zealand: Pearson Education.

O'Brien, M. (2001). Social work in context: Economics, organisation, politics, and ideology. In M. Connolly (Ed.), *New Zealand social work: Contexts and practice* (pp. 44–53). Melbourne, Australia: Oxford University Press.

O'Brien, M. (2003). Social policy and sociology: A diverging convergence? *New Zealand Sociology, 18*(1), 33–45.

O'Brien, M. (2007). Social and economic exclusion/inclusion: A complex paradox. In L. Harrysson & M. O'Brien (Eds.), *Social welfare, social exclusion: A life course frame* (pp. 33–56). Lund, Sweden: Varpinge Ord & Text.

O'Brien, M. (2008). Social security in a globalised New Zealand. In N. Lunt, M. O'Brien, & R. Stephens (Eds.), *New Zealand, new welfare* (pp. 137–145). Melbourne, Australia: Cengage Learning Australia.

O'Brien, M. (2008). Work-first and active labour markets. In N. Lunt, M. O'Brien, & R. Stephens (Eds.), *New Zealand, new welfare* (pp. 51–59). Melbourne, Australia: Cengage Learning Australia.

O'Brien, M. (2009). Social work, policy and disadvantage. In M. Connolly & L. Harms (Eds.). *Social work: Contexts and practice* (2nd ed.) (pp. 68–80). Melbourne,

Australia: Oxford University Press.

O'Brien, M. (2009). Social work and the practice of social justice: An initial overview. *Aotearoa New Zealand Social Workers Review, 21*(1& 2), 3–10.

O'Brien, M. (2010). 'Relative poverty' — raw statistics for children in New Zealand. *Children's Commissioner, 72*, 11–12.

O'Brien, M., & de Haan, I. (2002). Empowerment research with a vulnerable group — homelessness and the social services: The story of a research project. *Social Work Review, 14*(1), 29–35.

O'Brien, M., & Wilkes, C. (1993). *The tragedy of the market.* Palmerston North, New Zealand: Dunmore Press.

O'Brien, M., Wynd, D., & Humpage, L. (2008). Work, families and poverty: Overview of social welfare reforms. In S. St John & D. Wynd (Eds.), *Left behind: How social and income inequalities damage New Zealand children* (pp. 27–44). Auckland, New Zealand: Child Poverty Action Group Inc.

O'Donoghue, K. (2001). The future of social work supervision within New Zealand. *Social Work Review, 13*(1), 29–35.

O'Donoghue, K. (2001). Surfing the worldwide web and social work practice in Aotearoa New Zealand. *Social Work Review, 13*(2), 43–49.

O'Donoghue, K. (2012). Windows on the supervisee experience: An exploration of supervisees' supervision histories. *Australian Social Work, 65*(2), 214–231.

O'Donoghue, K. (2014). Towards an evidence-informed approach to clinical social work supervision. In M. Pack & J. Cargill (Eds.), *Evidence, discovery and assessment in social work practice* (pp. 295–308). Hershey, PA: IGI Global. doi: 10.4018/978-1-14666-6563-7.ch014

O'Donoghue, K., Nash, M., & Munford, R. (2005). Conclusion: Integrated theory in action. In M. Nash, R. Munford, & K. O'Donoghue (Eds.), *Social work theories in action* (pp. 251–260). London, England: Jessica Kingsley Publishers.

O'Donoghue, K., & Tsui, M. (2012). Towards a professional supervision culture: The development of social work supervision in Aotearoa New Zealand. *International Social Work, 55*(1), 5–28.

O'Donoghue, K., & Tsui, M. S. (2015). Social work supervision research (1970–2010): The way we were and the way ahead. *British Journal of Social Work, 45*(2), 616–633. doi: 10.1093/bjsw/bct115

O'Donoghue, K. B. (2014). Towards an interactional map of the supervision session: An exploration of supervisees' and supervisors' experiences. *Practice: Social Work in Action, 26*(1), 53–70. doi: 10.1080/09503153.2013.869581

O'Donoghue, K. B., & Tsui, M. S. (2012). In search of an informed supervisory practice: An exploratory study. *Practice: Social Work in Action, 24*(1), 3–20.

Office for Disability Issues. (2016). United Nations Convention on Rights of Persons with Disabilities and Optional Protocol. http://www.odi.govt.nz/what-we-do/un-convention/index.html

Office of Treaty Settlements. (2015). Healing the past, building a future: A guide to Treaty of Waitangi claims and negotiations with the Crown. Wellington, New Zealand: Office of Treaty Settlements. https://www.govt.nz/assets/Documents/Red-Book-Healing-the-past-building-a-future.pdf

O'Neill, K. L. (2004). *Measuring social well-being: A critical review of the development, reliability and validity of social well-being measures with particular reference to selected measures in New Zealand.* (MA (Social Policy) thesis, Palmerston North, New Zealand: Massey University.) http://mro.massey.ac.nz/handle/10179/6465

Opie, A., & Munford, R. (1996). *Beyond good intentions: Support work with older people.* Wellington, New Zealand: Health Services Research Centre, University of Victoria.

Ord, N. (2000). *Partnerships with the community sector as a strategy for good practice and effective governance for local government.* (MA (Social Policy) thesis, Palmerston North, New Zealand: Massey University.) http://mro.massey.ac.nz/handle/10179/6761

Panelli, R., Mongston, T., & Young, F. (2015). 'Moving beyond violence': Exploring new ways to support women and develop networked approaches following intimate partner violence. *Aotearoa New Zealand Social Work, 27*(3), 14–28.

Parker, W. (1997). New lamps for old? Proposals to reform family property law. *Butterworths Family Law Journal, 2*(8), 189–196.

Parker, W., & Pedley, J. (1996). Legal aspects of goodwill in matrimonial property cases. *New Zealand Valuer's Journal,* (November), 35–42.

Parker, W. E., & Pedley, J. (1996). Goodwill as matrimonial property. *New Zealand Law Journal,* (August), 309–310.

Parsons, J. (2009). Perinatal health of young women. *Aotearoa New Zealand Social Work Review, 21*(3), 14–25.

Parsons, J. E. (2008). *Perinatal mental health policy: Young women's mental health support during pregnancy.* (MPhil thesis, Palmerston North, New Zealand: Massey University.)

Patterson, L., & Briar, C. (2005). Lone mothers in liberal welfare states: Thirty years of change and continuity. *Hecate, 31*(1), 46.

Patterson, V. E. K. (1997). *Who cares? Making elder carers visible — eleven women talk about the implications of the caregiving role.* (MSW thesis, Auckland, New Zealand: Massey University. http://mro.massey.ac.nz/handle/10179/6458

Payne, C. L. (2007). *'Sometimes we are everything and nothing in the same breath': Beginning social work practitioners' constructions of professional identity.* (MSW thesis, Wellington, New Zealand: Massey University.) http://mro.massey.ac.nz/handle/10179/4976

Pearce, J. L. M. (2008). *Is there an appropriate model of community wind turbine ownership for New Zealand?* (MA (Social Policy) thesis, Palmerston North, New Zealand: Massey University.) http://mro.massey.ac.nz/handle/10179/798

Pearce, K. (2008) Te matauranga o ko wai au. *Aotearoa New Zealand Social Work Review/Te Kōmako, 20*(4), 46–51.

Pepworth, J., & Nash, M. (2009). Finding 'a safe place to cry': A review of research and evidence informing social work with refugees and new settlers in Aotearoa New Zealand. *Aotearoa New Zealand Social Work Review, 21*(1&2), 48–59.

Perkins, J. (1996). *Days of our lives: People with intellectual disabilities describe their experience and viewpoints of services.* (MSW thesis, Palmerston North, New Zealand: Massey University.) http://mro.massey.ac.nz/handle/10179/6040

Perkins, J. (2000). Partners in change: A community-based response for people with intellectual disability whose behaviour challenges. *Social Work Review, 12*(2), 23–25.

Pernice, R. & Lunt, N. (1998) *International Research Project on Job Retention and Return to Work Strategies for Disabled Workers. Study Report: New Zealand.* Geneva: International Labour Organization.

Phillips, C. (2014). Spirituality and social work: Introducing a spiritual dimension into social work education and practice. *Aotearoa New Zealand Social Work Review, 26*(4), 65–77.

Phillips, C. A. (2010). *Spirituality in social work education and practice in Aotearoa New Zealand.* (MSW thesis, Palmerston North, New Zealand: Massey University.) http://mro.massey.ac.nz/handle/10179/2487

Phillips, R. (2008). *A right to a risk filled life: Understanding and analysis of the risk discourse for consumers in mental health.* (MA (Social Policy) thesis, Auckland, New Zealand: Massey University.)

Phillips, S., & Pitt, L. (2011). Maternal mental health making a difference. *Aotearoa New Zealand Social Work, 23*(3), 31–37.

Pilalis, J. (1980). Challenges for social workers with family groups. *New Zealand Social Work, 6*(1), 6–8.

Pilalis, J. K. (1981). 'Why do we need to bring all the children?' *Australian Social Work,*

34(1), 21–25. doi:10.1080/03124078108549690

Pilalis, J. K. (1982). Consumer feedback from short courses in family therapy: A New Zealand report. *Australian Journal of Family Therapy, 3*(4), 211–216.

Pitt, L. (2005). Social work registration knowledge and power. *Social Work Review, 17*(3), 41–42.

Pitt, L. (2010). Woolsheds, wet weather gear, and the west coast: Social work practice in Taranaki. *Aotearoa New Zealand Social Work, 22*(3), 39–47.

Pitt, L. (2013). What's happening in Taranaki? Social workers and the environment. *Aotearoa New Zealand Social Work Review, 25*(4), 52–61.

Pitt, L. N. (1998). *Patriarchs, paddocks and the personal: Five women from the Wharehuia/Te Popo District talk about their lives.* (MSW thesis, Palmerston North, New Zealand: Massey University.) http://mro.massey.ac.nz/handle/10179/6014

Poindexter, C. D., Henrickson, M., Fouché, C., Brown, D. B., & Scott, K., (2013). 'They don't even greet you': HIV stigma and diagnosis disclosure experienced by HIV-positive African immigrants and refugees in New Zealand. *Journal of HIV and Social Services, 12*(1), 44–65. doi: 10.1080/15381501.2013.765715

Pollock, K. (2016). Childhood: Children's rights, *Te Ara — the Encyclopedia of New Zealand.* http://www.TeAra.govt.nz/en/ephemera/26292/international-year-of-the-child-1979

Powell, T. W. (1999). *Sexual orientation diversity programmes: An evaluation.* (MA (Social Policy) thesis, Auckland, New Zealand: Massey University.) http://mro.massey.ac.nz/handle/10179/6113

Prasad, R. (1984). *A journey into foster care: An essential preparation programme.* Palmerston North, New Zealand: Massey University.

Prasad, R. (1984). *For less than $399 per week: Evaluation of the Masterton Christian Child Care Programme.* Palmerston North, New Zealand: Social Work Unit, Massey University.

Pratt, J. (1987). Dilemmas of the alternative to custody concept: Implications for New Zealand penal policy in the light of international evidence and experience. *Australian and New Zealand Journal of Criminology, 20,* 148–162.

Pratt, J. (1987). Power and resistance in the 'social': The critical theory of Michel Foucault. *Sites: A Journal for Radical Perspectives on Culture, 14*(1), 3–16.

Pratt, J. (1987). A revisionist history of intermediate treatment. *British Journal of Social Work, 17*(4), 417–436.

Pratt, J. (1987). 'Taking crime seriously: Social work strategies for law and order climates'. *New Zealand Sociology, 2,* 36–50.

Pratt, J., & Sparks, R. (1987). New voices from the ship of fools: A critical commentary on the renaissance of 'permissiveness' as a political issue. *Contemporary Crises, 11,* 3–23.

Property Relationships Act 1976. Wellington, New Zealand: Government Printer.

Public Finance Act 1989. Wellington, New Zealand: Government Printer.

Puharich, E. J. (2000). *Let's do it better: A look at how the Department of Child, Youth and Family Services works with adolescent girls with problem behaviour.* (MPhil research report, Palmerston North, New Zealand: Massey University.) http://mro.massey.ac.nz/handle/10179/6257

Radio New Zealand. (2009). New association for Maori social workers. http://www.radionz.co.nz/news/national/16501/new-association-for-maori-social-workers.

Rains, E. (2007). Interdisciplinary supervisor development in community health service. *Aotearoa New Zealand Social Work, 19*(3), 58–65.

Ralph, L. T. (2003). *Medical misadventure, legislation, reporting, and injury prevention: An evaluation of the process of ACC's reporting of medical error findings with regard to injury prevention.* (MPhil (Social Policy) thesis, Palmerston North, New Zealand: Massey University.)

Ramacake, S. (2010). Fijian social work practice. *Aotearoa New Zealand Social Work, 22*(4), Tu Mau, 38–43.

Raven, A. (1991). *The significance of gender and sexuality: A study of discrimination and equal employment opportunities policy in the state sector.* (MSW thesis, Palmerston North, New Zealand: Massey University.)

Read, L, (1983). Supervision in social work — some thoughts. *New Zealand Social Work, 10*(2), 7–8.

Research and Publishing Group of the New Zealand Ministry for Culture and Heritage. (2016). New Zealand history. http://www.nzhistory.govt.nz/

Rennie, G. (2006). Review. *Community Development Journal, 41*(4), 528–531. doi: 10.1093/cdj/bsl033

Rickard, T. (2014). *He iwi moke, he whanokē: iwi social services, policy and practice.* (MA (Social Policy) thesis, Palmerston North, New Zealand: Massey University.) http://mro.massey.ac.nz/handle/10179/5768

Riffe, H., & Fouché, C. (2007). Does anyone die from AIDS in South Africa? *Journal of HIV/AIDS and Social Services, 6*(4), 23–36.

Rivera, M. A. (1997). *Contra viento y marea = Against the wind and the tide: Latin American women in New Zealand — resettlement experiences and issues.* (MPhil thesis, Palmerston North, New Zealand: Massey University.) http://mro.massey.ac.nz/handle/10179/6039

Robinson, J. F. (1994). *Mothers' experience of family therapy: 'you're not human, you're*

Mum'. (MSW thesis, Palmerston North, New Zealand: Massey University.) http://mro.massey.ac.nz/handle/10179/6734

Roche, B., & Baskerville, M. A. (2007). A balancing act! Social workers' experiences of work–life balance while combining work and study. *Aotearoa New Zealand Social Work Review, 19*(2), 59–67.

Roe, S. (2014). *Sea-change: Negotiating the United Nations Convention on the Rights of Persons with Disabilities — a New Zealand perspective*. (MPhil thesis, Palmerston North, New Zealand: Massey University.) http://mro.massey.ac.nz/handle/10179/6981

Ross, A. K. (2011). *Justice in action? Social work and social justice in the 21st century*. (MSW thesis, Palmerston North, New Zealand: Massey University.) http://mro.massey.ac.nz/handle/10179/3414

Ruka, R. (1998). *Perceptions of the Treaty/Te Tiriti: A study of how education changes students' perceptions of the current relevance of the Treaty of Waitangi/Te Tiriti o Waitangi*. (MSW thesis, Auckland, New Zealand: Massey University.)

Ruston, J. (2015). Volunteer peer supervision: In an ever-changing social service environment. *Aotearoa New Zealand Social Work, 27*(3), 68–77.

Ruwhiu, L. (1995). Home fires burn so brightly with theoretical flames. *Social Work Review/Te Kōmako, 7*(1), 21–24.

Ruwhiu, L. (1999), Ko Tane pupuke. *Social Work Review/Te Kōmako, 11*(4), 32–37.

Ruwhiu, L. (2001). Bicultural issues in Aotearoa New Zealand. In M. Connolly (Ed.), *New Zealand social work: Contexts and practice* (pp. 54–71). Melbourne, Australia: Oxford University Press.

Ruwhiu, L. (2002). It's time . . . Ko tenei te wa. *Social Work Review/Te Kōmako, 14*(2), 8–9.

Ruwhiu, P., & Ruwhiu, L. (2005). Ko te pae o te atua mai i nga whakaaro hohonu nei, hei oranga mo te ira tangata. *Social Work Review/Te Kōmako, 17*(2), 4–19.

Ruwhiu, P., Ruwhiu, L. A., & Ruwhiu, L. L. H. (2008). To tatou kupenga: Mana tangata supervision a journey of emancipation through heart mahi for healers. *Aotearoa New Zealand Social Work Review/Te Kōmako, 20*(4), 13–34.

Ruwhiu, L., & Walsh-Tapiata. W. (1995). He Kōrerorero: An interview with Puti Geilding, Te Kore (Fleur) Rogers and Margaret Walsh. *Social Work Review/Te Kōmako, 7*(1), 31–35.

Salmond, P. (1997). Attachment and family therapy including a narrative approach. *Social Work Review, 9*(3), 27–32.

Samuelu, T. F. (1999). *E mamae le tava'e i lona fulu: A study of the impact of the Congregational Christian Church of Samoa on Vaigaga's social structure*. (MSW thesis, Palmerston North, New Zealand: Massey University.) http://mro.massey. ac.nz/handle/10179/7826

Sanders, J., & Munford, R. (2003). Strengthening practice through research: Research in organisations. In R. Munford & J. Sanders, *Making a difference in families: Research that creates change* (pp. 151–171). Crows Nest, NSW, Australia: Allen and Unwin.

Sanders, J., & Munford, R. (2005). Activity and reflection: Research and change with diverse groups of young people. *Qualitative Social Work: Research and practice. 4*(2), 197–209.

Sanders, J., & Munford, R. (2005). Authentic relationships: Possibilities for social work to make a difference for children and young people. *Childrenz Issues: Journal of the Children's Issues Centre, 9*(1), 12–16.

Sanders, J., Munford, R., Liebenberg, L., & Ungar, M. (2014). Multiple service use: The impact of consistency in service quality for vulnerable youth. *Child Abuse and Neglect, 38*(4), 687–697. doi: 10.1016/j.chiabu.2013.10.024

Sanders, J., Munford, R., & Maden, B. (2009). Enhancing outcomes for children and young people: The potential of multi-layered interventions. *Children and Youth Services Review, 31*(10), 1086–1091.

Sanders, J., Munford, R., & Thimasarn-Anwar, T. (2016). Staying on-track despite the odds: Factors that assist young people facing adversity to continue with their education. *British Educational Research Journal, 42*(1), 56–73. doi:10.1002/ berj.3202

Sanders, J., Munford, R., Thimasarn-Anwar, T., Liebenberg, L., & Ungar, M. (2015). The role of positive youth development practices in building resilience and enhancing wellbeing for at-risk youth. *Child Abuse and Neglect, 42*, 40–53. doi: http://dx.doi.org/10.1016/j.chiabu.2015.02.006

Sayers, J. (2014). Reminiscences of anti-racism training in the 1980s. *Aotearoa New Zealand Social Work Review, 26*(2&3), 81–85.

Schorer, M. T. M. (2012). *From the New Zealand Crippled Children Society to CCS Disability Action: A social and political history of a disability organisation in Aotearoa New Zealand moving from charity to social action.* (MPhil thesis, Palmerston North, New Zealand: Massey University.) http://mro.massey.ac.nz/ handle/10179/3844

Scott, R. (1997). *An assessment of community care service provision for older people residing in Feilding.* (MPhil thesis, Palmerston North, New Zealand: Massey University.) http://mro.massey.ac.nz/handle/10179/6369

Selby, R. (1999). *Still being punished.* Wellington, New Zealand: Huia Publishers.

Selby, R. (Ed.). (2001). *Reflections: Otaki women looking back in 2000.* Otaki, New

Zealand: Otaki Women's Health Centre, Kainga o te toko i te ora mo nga wahine.

Selby, R. (2001). Women writing history. In R. Selby (Ed.), *Reflections: Otaki women looking back in 2000* (pp. 5–12). Otaki, New Zealand: Otaki Women's Health Centre, Kainga o te toko i te ora mo nga wahine.

Selby, R. (2003). Getting on board with the Treaty in the boardroom. *Te Whakahaere, 1*, 75–82.

Selby, R. (2003). Whistleblower — abuse of power in the church. A New Zealand story by Louise Deans. *Mai i Rangiatea, 1*, 106–108.

Selby, R. (2004). Tararua is my mountain. In S. Greymorning (Ed.), *A will to survive: Indigenous essays on the politics of culture, language, and identity* (pp. 171–180). New York, NY: McGraw-Hill.

Selby, R. A. (2005). Partnership and protection of participants: Collecting and using Māori oral histories. In R. Selby & A. Laurie (Eds.), *Maori and oral history: A collection* (pp. 70–73). Wellington, New Zealand: National Oral History Association of New Zealand.

Selby, R. A. (2005). Still being punished: Corporal punishment's lifelong effects. In R. Selby & A. Laurie (Eds.), *Maori and oral history: A collection* (pp. 74–77). Wellington, New Zealand: National Oral History Association of New Zealand.

Selby, R., Rosier, J., & Garrett, E. M. (2002). *Te korowai aroha: Ephra's quilt*. Palmerston North, New Zealand: School of Sociology, Social Policy and Social Work, College of Humanities and Social Sciences, Massey University.

Selby, R. A (1996) *A study of the factors which contribute to success for Māori women in tertiary education*: (MPhil thesis, Palmerston North, New Zealand: Massey University.) http://mro.massey.ac.nz/handle/10179/5860

Selby, R. A. (2005). Maori times, Maori places prophetic histories. *New Zealand Geographer, 61*(2), 177–178.

Selby, R. A. (2006). New perspectives on learning in the Fiji context. *Fiji Social Workers Journal, 2*, 19–26.

Selby, R. A. (2007). The Waitohu Stream, providing abundantly — an interview with Betty Raureti. *Indigenous Voices, Indigenous Visions, 3*, 37–41.

Selby, R. A., & Barnes, A. (2013) *Māori mentoring and pathways to wellbeing: Te Huarahi o te Ora*. Ōtaki, New Zealand: Te Tākupu Te Wānanga o Raukawa.

Selby, R. A., & Laurie, A. (2005). Introduction. In R. Selby & A. Laurie (Eds.), *Maori and oral history: A collection* (pp. ii–iv). Wellington, New Zealand: National Oral History Association of New Zealand.

Selby, R. A., & Moore, P. J. (2004). Where have all the eels gone? *Historical Journal: Otaki Historical Society, 26*, 49–54.

Selby, R. A., & Moore, P. J. (2006). Eels, eels and more eels: The most versatile food. *Words and Silences, 3*(1), 50–57.

Selby, R. A., & Moore, P. J. (2006). Guardians of the land: A Maori community's environmental battles. In S. H. Washington, P. C. Rosier, & H. Goodall (Eds.), *Echoes from the poisoned well: Global memories of environmental injustice* (pp. 299–309). Lanham, MD: Lexington Books.

Selby, R. A., & Moore, P. J. (2007). Maori research in Maori communities: No longer a new phenomenon. *AlterNative: An International Journal of Indigenous Peoples, 2007,* 96–107.

Selby, R. A., & Nomfundo Mlisa, L. (2007). Why Lily-Rose? Naming children in Maori and Xhosa families. *Women's Studies Journal, 21*(2), 20–29.

Selby, R. A., & Walsh-Tapiata, W. W. (2005). Reflections on teaching and learning in Fiji. In K. Sanga, C. Chu, C. Hall, & L. Crowl (Eds.), *Re-thinking aid relationships in Pacific education* (pp. 251–260). Wellington, New Zealand: Victoria University of Wellington, He Parekereke.

Semmons, W. V. (2006). *Ko au te wahine Māori: A phenomenological study of Māori women diagnosed with a mental illness and their experiences of pregnancy and childbirth.* (MSW thesis, Auckland, New Zealand: Massey University.) http://mro.massey.ac.nz/handle/10179/6182

Shadbolt, M. P. (1996). *The longest journey: The resettlement of Ethiopian and Eritrean refugees in Auckland.* (MPhil thesis, Auckland, New Zealand: Massey University.) http://mro.massey.ac.nz/handle/10179/5888

Sharland, L. (1999). *Promoting safer sex: An examination of agencies within the New Plymouth area providing sexual health education programmes for adolescents.* (MPhil thesis, Palmerston North, New Zealand: Massey University.)

Shaw, B. (1997). An investigation into the training need of managers in the voluntary sector. *Social Work Review, 9*(1&2), 31–38.

Shaw, R. (1996). *Unbridled optimism: Public choice, the public service and electoral law reform.* (MA (Social Policy) thesis, Palmerston North, New Zealand: Massey University.) http://mro.massey.ac.nz/handle/10179/5852

Shaw, R., & Sullivan, M. J. (2003). Towards disability ethics: A social science perspective. *New Zealand Bioethics Journal, 4*(2), 7–14.

Shaw, R. H. (2003). Advisers and consultants. In R. Miller (Ed.), *New Zealand government and politics* (3rd ed.) (pp. 148–160). Melbourne, Australia: Oxford University Press.

Shaw, R. H. (2004). Electoral law reform and the work of the New Zealand parliament. *Australasian Parliamentary Review, 19*(1), 18–31.

Shaw, R. H. (2004). Shaping bureaucratic reform down-under. *Commonwealth and Comparative Politics, 42*(2), 169–183. doi: 10.1080/1466204042000299245

Shaw, R. H. (2005). New Zealand: Public management reform and the partnership for quality agreement. In D. Farnham, A. Hondeghem, & S. Horton (Eds.), *Staff participation and public management reform: Some international comparisons* (pp. 214–229). Basingstoke, England: Palgrave Macmillan.

Sheafor, B. W., Teare, T., Hancock, M. W., & Gauthier, T. P. (1985). Curriculum development through content analysis. *Journal of Education in Social Work, 20–21*(3), 113–124.

Shirley, I. F. (1982). Social policy and social planning. In P. Spoonley., D. Pearson, & I. Shirley (Eds.), *New Zealand: Sociological perspectives* (pp. 239–262). Palmerston North, New Zealand: Dunmore Press.

Shirley, I. (1982). Professional education: Is there an alternative for social work? *New Zealand Social Work, 7*(4), 6–8.

Shirley, I. (1987). 'Lessons in full employment'. *New Zealand Social Work 12*(1), 12–13.

Shirley, I. (1988). The New Zealand experiment. *Accent, 3*(1), 10–13.

Shirley, I. (1988). State policy and employment. In D. Corson (Ed.), *Education for work* (pp. 146–163). Palmerston North, New Zealand: Dunmore Press.

Shirley, I. (1989). Community development: A personal viewpoint. *Social Work Review, 1*(3&4), 13–16.

Shirley, I. (1990). New Zealand: The advance of the new right. In I. Taylor (Ed.), *The social effects of free market policies: An international text* (pp. 351–390). London, England: Harvester Wheatsheaf.

Shirley, I. (1990). Social policy. In P. Spoonley, D. Pearson, & I. Shirley, (Eds.), *New Zealand society* (pp. 132–147). Palmerston North, New Zealand: Dunmore Press.

Shirley, I. (1991). Unemployment: Containing the epidemic. *Management,* (May), 48–49.

Shirley, I. (1991). Unemployment — its realities and human costs. In R. Pelly (Ed.), *Towards a just economy* (pp. 21–42). Wellington, New Zealand: Victoria University of Wellington.

Shirley, I. (1992). Social policy: Beyond the welfare state. In P. Saunder & D. Encel (Eds.), *Social policy in Australia: Options for the 1990s. Proceedings, National Social Policy Conference, Sydney, New South Wales, 3–5 July, 1991,* (pp. 61–84). Sydney, NSW, Australia: University of New South Wales, Social Policy Research Centre.

Shirley, I. (1997). Educating social workers in a changing cultural context. Response: a New Zealand perspective. *Social Work Review 9*(4), 12 13.

Shirley, I. (1997). *The Hawkes Bay labour market: General report — 1997.* Palmerston

North, New Zealand: Massey University Printery.

Shirley, I. (1998). *Dealing with crime: A crime profile commissioned by the Auckland City Council for safer Auckland City.* New Zealand: Crime Profile Research Team, Massey University.

Shirley, I. (2000). *The South Waikato labour market: General report — 1998/99.* Palmerston North & Auckland, New Zealand: Labour Market Dynamic Research Programme, Massey University.

Shirley, I. (2001). *Transitions in the Hawkes Bay labour market: Education and training.* Palmerston North & Auckland, New Zealand: Labour Market Dynamic Research Programme, Massey University.

Shirley, I. (2001). *Transitions in the Hawkes Bay labour market: Unpaid work and paid work.* Palmerston North & Auckland, New Zealand: Labour Market Dynamic Research Programme, Massey University.

Shirley, I. (2001). *Transitions in the Hawkes Bay labour market: Welfare and unemployment.* Palmerston North & Auckland, New Zealand: Labour Market Dynamic Research Programme, Massey University.

Shirley, I. (2001). *Transitions in the South Waikato labour market: An ethnographic study.* Palmerston North & Auckland, New Zealand: Labour Market Dynamic Research Programme, Massey University.

Shirley, I. (2001). *Transitions in the Waitakere labour market: An ethnographic study.* Palmerston North & Auckland, New Zealand: Labour Market Dynamic Research Programme, Massey University.

Shirley, I., Koopman-Boyden, P., Pool, I., & St. John, S. (1997). Conclusion. In S. Kammerman & A. Khan, (Eds.).*Family change and family policies in Great Britain, Canada, New Zealand and the United States* (pp. 300–304). Oxford, England: Clarendon Press.

Shirley, I., Koopman-Boyden, P., Pool, I., & St. John, S. (1997). Families and social services. In S. Kammerman & A. Khan, (Eds.), *Family change and family policies in Great Britain, Canada, New Zealand and the United States* (pp. 270–285). Oxford, England: Clarendon Press.

Shirley, I., Koopman-Boyden, P., Pool, I., & St. John, S. (1997). Family change and family policies: New Zealand. In S. Kammerman & A. Khan, (Eds.), *Family change and family policies in Great Britain, Canada, New Zealand and the United States* (pp. 209–216). Oxford, England: Clarendon Press.

Shirley, I., Koopman-Boyden, P., Pool, I., & St. John, S. (1997). Family policy and political economy. In S. Kammerman & A. Khan, (Eds.), *Family change and family policies in Great Britain, Canada, New Zealand and the United States* (pp. 286–299). Oxford, England: Clarendon Press.

Shirley, I., Koopman-Boyden, P., Pool, I., & St. John, S. (1997). Financial assistance to families. In S. Kammerman & A. Khan, (Eds.), *Family change and family policies in Great Britain, Canada, New Zealand and the United States* (pp. 253–269). Oxford, England: Clarendon Press.

Shirley, I., Koopman-Boyden, P., Pool, I., & St. John, S. (1997). The formation of families. In S. Kammerman & A. Khan, (Eds.), *Family change and family policies in Great Britain, Canada, New Zealand and the United States* (pp. 217–235). Oxford, England: Clarendon Press.

Shirley, I. F. (1980). The administration and the community. In R. M. Alley (Ed.), *State services and the public in the 1980s* (pp. 102–112). Wellington, New Zealand: New Zealand Institute of Public Administration.

Shirley, I. F. (1980). Beneath the surface: Social relationships and the costs of unemployment. In P. Shannon & B. Webb (Eds.), *Unemployment and New Zealand's future* (pp. 59–68). Dunedin, New Zealand: University Extension, University of Otago.

Shirley, I. F. (1981). The nature of social work. *New Zealand Social Work Journal, 6*(2), 14–15.

Shirley, I. F. (1981). The social sciences: An example of social irresponsibility. In W. Green (Ed.), *Focus on social responsibility in science* (pp. 107–116). Wellington, New Zealand: Association of Scientists.

Shirley, I. F. (1982). Conclusion: Critical practice as a model for development. In I. F. Shirley (Ed.), *Development tracks: The theory and practice of community development* (pp. 271–291). Palmerston North, New Zealand: Dunmore Press.

Shirley, I. F. (1982). Introduction: Development tracks. In I. F. Shirley (Ed.), *Development tracks: The theory and practice of community development* (pp. 9–27). Palmerston North, New Zealand: Dunmore Press.

Shirley, I. F. (1987). In search of a social policy. *NZ Disabled, 7*(4), 56–58.

Shirley, I. F. (1993). The culture of violence. *Community Mental Health in New Zealand, 7*(2), 3–9.

Shirley, I. F. (1993). *Social and economic trends in New Zealand.* In a seminar for social service personnel organised by the Justice, Peace and Development Commission of the combined churches. February 20, 1993. Christchurch, New Zealand. Working paper. Palmerston North, New Zealand: Social Policy Research Centre.

Shirley, I. F. (1994). Managerial determinism. *Social Work Review, 6*(3), 1–2.

Shirley, I. F. (1994). Social policy. In P. Spoonley, D. Pearson, & I. Shirley, *New Zealand society: A sociological introduction* (2nd ed.) (pp. 130–145). Palmerston North, New Zealand: Dunmore Press.

Siaosi Sumeo, K. (2004). *A research on processes used to address the physical and sexual abuse of children in Samoa*. (MSW thesis, Auckland, New Zealand: Massey University.) http://mro.massey.ac.nz/handle/10179/7138

Simmons, H., Mafile'o, T., Webster, J., Jakobs, J., & Thomas, C. (2008). He wero: The challenge of putting your body on the line: Teaching and learning in anti-racist practice. *Social Work Education. 27*(4), 366–379. doi: 10.1080/02615470701380154

Simmons, H., & Wheeler, C. (2010). Serendipity — surprises in critical reflection on supervision. *Aotearoa New Zealand Social Work Review, 22*(2), 53–61.

Sion, K. (1997). *The social and cultural context of domestic violence in Papua New Guinea: Effectiveness of past and current social work practice in helping victims*. (MSW thesis, Palmerston North, New Zealand: Massey University.)

Slatter, C. (2004). *The politics of economic restructuring in the Pacific with a case study of Fiji*. (PhD thesis, Auckland, New Zealand: Massey University.) http://mro.massey.ac.nz/handle/10179/1646

Smith, P. (2001). Statutory social work: A study of social workers expectations and realisations. *Social Work Review, 13*(4), 22–24.

Smith, P. (2004). Defensive social work: Square peg-round hole. *Social Work Review, 16*(3), 22–25.

Smith, P. (2010). Whatever happened to Tuatapere? A study of a small rural community. *Aotearoa New Zealand Social Work, 22*(3), 27–38.

Smith, P. (2013). Whose culture is it anyway? Social working in a rural community. *Aotearoa New Zealand Social Work Review, 25*(1), 14–23.

Smith, P. (2013). Registration: Ten years on within a non-government organisation. *Aotearoa New Zealand Social Work Review, 25*(3), 19–24.

Smith, P. (2014). The why, what, where of social work: A personal reflection on the social work role over a thirty-year period. *Aotearoa New Zealand Social Work Review, 26*(2&3), 75–80.

Smith, P. A. (2009). *Whatever happened to Tuatapere: Are we doing very nicely thank you?* (MPhil thesis, Palmerston North, New Zealand: Massey University.) http://mro.massey.ac.nz/handle/10179/1322

Smith, R. J. (2000). *Behaviour change: Identifying the external factors which help direct the effective management of stopping reoffending or help maintain recidivism — a study of driver offenders who have made a decision to stop driving while disqualified*. (MSW thesis, Palmerston North, New Zealand: Massey University.) http://mro.massey.ac.nz/handle/10179/6019

Sorrenson, D. (1996). *Kaupapa Maori and responsiveness: New Zealand Children and Young Persons Service management responsiveness to Maori in the restructured state sector*. (MSW thesis, Palmerston North, New Zealand: Massey University.) http://mro.massey.ac.nz/handle/10179/5563

Spoonley, P. (2011). Ethnic and religious intolerance: Intolerance towards Pacific migrants. *Te Ara — the Encyclopedia of New Zealand*. http://www.TeAra.govt.nz/en/ethnic-and-religious-intolerance/page-4

Staniforth, B. (2010). Counselling in social work in Aotearoa New Zealand: The historical, political and socio-cultural evolution. *Aotearoa New Zealand Social Work Review, 22*(3), 3–14.

Staniforth, B. (2010). Counselling in social work in Aotearoa: Social workers' perspectives and practice. *Aotearoa New Zealand Social Work Review, 22*(2), 15–26.

Staniforth, B. L. (2007). Ruth and Brian Manchester: Social work's dynamic duo. *Social Work Review, 19*(1), 55–65.

Staniforth, B. L. (2007). Their stories, our history: Judith MacKenzie. *Aotearoa New Zealand Social Work, 19*(4), 40–51.

Staniforth, B. L., Butterfield, E., & Fenaughty, J. (2006). Cyberspace and young people. *Social Work Now, 33*, 4–11. http://www.cyf.govt.nz/documents/about-us/publications/social-work-now/social-work-now-33-april06.pdf

Staniforth, B. L., & Larkin, R. (2006). Documentation in social work: Remembering our ABCs. *Social Work Review, 18*(3), 13–20.

Stanley-Clarke, N. (2000). *Returning to paid work: Mothers and the impact of student loan debt*. (MSW thesis, Palmerston North, New Zealand: Massey University.) http://mro.massey.ac.nz/handle/10179/6047

Stanley-Clarke, N., Sanders, J., & Munford, R. (2014). The role of government policy in service development in a New Zealand statutory mental health service: Implications for policy planning and development. *Australasian Psychiatry, 22*(6), 557–559. doi: 10.1177/1039856214555890

Stanley-Clarke, N., Sanders, J., & Munford, R. (2016) Implementing a new governance model: Lessons from a New Zealand statutory mental health organisation. *Journal of Health Organization and Management, 30*(3): 498–508.

State Sector Act 1988. Wellington, New Zealand: Government Printer.

Stevens, K., Munford, R., Sanders, J., Liebenberg, L., & Ungar, M. (2014). Change, relationships and implications for practice: The experiences of young people who use multiple services. *International Journal of Child, Youth and Family Studies, 5*(3), 447–465.

Stewart, B. W. (1999). *Spirituality in counselling: Assisting counsellors and the depressed*. (MPhil thesis, Palmerston North, New Zealand: Massey University.) http://mro.massey.ac.nz/handle/10179/5819

Stewart, K. (2001). The evolution of critical stress incident management within secondary schools in Aotearoa New Zealand. *Social Work Review, 13*(2), 37–42.

Stewart, K. (2004). Critical incident responses in secondary schools in Aotearoa New Zealand: Are we doing justice to our adolescents. *Social Work Review, 16*(1), 13–18.

Stewart, K. (2005). Adult experts and adolescence voices in the field of critical incident responses. *Social Work Review, 17*(1), 31–37.

Stewart, K. (2009). The development of a critical incident student team. *Aotearoa New Zealand Social Work Review, 21*(3), 46–54.

Stokes, K. (2003). *The tensions facing a board of trustee model within the cultural framework of kura kaupapa Māori.* (MA (Social Policy) thesis, Auckland, New Zealand: Massey University.) http://mro.massey.ac.nz/handle/10179/910

Storer, F. (1996). *Realising their governance role: Community boards in New Zealand.* (MPhil thesis, Palmerston North, New Zealand: Massey University.)

Strahern, B. (1995). Risk assessment: Structured decision-making. *Social Work Review, 7*(3), 2–5.

Sullivan, M. (1997). Thinking about disability policy in the 1990s. *Disinformation, 4*(5), 12.

Sullivan, M. (1997). What's gone wrong with the 'new deal'? Neo-liberal approaches to disability support services: Markets and disempowerments. *Disinformation, 4*(6), 14.

Sullivan, M. (1998). Contemporary policy developments in disability support services: Social work practice under difficult circumstances. *Social Work Review, 10*(2), 9–12.

Sullivan, M. (2000). Does it say what we mean, do we mean what it says, do we know what we are doing? Problematising the way disability is conceptualised, written and spoken about. *New Zealand Journal of Disability Studies, 8,* 36–46.

Sullivan, M. (2003). The disabled god. Towards a liberatory theology of disability. *New Zealand Journal of Disability Studies, 10,* 162–169.

Sullivan, M. (2005). Subjected bodies: Paraplegia, rehabilitation and the politics of movement. In S. Tremain (Ed.), *Foucault and the government of disability* (pp. 27–44). Ann Arbor, MI: University of Michigan Press.

Sullivan, M. (2006). Changing the relations of research production? The emancipatory research paradigm: Towards resolution of some contradictions. *New Zealand Journal of Disability Studies, 12,* 178–195.

Sullivan, M. (2016). Towards emancipation: Disability policy in Aotearoa New Zealand. In J. Maidment & L. Beddoe (Eds.), *Social policy for social work and human services in Aotearoa New Zealand: Diverse perspectives* (pp. 164–179).

Christchurch, New Zealand: Canterbury University Press.

Sullivan, M., Derrett, S., Paul, C., Beaver, C., & Stace, H. (2014). Using mixed methods to build research capacity in the spinal cord injured population in New Zealand. *Journal of Mixed Methods Research, 8*(3), 234–244. doi: 10.1177/1558689814527942

Sullivan, M., & Munford, R. (1996). Social theories of disability. In P. O'Brien & R. Murray (Eds.), *Working in human services.* Palmerston North, New Zealand: Dunmore Press.

Sullivan, M., & Munford, R. (1998). The articulation of theory and practice: Critique and resistance in Aotearoa New Zealand. *Disability and Society, 13*(2), 183–198.

Sullivan, M., & Munford, R. (2005). Disability and support: The interface between disability theory and support — an individual challenge. In P. O'Brien & M. Sullivan (Eds.), *Allies in emancipation: Shifting from providing service to being of support* (pp. 19–35). Melbourne, Australia: Cengage Learning.

Sullivan, M. J. (1996). *Paraplegic bodies: Self and society.* (PhD thesis, Auckland, New Zealand: University of Auckland.) https://researchspace.auckland.ac.nz/handle/2292/1917

Sullivan, M. J. (2001). Disabled people and the politics of partnership in Aotearoa New Zealand. In L. Barton (Ed.), *Disability, politics and the struggle for change* (pp. 93–109). London, England: David Fulton Publishers.

Sullivan, M. J. (2003). The disabled god. Towards a liberatory theology of disability. *New Zealand Journal of Disability Studies. 10,* 162–169.

Sullivan, M. J. (2009). Philosophy, ethics, and the disability community. In D. Mertens & P. Ginsberg (Eds.), *The handbook of social research ethics* (pp. 69–84). Thousand Oaks, CA: Sage Publications.

Sullivan, M. J., & O'Brien, P. (2005). Being of support — a final reflection. In P. O'Brien, & M. Sullivan (Eds.), *Allies in emancipation: Shifting from providing service to being of support* (pp. 213–219). Melbourne, Australia: Cengage Learning.

Sullivan, M. J., Paul, C. E., Herbison, G. P., Tamou, P., Derrett, S., & Crawford, M. (2010). A longitudinal study of life histories of people with spinal cord injury. *Injury Prevention, 16*(6), 1–9. doi:10.1136/ip.2010.028134

Sullivan, M. J., & West Newman, C. L. (2007). Being: Identity. In S. Matthewman, C. West Newman, & B. Curtis (Eds.), *Being sociological* (pp. 233–252). New York, NY: Palgrave Macmillan.

Swain, P. M. (1983). *Inservice social work education: An analysis of policies and programmes.* (MPhil (Social Work), Palmerston North, New Zealand: Massey University.

Switzer, P. K. (1998). *Yours, mine or ours? A study of intra family income distribution.*

(MA (Social Policy) thesis, Auckland, New Zealand: Massey University.)

Teine, M. I. (1998). *Health care services delivery in Papua New Guinea: An argument for policy change*. (MA (Social Policy) thesis, Auckland, New Zealand: Massey University.)

Te Kōhanga Reo, National Trust. (2016). *History*. http://www.kohanga.ac.nz/history/

Te Momo, F. H. (2004). A Maori third way: What does it mean in New Zealand today? *Social Work Review/ Te Kōmako, 16*(2), 5–11.

Te Momo, O. H. (2007). Biotechnology: The language of multiple views in Maori communities. *Biotechnology Journal, 2*, 1179–1183. doi: 10.1002/biot.200700123

Te Momo, O. H. (2007). Maori volunteerism from 1800 to 1900: A recognition of community services in Aotearoa/New Zealand. *e-Volunteerism, 7*(4).

Te Momo, O. H. (2007). Te poi poroiti — the circle of work life for Maori academic women. In M. Waring & C. Fouché (Eds.), *Managing mayhem: Work–life balance in New Zealand* (pp. 86–103). Wellington, New Zealand: Dunmore Press.

Te Momo, O. H. (2012). *Whānau evolution: Introducing the different perspectives in Aotearoa/New Zealand*. Palmerston North, New Zealand: Office of the AVC Maori and Pasifika, Massey University.

Teppett, R. B. G. (1999). *'To speak of unspeakable acts'*. (MA (Social Policy) thesis, Palmerston North, New Zealand: Massey University.) http://mro.massey.ac.nz/handle/10179/8288.

Thomas, G. (2007). The power of the therapeutic relationship: Bringing to evidence-based practice. *Aotearoa New Zealand Social Work, 19*(4), 55–66.

Thompson, A. P. (2009). *Whanau/family meetings in the paediatric intensive care unit: Content, process, and family satisfaction*. (MPhil thesis, Auckland, New Zealand: Massey University.) http://mro.massey.ac.nz/handle/10179/1102

Thompson, P., & Yeung, P. (2015). Is a funeral a right? Exploring indigent funerals from social work perspectives. *Aotearoa New Zealand Social Work, 27*(1&2), 73–86.

Thomson, C. (2014). Reflections on the social work profession on the 50th anniversary of ANZASW: Those who fail to learn from history are doomed to repeat it. *Aotearoa New Zealand Social Work Review, 26*(2&3), 3–5.

Thomson, J. B. (1995). *Indigence to independence: The development of social policy in New Zealand for people with learning disabilities*. (MSW thesis, Palmerston North, New Zealand: Massey University.) http://mro.massey.ac.nz/handle/10179/6344

Thorburn, N., & De Hann, I. (2014). Children and survival sex: A social work agenda. *Aotearoa New Zealand Social Work Review, 26*(4), 14–21.

Thornton, P., & Lunt, N. (1997). *Employment policies for disabled people in eighteen countries: A review*. York, England: Social Policy Research Unit.

Thorpe, A. (2004). *Negotiating infertility treatment decisions.* (MSW thesis, Palmerston North, New Zealand: Massey University.) http://mro.massey.ac.nz/handle/10179/7241

Tie, W. (1993). *Managing the irresistible force: An analysis of the means by which the Corrections Division of the Department of Justice relates to voluntary sector agencies.* (MSW thesis, Palmerston North, New Zealand: Massey University.) http://mro.massey.ac.nz/handle/10179/6808

Titchener, S. (2010). *Entering unknown territory: Exploring the impact on indigenous field researchers when conducting gender based violence and child abuse research in the Solomon Islands.* (MPhil thesis, Auckland, New Zealand: Massey University.) http://mro.massey.ac.nz/handle/10179/1318

Todman, A., & Mulitalo-Lauta, P. (2010). The social work alert system: An account of a new initiative in the emergency department at Middlemore hospital. *Aotearoa New Zealand Social Work, 21*(4) & 22(1), 44–45.

Tolich, M., & Briar, C. (1999). Just checking it out: Exploring the significance of informal gender divisions amongst American supermarket employees. *Gender, Work and Organization, 6*(3), 129–133.

Trlin, A. (1992). Bibliography. In A. Trlin & P. Spoonley (Eds.), *New Zealand and international migration: A digest and bibliography* (pp. 99–161). Palmerston North, New Zealand: Massey University, Department of Sociology.

Trlin, A. (1992). Change and continuity: New Zealand's immigration policy in the late 1980s. In A. Trlin & P. Spoonley (Eds.), *New Zealand and international migration: A digest and bibliography* (pp. 1–28). Palmerston North, New Zealand: Massey University, Department of Sociology.

Trlin, A., & Kang, D. (1992). The business immigration policy and the characteristics of approval — Hong Kong and Taiwanese applicants, 1986–1988. In A. Trlin & P. Spoonley (Eds.), *New Zealand and international migration: A digest and bibliography* (pp. 48–64). Palmerston North, New Zealand: Massey University, Department of Sociology.

Trlin, A. (1997). For the promotion of economic growth and prosperity: New Zealand's immigration policy, 1991–1995. In A. Trlin & P. Spoonley, *New Zealand and international migration: A digest and bibliography* (3rd ed.) (pp. 93–178). Palmerston North, New Zealand: Massey University.

Trlin, A., & Spoonley, P. (Eds.). (1992). *New Zealand and international migration: A digest and bibliography.* Palmerston North, New Zealand: Massey University, Department of Sociology.

Tsui, M.-S., O'Donoghue, K., & Ng, A. K. (2014). Diversity-sensitive clinical supervision: An international perspective. In C. Watkins & D. Milne (Eds.), *The*

Wiley international handbook of clinical supervision (pp. 238–254). Chichester, England: John Wiley & Sons. doi: 10.1002/9781118846360.ch10

Tucker, P. (2004). *Raising a child with high care needs: The parental experience of caring for a child who experiences disability and has high care needs.* (MSW thesis, Auckland, New Zealand: Massey University.) http://mro.massey.ac.nz/handle/10179/6349

Turner, C. J. (1994). *Sweden and New Zealand: A comparative analysis of an alternative to the Employment Contracts Act 1991.* (MPhil thesis, Palmerston North, New Zealand: Massey University.) http://mro.massey.ac.nz/handle/10179/6269

Uddy, D. (1987). Violence: An occupational hazard for social workers. *New Zealand Social Work, 12*(1&2), 2–5.

United Nations. (2003–4). UN Enable: The International Year of Disabled Persons 1981. http://www.un.org/esa/socdev/enable/disiydp.htm

Urry, Y., Sanders, J., & Munford, R. (2015). The 'right time' — negotiating the timing of interviews with vulnerable young people. *Journal of Youth Studies, 18*(3), 291–304. doi: 10.1080/13676261.2014.944120

Vere-Jones, M. (2005). *Ready to practice? Graduates' experiences of competency-based social work education.* (MPhil thesis, Palmerston North, New Zealand: Massey University.) http://mro.massey.ac.nz/handle/10179/7318

Virtue, C. (2007). *Multiple holding: Clinical supervision in the context of trauma and abuse.* (MSW thesis, Auckland, New Zealand: Massey University.) http://mro.massey.ac.nz/handle/10179/7443

Virtue, C., & Fouché, C. (2010). Multiple holding: A model for supervision in the context of trauma and abuse. *Aotearoa New Zealand Social Work, 21*(4) & 22(1), 64–72.

Wainwright, B., Jülich, S. J., Waring, M. J., Yeung, P. H. Y., & Green, J. K. (2016). Leaving the experts: Experiences of liver transplant recipients in New Zealand. *Nursing Praxis in New Zealand, 32*(3), 7–19.

Walsh-Tapiata, W. (1999). The more we go into the future the more we depend on the past: Strategic planning Maori style. *Social Work Review/Te Kōmako, 11*(4), 21–24.

Walsh-Tapiata, W. (2000). Te Tau Rua Mano. He aha nga wero inaianei? The year 2000. What are the challenges for Maori social workers now? *Social Work Review/Te Kōmako, 12*(4), 9–12.

Walsh-Tapiata, W. (2002). A question of identity for our rangatahi. *Social Work Review/Te Kōmako, 14*(2), 24–27.

Walsh-Tapiata, W. (2003). A model for Maori research: Te whakaeke i te ao rangahau o te Maori. In R. Munford & J. Sanders (Eds.), *Making a difference in families:*

Research that creates change (pp. 55–73). Crows Nest, NSW, Australia: Allen and Unwin.

Walsh-Tapiata, W. (2003). The praxis of research — what can social services learn from the practice of research in an iwi setting? *Social Work Review/Te Kōmako, 15*(3), 25–29.

Walsh-Tapiata, W. (2004). The past, the present and the future: The New Zealand indigenous experience of social work. *Social Work Review, 16*(4), 30–37.

Walsh-Tapiata, W. (2008). The past, the present and the future: The New Zealand indigenous experience of social work. In M. Gray, J. Coates, & M. Yellow Bird (Eds.), *Indigenous social work around the world: Towards culturally relevant education and practice*. Aldershot, England; Burlington, VT: Ashgate.

Walsh-Tapiata, W., Metuamate, A., Rikihana, T., Webster, J., Warren, T. R., & Kiriona, D. (2006). Māori youth (rangatahi) lead positive social change in identifying health issues. *Commonwealth Youth and Development, 4*(1), 2–16.

Ward, A. E. (2007). *Does this fit? A study of the perspectives of home detention probation officers*. (MPhil thesis, Palmerston North, New Zealand: Massey University.) http://mro.massey.ac.nz/handle/10179/10365

Ward, J., & Asher, B. (1984). Organisation and financing of health care in New Zealand. In C. Wilkes & I. Shirley (Eds.), *In the public interest: Health work and housing in New Zealand society* (pp. 90–101). Auckland, New Zealand: Benton Ross.

Ware, F., & Walsh-Tapiata, W. (2010). Youth development: Maori styles. *Youth Studies Australia, 29*(4), 18–29.

Waring, M. (1996). A woman's reckoning. In G. Argyrous & F. Stilnell (Eds.), *Economics as a social science* (pp. 184–189). New South Wales, Australia: Pluto Press.

Waring, M. (1997). If women counted. In W. Moorman & N. Goodwin, *Frontier issues in economic thought*. (Medford Global Development and Environmental Institute). Medford, MA: Tufts University.

Waring, M. (1997). Introduction. In M. Moir, *New Zealand country women*. Auckland, New Zealand: Tandem Press.

Waring, M. (1997). The invisibility of women's work: The economics of local and global 'shitwork'. *Canadian Women's Studies Journal, 17*(2), 31–40.

Waring, M. (1997). *Three masquerades*. Toronto, Canada: Toronto University Press.

Warner, G. J. (2001). *Social policy in a Christian frame of meaning: A world-view, ethic and theoretical framework for the analysis, choice, and design of social policy*. (MA (Social Policy), Palmerston North, New Zealand: Massey University.) http://

mro.massey.ac.nz/handle/10179/8422

Watkins, L. A. (2007). 'In her shoes': The experience of mothers living with mental illness. (MSW thesis, Palmerston North, New Zealand: Massey University.) http://mro.massey.ac.nz/handle/10179/7347

Wealleans, N. (1994). Consumer rights and empowerment under the Health and Disability Commissioner Act 1994. Social Work Review, 9(3), 13–15.

Wealleans, N. (1998). The quest for consumer voice: An evaluation of the implementation and outcomes of the Health and Disability Commissioner Act (1994). (MSW thesis, Palmerston North, New Zealand: Massey University.) http://mro.massey.ac.nz/handle/10179/6099

Webb, L. (1999). Can severe behaviour problems be prevented? (MSW thesis, Auckland, New Zealand: Massey University.) http://mro.massey.ac.nz/handle/10179/6203

Webber-Dreadon, E., & Mollard-Wharepapa, M. (2002). What has marine science got to do with social work? Social Work Review/Te Kōmako, 14(2), 10–13.

Webber-Dreadon, E. T. P. (2012). Ngamotu me Kihitu nga whenua, Ngamotu me Kihitu nga turangawaewae: 'Aue Te Ariki aue', kei whea ra nga tangata o te hau kainga nei? A personal journey — where have all the people gone? (MPhil thesis, Palmerston North, New Zealand: Massey University.) http://mro.massey.ac.nz/handle/10179/4252

Webster, J., & Bosmann-Watene, G. (2003). Walking in two worlds: A critique of the diagnostic and statistical manual of mental disorders from a te ao Maori perspective. Social Work Review/Te Kōmako, 15(3), 8–11.

Webster, J., Warren, T., Walsh-Tapiata, W., & Kiriona, D. (2002). How rangatahi lead positive social change in identifying their hauora issues. Otaki, New Zealand: Whāia te Hauora o ngā Rangatahi Research Unit, Te Rūnanga o Raukawa Inc.

Wei, V. H. (2003). Whose paradise is New Zealand, female or male? An investigation into the different perspectives of the immigration experience between professional Chinese females and males. (MA (Social Policy) thesis, Auckland, New Zealand: Massey University.) http://mro.massey.ac.nz/handle/10179/6814

Wepa, D., & Te Huia, J. (2006). Cultural safety and the birth culture of Maori. Social Work Review/Te Kōmako, 18(2), 9, 26–31.

Whibley Smith, A., Selby, R. A., & Baskerville Davies, M. A. (2002). Reviewing the review: A review of the ANZASW Social Work Review journal from 1988–2000. Social Work Review, 14(3), 6–9.

Wicks, W. (1998). Edges, margins and rocky perches: Life stories of older disabled women. (MSW thesis, Palmerston North, New Zealand: Massey University.) http://mro.massey.ac.nz/handle/10179/7022

Wilkes, C., & Shirley, I. (Eds.). (1984). *In the public interest: Health work and housing in New Zealand society*. Auckland, New Zealand: Benton Ross.

Wilkes, C., & Shirley, I. (1984). An introduction to social policy. In C. Wilkes & I. Shirley (Eds.), *In the public interest: Health work and housing in New Zealand society* (pp. 7–50). Auckland, New Zealand: Benton Ross.

Williams, L. K., Labonte, R., & O'Brien, M. A. (2003). Empowering social action through narratives of identity and culture. *Health Promotion International, 18*, 33–40.

Williams, T., & McMaster, K. (1984) Anger management: A course for aggressive men. *New Zealand Social Work, 9*(2), 2–7.

Wills, R. M. C. (2003). *Special education 2000: The implementation experience*. (MA (Social Policy) thesis, Auckland, New Zealand: Massey University.)

Wilson, C. M. (2001). *The process of an intercountry adoption: The role of the women within the couples involved*. (MSW thesis, Palmerston North, New Zealand: Massey University.) http://mro.massey.ac.nz/handle/10179/6670

Wilson, W. J., & Baskerville, M. A. (2000). *Safety and access issues in Feilding: A pilot study*. Palmerston North, New Zealand: Massey University, School of Social Policy and Social Work.

Winbush, C., & Selby, R. (2015). Finding home: South African migration to New Zealand. *Aotearoa New Zealand Social Work Review, 27*(1&2), 46–58.

Winkelmann, G. (2013). Social work in health — the way ahead. *Aotearoa New Zealand Social Work Review, 25*(4), 85–88.

Wood, P. (2013). *Citizenship and participation of young people in Aotearoa/New Zealand*. (MA (Social Policy) thesis, Palmerston North, New Zealand: Massey University.) http://mro.massey.ac.nz/handle/10179/4979

Worrall, J. (1996). *Because we're family: A study of kinship care of children in New Zealand*. (MSW thesis, Auckland, New Zealand: Massey University.) http://mro.massey.ac.nz/handle/10179/5569

Worrall, J. (2001). Kinship care of the abused child: The New Zealand experience. *Child Welfare, 80*(5), 497–511.

Worrall, J. (2002). Turning around: An ecological approach to recidivist youth offending. *Developing Practice: The Child, Youth and Family Work Journal, 3*(Autumn), 36–42.

Yates, D. (2000). *Sink or swim: leaving care in New Zealand*. (MA (Social Policy) thesis, Auckland, New Zealand: Massey University.) http://mro.massey.ac.nz/handle/10179/5772

Yeung, P., & Breheny, M. (2016). Using the capability approach to understand the determinants of subjective well-being among community-dwelling older people in New Zealand. *Age & Ageing, 45*(2), 292–298. doi: 10.1093/ageing/afw002

Yeung, P., Cooper, L., & Dale, M. (2015). Prevalence and associated factors of elder abuse in a community-dwelling population of Aotearoa New Zealand: A cross-sectional study. *Aotearoa New Zealand Social Work Review, 27*(3), 29–43.

Yeung, P., & English, A. N. R. (2012). A survey of knowledge, attitudes and behaviours regarding sexual wellbeing among Chinese women living in New Zealand — a pilot study. *Aotearoa New Zealand Social Work Review, 24*(1), 14–30.

Yeung, P., Passmore, A., & Packer, T. (2010). Active citizens or passive recipients: How Australian young adults with cerebral palsy define citizenship. *Journal of Intellectual and Developmental Disability, 33*, 65–75.

Yeung, P., Rodgers, V., Dale, M., Spence, S., Ros, B., Howard, J., & O'Donoghue K. (2016). Psychometric testing of a person-centred care scale — the Eden Warmth Survey in a long-term care home in New Zealand. *Contemporary Nurse, 52*(2&3), 176–190. doi: 10.1080/10376178.2016.1198236

Yeung, P., Towers, A., La Grow, S., Philipp, M., Alpass, F., & Stephens, C. (2015). Mobility, satisfaction with functional capacity and perceived quality of life (PQOL) in older persons with self-reported visual impairment: The pathway between ability to get around and PQOL. *Disability and Rehabilitation, 37*(2), 113–120. doi:10 .3109/09638288.2014.910559

About the authors

DR MICHAEL DALE is a senior lecturer at Massey University's Social of Social Work, Palmerston North. Michael has extensive work experience within the social services sector as a practitioner, trainer, project leader, policy adviser and manager. He has worked for central government, local government and the NGO sector.

HANNAH MOONEY (Ngāti Raukawa ki te tonga, Te Ātiawa, Te Atihaunui a Pāpārangi, Ngā Rauru) is a lecturer at Massey University's School of Social Work, Palmerston North. She completed her Bachelor of Social Work with Massey in 2004 and went on to work for Māori mental health with children, youth and their families. She completed her Master in Social Work at Massey, and in late 2011 was employed as a member of staff.

KIERAN O'DONOGHUE is an associate professor and head of the School of Social Work at Massey University. His work in the areas of social work theory and practice and social work supervision has been published internationally.

Acknowledgements

My association with Massey began in 1972 as an undergraduate. Over many years I have retained an association with the social work programme, joining the staff in 2011. Preparing this book has been a journey of reflection on both the Massey social work programme and my own social work practice. In particular, I would like to acknowledge the influence of Andrew Trlin, who supported me through my doctoral research and challenged me to develop a critical perspective.
— Michael Dale

I would like to thank Michael and Kieran for asking me to join the team for this book; it has been an enjoyable experience 'reliving' aspects of my own study with the social work programmes at Massey. I have also felt privileged to hear stories about the conception of the programme and how it has changed over time. I would like to thank my aunt, Wheturangi Walsh-Tapiata, and Leland Ruwhiu and Rachael Selby for being generous with their time and sharing experiences of their work with Massey, and for their ideas around how to always improve and work towards higher bicultural aspirations. I will always appreciate opportunities to be in the same space with the three of you. Thanks also to Sheryl Kirikiri and the Practice Research and Professional Development Hub for transcribing the interviews and supporting this project.
— Hannah Mooney

I wish to acknowledge all of the people across the years who have contributed to the social work programme at Massey University, particularly the administrative and professional services staff who worked behind the scenes to ensure that the wheels of the programme turn efficiently and effectively. I also acknowledge all of the guest lecturers, placement supervisors, casual tutors and markers whose contribution is invaluable. I wish to especially thank Professor Robyn Munford for her encouragement and support, and for peer-reviewing the manuscript of this book. To Nicola Legat and the team at Massey University Press, thank you for your help in the commissioning and production of the book.
— Kieran O'Donoghue

Index

For more information about our books please visit
www.masseypress.ac.nz

MASSEY UNIVERSITY PRESS